THE Early Childhood Coaching Handbook

THE Early Childhood Coaching Handbook

by

Dathan D. Rush, Ed.D., CCC-SLP

and

M'Lisa L. Shelden, PT, Ph.D.

Family, Infant and Preschool Program
J. Iverson Riddle Development Center
Morganton, NC

·P·A·U·L·H·
BROOKES
PUBLISHING Co.®

Baltimore • London • Sydney

Paul H. Brookes Publishing Co.
Post Office Box 10624
Baltimore, Maryland 21285-0624
USA

www.brookespublishing.com

Typeset by Aptara, Inc., Falls Church, Virginia.
Manufactured in the United States of America by
Versa Press, Inc., East Peoria, Illinois.

The individuals described in this book are composites or real people whose situations are masked and are based on the authors' experiences. In all instances, names and identifying details have been changed to protect confidentiality.

Library of Congress Cataloging-in-Publication Data

Rush, Dathan D.
    The early childhood coaching handbook / Dathan D. Rush, M'Lisa Shelden.
        p.   cm.
    Includes bibliographical references and index.
    ISBN-13: 978-1-59857-067-0
    ISBN-10: 1-59857-067-6
    1. Early childhood teachers—Handbooks, manuals, etc.   2. Early childhood special education—Handbooks, manuals, etc.   3. Early childhood education—Handbooks, manuals, etc.   4. Child development—Handbooks, manuals, etc.   I. Shelden, M'Lisa L.   II. Title.

    LB1775.6.R87 2011
    372.21—dc22   2010052344

British Library Cataloguing in Publication data are available from the British Library.

2020   2019   2018   2017   2016
10   9   8   7   6   5

Contents

About the Authors

Dathan D. Rush, Ed.D., CCC-SLP, has a doctoral degree in child and family studies from Nova Southeastern University, Fort Lauderdale, Florida, and a master's degree in speech-language pathology from Oklahoma State University. Dr. Rush is currently Associate Director/Researcher at the Family, Infant and Preschool Program (FIPP) in Morganton North Carolina. He provides ongoing technical assistance to several statewide early intervention programs to implement evidence-based early intervention practices in natural settings. Dr. Rush previously served as Clinical Assistant Professor at the University of Oklahoma Health Sciences Center, teaching early childhood intervention in the graduate program. He has more than 25 years of experience as a practitioner and early intervention program director and has managed a number of training contracts with various state agencies and organizations. He served as an editorial board member of *Infants and Young Children* until 2002 and has published articles in the area of coaching families in early intervention, in-service training, and teaming in early intervention. He is also a past president and former executive council member of the Oklahoma Speech-Language-Hearing Association. Dr. Rush has presented numerous workshops nationally on topics related to writing and implementing individualized family service plans, team building, using a primary service provider approach to teaming, coaching, and supporting young children with disabilities and their families in natural learning environments. Dr. Rush has also co-authored a previous book on coaching in early childhood intervention as well as a chapter on using a primary coach approach to teaming in *Working with Families of Young Children with Special Needs* (McWilliam, 2010; Guilford Press).

M'Lisa L. Shelden, PT, Ph.D., has a doctoral degree in special education from the University of Oklahoma. She also has a bachelor's degree in physical therapy from the University of Oklahoma Health Sciences Center and a master's degree in early childhood special education from the University of Oklahoma (Norman Campus). Dr. Shelden currently serves as Director/Researcher of the Family, Infant and Preschool Program (FIPP) in Morganton, North Carolina. She works alongside Dr. Rush providing ongoing technical assistance to several statewide early intervention programs to implement evidence-based early intervention practices in natural settings. Dr. Shelden has 28 years of experience as a physical therapist and special educator. In addition, she received a 2000 National Institute on Disabilities and Rehabilitation Research (NIDRR) Mary E. Switzer Merit Fellowship. She is a graduate Fellow of the ZERO TO THREE National Center for Infants, Toddlers, and Families. Dr. Shelden has co-authored several articles related to early intervention teamwork, writing individualized family service plans (IFSPs), coaching, and supporting young children with disabilities and their families in natural learning environments. She has also written a chapter related to physical therapy personnel preparation and service delivery and co-authored a book titled *Physical Therapy under IDEA* (McEwen, Arnold, Jones, & Shelden, 2000; American Physical Therapy Association, Section on Pediatrics). Dr. Shelden has co-authored a previous text *Coaching Families and Colleagues in Early Childhood* (with Barbara E. Hanft & Dathan D. Rush; 2004, Paul H. Brookes Publishing Co.) as well as a chapter on using a primary coach approach to teaming in *Working with Families of Young Children with Special Needs* (McWilliam, 2010; Guilford Press). Dr. Shelden has made numerous presentations nationally on the topics related to IFSP development and implementation, transition, inclusion, evaluation and assessment, coaching, primary service provider approach to teaming, and provision of supporting children with disabilities and their families in natural learning environments.

Foreword

I am beginning to see why careers need to last across decades. The truth is that it takes a long time to really understand how our professional work "works." We begin fueled by passion and energy, doing the best we know how to do. However, at the beginning there is only so much we can actually know because we are novices, so as we encounter children, families, colleagues, and settings, we build on our knowledge and channel our passion according to what we continue to learn as we practice. I find myself sitting here looking back on *many* iterations of this process of knowing, doing, reflecting, and knowing anew.

When I began practicing nearly 4 decades ago, I was proud to have a full schedule of children sequentially marching into my special room to receive my services. I was the expert! I needed to *know* what to do and direct the implementation of that perfect strategy. As a therapist, I believed that what I *did* with a child was the most important focus; we wouldn't have considered an emphasis on the process of discovery with a parent or teacher. In fact, such a focus would have been seen as a weakness of professionalism. We needed to know the answers. *Sigh* . . .

This was the time in our country's history when we were just beginning to serve children in community and neighborhood settings. Prior to this time we had served them primarily in institutions or special segregated schools. We did not make this transition easily; at first we imported our strategies from the institutions and continued to have special therapy times scheduled for each child. Our "institution" strategies did not fit so well into these new community settings, so slowly we experimented with new ideas.

And here we are; 4 decades later, we understand a lot of things about serving young children, their families, and their teachers. We see the children's strengths and build on them. We acknowledge the influence of context. We recognize the power within children, families, and teachers to identify and implement solutions that fit with their personal styles. We understand that our professional expertise is reflected in our approaches to problem solving rather than in implementation of techniques. We emphasize the importance of using evidence to guide our practices. That is a substantial distance to travel, so taking 40 years to get here makes sense.

The topic of coaching for early childhood intervention is a perfect reflection of this iterative process. Coaching principles developed on the basis of the evidence from all these decades of practice and research clearly outline our responsibilities. In my early years, the idea of facilitating another person to identify a solution would have seemed, well, crazy. Now we know that children, families, and teachers practice more, become more competent, build their own capacity, and generalize their skills when we employ coaching principles to deploy our expertise.

But having evidence that new practices are effective is not sufficient to change practices. Someone has to translate the evidence, integrate the interdisciplinary knowledge, and illustrate what practices look like when actual therapists, teachers, families, and children are the focus of a team's attention. Thankfully, that is what Drs. Rush and Shelden provide in this new handbook. They are the perfect conduit for this knowledge translation. As they describe in the beginning of their book, they both went through professional journeys in their early careers that were similar to the one that I have just described. Having had the experience of changing one's practices due to both pressure and a desire to learn more creates awareness about how current practitioners might be feeling about making their own changes.

Drs. Rush and Shelden illustrate their understanding of the challenges of transitioning by sharing stories about traditional practices and how they can be transformed into coaching practices. For example, they address the real fears that professionals experience when it seems that they must abandon their current expertise to employ new practices. They make it clear that one's expertise remains critical and that professionals need only learn new methods for interacting in order to use their expertise. Their approach is reassuring to even the most cautious colleagues; they offer small steps to try out coaching so that one can make a smooth transition from traditional practices.

This handbook contains all the tools that professionals will need to become effective coaching practitioners. The authors provide conceptual background and summarize the evidence that indicates the effectiveness of the coaching practices so that professionals can back up their professional decisions and plans with appropriate literature. They compare and contrast a coaching style of interaction with other approaches to interdisciplinary communication and offer a step-by-step method for learning the coaching strategies. The handbook also contains entire chapters on coaching the unique groups of families and teachers. Because Drs. Rush and Shelden understand the continuing evolution of knowledge, they also hypothesize how coaching practices will evolve in early childhood programs of the future. Their vision will guide us toward even better ways to serve.

Forty years from now, we will be talking about these "early years" of implementing coaching practices, just as today we reflect on how our segregated practices evolved into community-based services. Readers who are just beginning their careers today will be the ones telling this next set of stories. They must ensure that we continue to make as much progress in respectfully serving children, families, and teachers as we have up to this point. I look forward to seeing where coaching leads us; with the leadership of Drs. Rush and Shelden, I know it will be an enjoyable and thought-provoking journey!

Winnie Dunn, Ph.D., OTR
Professor and Chair
Department of Occupational Therapy Education
School of Allied Health
University of Kansas Medical Center

Preface

We were standing in the middle of a hotel lobby during a break in a conference we were attending in Washington, D.C., in 2001, when our friend and colleague, Barbara E. Hanft, approached us and said, "We need to write a book on coaching." Barbara had been asked to update a text that she had written on consultation, but she told us that what she was doing in her own practice and what she was training others to do at that time was really more like coaching. We, too, had been studying the literature on coaching and examining how it could be applied in early intervention programs to work with families in natural environments as well as with colleagues in the course of using a primary service provider approach to teaming. In the work that we had all been doing with programs around the country, we were starting to teach our colleagues how to use a coaching interaction style in early intervention and pre-school programs, but we lacked a comprehensive guide to assist new learners.

Immediately, we agreed to put our collective experience and thinking about this topic into words to produce *Coaching Families and Colleagues in Early Childhood* (Hanft, Rush, & Shelden, 2004; Paul H. Brookes Publishing Co.). In our first text on this topic, the three of us worked to describe coaching in early childhood and define the coaching process in a way that we hoped would be immediately applicable and helpful to early childhood practitioners, administrators, and providers of professional development. We focused on coaching in the home, community, and group settings, the contexts in which all young children learn and develop. Our goal was to provide ample illustrations of coaching family members, other care providers, and colleagues.

The response to that volume far exceeded our expectations. Although coaching had been referenced in the early childhood intervention literature for quite some time, readers of the *Coaching Families and Colleagues in Early Childhood* commented about how much they appreciated having a guide to help them operationalize the coaching process. During the past 6 years, the use of coaching principles and practices has become more common, and references in the literature to coaching as an interaction style in early childhood have become more prevalent. At the same time, as individuals and programs became more aware of coaching, their requests for more of the research behind the practices to validate their use in various settings increased. We also have heard the term *coaching* mistakenly used to describe a service delivery model in early intervention and referred to as a hands-off method of intervention.

After *Coaching Families and Colleagues in Early Childhood* was published, the three of us continued to provide training for various programs about how to use the coaching process that was provided in the text. In addition, Dathan and M'Lisa continued to synthesize the research on coaching in order to further delineate the evidence-based characteristics of the practice, an effort that modified and in some ways simplified the process. Both by reviewing the research and through working with individuals and groups to apply the research-based characteristics, we have deepened and expanded on our initial understanding of coaching as an interaction style for building the capacity of another person to achieve his or her desired outcomes.

This text follows up on *Coaching Families and Colleagues in Early Childhood*. Our intent is to further clarify coaching practices for use with parents, other care providers, teachers, and colleagues across settings such as early intervention, early literacy, and early childhood programs. *The Early Childhood Coaching Handbook* also addresses questions, misperceptions, and needs for further explanation that we have experienced over the past 6 years. We also tried to fill this new book with examples from actual coaching situations that we have received from readers and individuals whom we have had the privilege to support in their learning and use of these practices. The names of the participants in the scenarios and examples in this book have been changed to protect the individuals' confidentiality. Although our vision was to provide as comprehensive a resource on this topic as possible, we have yet to stop learning about or applying this work. This handbook is our best compilation of what we know and can share with you about this topic at this point, based on the research that exists and on what we have learned from our own development and learning process.

Our hope is that you, the reader, will gain information that you can use in your work to support the learning and development of others. Just as coaching is a process, reading and operationalizing the information contained in this book is a process as well. For that reason, we hope that you will take time to observe, practice, reflect on, and remember key concepts as you move through the chapters and begin to apply the principles and practices that we have described and illustrated.

REFERENCE

Hanft, B.E., Rush, D.D., & Shelden, M.L. (2004). *Coaching families and colleagues in early childhood*. Baltimore: Paul H. Brookes Publishing Co.

Acknowledgments

We would like to thank the many teams of practitioners across the United States who have worked hard to use a coaching style of interaction with one another as well as the families and teachers they serve. We also extend special thanks to family members of young children who have been very understanding as the practitioners with whom they work refine their coaching skills. We appreciate the families' willingness to share how coaching has acknowledged and enhanced their abilities and confidence to achieve their desired outcomes. We would like to recognize the contributions of our colleagues in Western Australia who have expanded our thinking about the effectiveness of coaching across continents and cultures. Thanks to those who provided feedback on early versions of portions of this text.

To our families for their patience, support, and sacrifice
and to the staff members at the Family, Infant and Preschool Program,
who inspire us on a daily basis

Chapter 1

Introduction to Coaching

Once upon a time, long ago, a speech-language pathologist (SLP) and a physical therapist (PT) were happily working in their chosen professions. He, the SLP, was a speech-language services supervisor working in a state-funded child guidance clinic along with child development specialists, psychologists, and social workers. She, the PT, worked as a faculty member on the health sciences center campus of a highly respected state-funded university. He, the SLP, worked primarily with children from 2 to 8 years of age to conduct comprehensive speech-language evaluations and then remediate identified articulation and language disorders within a clinic-based setting. Parents usually waited in the reception area while he worked directly with the children. Following each session, he discussed the progress he had made with the child during the visit and provided worksheets for practice as part of the home program that he had carefully designed.

Little did he know that only a few years earlier, the Education of the Handicapped Act Amendments of 1986 (PL 99-457) had passed Congress and created the Part H early intervention program, now referred to as Part C of the Individuals with Disabilities Education Act (IDEA; PL 108-446). Since that time, the state had been working to create its own legislation to ensure that all eligible children from birth to 3 years of age with a developmental delay or a diagnosed syndrome or condition would receive comprehensive supports that were based on Part C of IDEA. State staff were working quickly, but thoughtfully, to create a system to provide these federally and state-mandated services and supports as envisioned by those who testified to Congress and wished to see these supports in place nationwide.

In the fall of 1989, the SLP became the first SLP in the state to start providing services under these new federal and state laws. He was not enthusiastic when he was informed that his services were to be provided in the children's "natural environments," meaning that he would be going to their homes to provide services and would be working with a team of other professionals that would now include PTs and occupational therapists (OTs).

The PT's responsibilities included teaching undergraduate physical therapy and occupational therapy students. One of her job duties was to give a portion of her time to the state agencies that were responsible for developing the Part C early intervention program across the state. She was to work on one of the newly formed teams and to train other therapists and educators to provide the services and supports in a manner that was consistent with state and federal regulations.

He, the SLP, first encountered her, the PT, as she dashed into the new team's meeting—late—wearing overalls that were short enough in the legs to show her creatively colorful stockings, over which she wore combat-style boots. In her ears she wore mismatched earrings, one of which was a peace sign. All of the seats in the meeting room had already been taken, so she plopped on the floor and began rummaging through a canvas tote bag that had a conference name and the year 1985 emblazoned on the side, looking for an evaluation that she had recently written of a child who she claimed was eligible for services. Dressed in a freshly starched shirt, sharply creased dress slacks, patterned socks, silk club tie, and wingtip shoes, he watched as she ran back out to her car to retrieve the report, which was actually in a similar tote bag that had a different color and conference name. She proceeded to try to smooth the wrinkles out of the report and declared the child's eligibility.

As the meeting progressed, the PT and SLP presented the work they had done with different families in the families' homes. Each felt somewhat frustrated by the compounding factors that were present in the homes and that appeared to impede their therapy sessions. These factors had probably existed when the therapy had been done in the clinic, but they had not kept the SLP and PT from successfully completing their clinic-based sessions. They found it equally disconcerting, although it was not completely different from their previous experience, that parents rarely found the time to practice the activities and exercises that they were supposed to do between therapy sessions. So in that moment across a somewhat crowded room, this unlikely and clearly mismatched twosome identified a common and compelling mission: to figure out how to make home visitation in early intervention work. It was, after all, the law, and perhaps even more important, neither of them could stand the thought of failure. They shared a driving need to get interventions right for the children and families who they were being paid to serve.

They began by searching the research and other literature from their own disciplines' perspectives. Next, they delved into the fields of early childhood and early childhood special education to ascertain how to provide early intervention services in home and community environments. They also wanted to come up with a plan to work closely with the adults in the children's lives to ensure that they understood how to support child learning when the PT or SLP was not present. This book summarizes the part of their collective journey that was related to interaction with the adults in young children's lives for optimum success.

In their literature search, both the PT and the SLP found several references which recommended that therapists or educators in early intervention serve as coaches to important adults in young children's lives. The references inspired them to develop an operational definition, characteristics of the practice, and the steps or process one would use to coach a parent or other important person in a child's life. Their initial purpose in using coaching was to build the adult's capacity to support child participation and learning beyond that in everyday life.

Coaching is most commonly associated with its use in athletic settings, in which the coach instructs and motivates the athletes and calls the plays that they should implement. Increasingly, however, the concept of coaching is being used more broadly in business, self-help, education, early childhood, and early literacy environments. Coaching emerged as an accepted practice in the development and supervision of educators in the 1980s (Ackland, 1991; Brandt, 1987; Joyce & Showers, 2002). Subsequently, coaching has continued to be used successfully in the fields of early childhood education (Peterson, Luze, Eshbaugh, Jeon, & Kantz, 2007); elementary, middle school, and high school education and school administration (Delany & Arredondo, 1998; Kohler, Crilley, Shearer, & Good, 1997; Kohler, McCullough, & Buchan, 1995; Munro & Elliott, 1987; Phillips & Glickman, 1991; Roberts, 1991; Sparks, 1986); and special education (Kohler et al., 1997; Miller, 1994; Miller, Harris, & Watanabe, 1991). Coaching has been used extensively in preservice preparation programs for special and general educators (Cegelka, Fitch, & Alvarado, 2001; Kurtts & Levin, 2000;

Morgan, Gustafson, Hudson, & Salzberg, 1992) and in medicine (Homa et al., 2008; Sekerka & Chao, 2003). Within these contexts, coaching is a relationship-based process that is used to improve existing skills, develop new skills, and build the competence and confidence of the coachee (the individual who is being coached) to achieve desired or intended outcomes (Ellinger, Hamlin, & Beattie, 2008; Hanft, Rush, & Shelden, 2004).

No commonly agreed upon definition of coaching exists for purposes other than athletics (Berg & Karlsen, 2007; Ives, 2008). The International Coach Federation (ICF) is a professional organization that was formed to establish and maintain standards for coaches across all types of coaching (e.g., executive coaching, leadership coaching, life coaching) and to advance the practice of coaching. The ICF defines coaching as "an ongoing relationship which focuses on coaches taking action toward the realization of their visions, goals or desires. Coaching uses a process of inquiry and personal discovery to build the coachee's level of awareness and responsibility and provides the coachee with structure, support, and feedback" (ICF, n.d.).

Current Definitions of Coaching in the Literature

"Coaching is a helping and facilitative process that enables individuals, groups/teams and organizations to acquire new skills, to improve existing skills, competence and performance, and to enhance their personal effectiveness or personal development or personal growth" (Ellinger et al., 2008, p. 4).

"Coaching is helping people increase their sense of self-direction, self-esteem, efficacy and achievement" (Cox & Ledgerwood, 2003, p. 4).

Coaching is "the process of challenging and supporting a person or a team to develop ways of being and ways of learning" (Berg & Karlsen, 2007, p. 4).

"A literacy coach is one who helps the teachers to recognize what they know and can do, assists the teachers as they strengthen their ability to make more effective use of what they know and do, and supports teachers as they learn more and do more" (Toll, 2005, p. 4).

More specifically, the use of coaching in early childhood has been described by special educators, OTs, PTs, and SLPs as a practice to support families of children with disabilities, as well as to support practitioners, in early childhood programs. Campbell (1997), a pediatric PT, suggested that the early intervention practitioner should be a *coach* rather than a direct therapy provider. Hanft and Pilkington, OTs, encouraged early childhood practitioners to reconsider their role and "to move to a different position alongside a parent as a *coach* rather than lead player" (2000, p. 2). Such a move allows more opportunities to promote child development and learning than does direct intervention by the therapist or educator. Rush (2000), an SLP, noted that a practitioner-as-coach approach provides the parent with the necessary supports to improve the child's skills and abilities. Dinnebeil, McInerney, Roth, and Ramasway examined the role of itinerant early childhood special education teachers and concluded that they "should be prepared to act not simply as consultants to early childhood teachers but as *coaches*" (2001, p. 42). By acting as coaches, early childhood special education teachers can offer a more structured system for jointly planning new learning, modeling effective practices, and engaging in feedback.

PURPOSE OF COACHING

Coaching is used to acknowledge and perhaps improve existing knowledge and practices, develop new skills, and promote continuous self-assessment and learning on the part of the coachee. The role of the coach is to provide a supportive and encouraging environment in which the coach and coachee jointly examine and reflect on current practices, apply new skills and competencies with feedback, and problem solve challenging situations. The coach's ultimate goal is sustained performance in which the coachee has the competence and confidence to engage in self-reflection, self-correction, and the generalization of new skills and strategies to other situations as appropriate (Flaherty, 1999; Kinlaw, 1999). Effective coaching can set the stage for lifelong learning on the part of the coachee.

Some individuals believe that coaching parents, teachers, colleagues, and others is similar to the type of coaching used in sports, in which the athletic coach trains the athletes, calls the plays, motivates the athletes, and helps the athletes evaluate their performance so that they can improve. The type of coaching described in this book, however, is used to support the coachee in specific ways that are related to his or her goals, not to make the person do what the *coach* wants or believes that the coachee should do. Support includes 1) helping the coachee become aware of and analyze current knowledge and performance, 2) developing alternatives and a plan for improved knowledge and performance with assistance as needed from the coach, and 3) helping the coachee conduct a self-evaluation of his or her own knowledge and performance, with feedback from the coach as needed, until the coachee is competent and confident that he or she can achieve personal goals. If the knowledge or performance of the coachee is contrary to the research on a particular topic, the coach must assist the coachee in accessing the research-based information and in analyzing his or her knowledge and performance in light of the information, in order to make an informed decision about any intended future actions.

RECIPIENTS OF COACHING

Anyone who desires knowledge, skills, or development and who enters into a coaching relationship willingly without being coaxed or coerced can be a recipient of coaching. In early intervention programs, parents and other primary care providers are often considered the only possible recipients of coaching. Child care providers, early childhood teachers, or early intervention team members may also benefit from coaching relationships. In early literacy programs, the classroom teachers typically are considered to be the primary beneficiaries of coaching, but parents, teacher assistants, principals, program directors, and other administrators may be interested in a coaching relationship in order to better support the classroom teacher. Supervisors may find that supervisees respond more positively and productively to a coaching relationship than to feedback given in the hierarchical format of most supervisor–supervisee interactions. Preservice students who are engaged in practicum or internship experiences may find coaching particularly helpful as they begin to apply their recently learned knowledge and skills.

Parents and Caregivers

Coaching of parents can promote their confidence and competence in supporting child learning and development. When coaching is used with parents, the role of the coach is to identify the parents' priorities for their child's development, determine what they already know and are doing in relation to their child's development, share new information and ideas, and then work together to support the child's participation and expression of interest within everyday activity settings to provide opportunities for learning. Coaching is also useful to support parents in identifying, accessing, and evaluating needed resources for their child and family.

Teachers

Coaching can be used with teachers in child care settings, preschools, early childhood intervention programs, Early Head Start, Head Start, early literacy programs, schools, and other settings. Within these environments, coaching may be used as follow-up to professional development activities to help teachers incorporate new skills into their current teaching practices. It may also be used to support teachers whose classes include students who have individualized family service plans or individualized education programs. Teachers may also serve as coaches to other teachers and adults, rather than focusing only on teacher–child interactions. Chapter 8 provides detailed information about coaching teachers to incorporate new skills, such as an early literacy curriculum, into their teaching practices and to foster the learning of children with disabilities. Chapter 9 describes how coaching can be used as part of professional development activities to help teachers and other learners immediately apply newly learned information within the context of their classroom activities and teaching practices.

Colleagues

For the purposes of this book, *colleagues* are defined as other professionals in the work setting or on early intervention teams who provide related services in educational settings. Colleagues may include, but may not necessarily be limited to, OTs, PTs, SLPs, psychologists, social workers, teachers, nurses, nutritionists, and audiologists. Coaching can help colleagues develop and use new knowledge and skills that are related to a specific practice or as a follow-up to a professional development opportunity. Coaching may also be the preferred interaction style for assisting a colleague who is working with a particular child or family situation. Coaching is a viable option any time a colleague wants to build his or her knowledge and skills regarding a particular issue.

Supervisees and Mentees

Chapter 4 will define the differences between coaching and other forms of adult interaction, including supervision and mentoring. Although the overall purposes of supervision and mentoring differ from the purpose of coaching, supervisors and mentors may use a coaching interaction style with supervisees and mentees to promote their learning and problem solving so that they may build their capacity and decrease dependence on the supervisor or mentor.

Students

Coaching may be used with university students who are completing their practicum or internship requirements in a school, an early intervention program, or some other educational setting. When coaching is used with students, the students must compare what they have learned in their university coursework with what they now see or do in practice. Coaching provides the opportunity for the students to identify gaps in their knowledge and skills, develop plans to obtain the necessary knowledge and skills, begin to apply their new skills to real-life contexts, reflect on how the skills worked, and plan for continuous improvement of those abilities.

COACHING APPROACHES

Various approaches to coaching have conflicting paradigms, depending on the intent of the coach and coachee (Ives, 2008). Some of the approaches described in the literature are behavioral (Forunies, 2000; Peterson, 2006), humanistic (Stober, 2006; Whitmore, 2002), cognitive (Auerbach, 2006; Costa & Garmston, 1994), goal focused (Grant, 2006), and adult learning (Cox, 2006). A behavioral or behavior-based approach focuses on creating change and promoting learning within the context of real-life activities. Such an approach promotes the coachee's ability to determine what to do differently in order to achieve the intended outcomes (Berg & Karlsen, 2007; Ives, 2008). On the basis of a review of the literature related to behavioral coaching, Berg and Karlsen indicated that the techniques used include modeling, feedback, reinforcement, and self-management. They noted that the humanistic approach to coaching relies on the coachee's desire to reach the intended goals. The coach is a facilitator and expert on the process of coaching, rather than on the subject matter that is being coached. The coaching relationship is central to this approach in order to assist the coachee in achieving self-actualization (Ives, 2008; Stober, 2006). Cognitive coaching centers on the thoughts that are related to perceptions, attitudes, and beliefs of the coachee and assists the coachee in overcoming challenges that may limit success (Ives, 2008). Goal-oriented coaching involves helping the coachee to develop goals and action plans that are necessary to improve overall performance (Grant, 2006; Ives, 2008). An adult learning approach to coaching builds on the adult learning theories of Knowles, Holton, and Swanson (1998), Kolb (1984), and others. It is intended for use with goal-focused, self-directed learners to help them reflect on previous knowledge and experiences and to address what is happening in current real-life situations (Ives, 2008).

In a highly referenced analysis of the types of coaching, Ackland (1991) divided coaching into two basic forms: coaching by experts and reciprocal peer coaching. As defined by Ackland, experts are individuals with particular areas of knowledge and skills who have been trained specifically to provide feedback and support to others. In contrast, reciprocal peer coaching involves two individuals observing and coaching each other on targeted skills. The most common type of coaching used in the fields of early intervention, early childhood, and early literacy is expert coaching. In this approach to coaching, an individual with knowledge and skills in a particular area applies a coaching interaction style to support the coachee in recognizing what he or she already knows and then builds on the previous knowledge or skills by sharing new information and developing new skills that are based on the coach's knowledge and experience.

Expert Coaching

As an example of expert coaching, suppose that a PT in an early intervention program has expertise in motor development, motor learning, and assistive technology that can support the motor development of young children. Suppose also that this therapist has specialized knowledge in typical child development and parenting supports. Finally, suppose that the PT serves as a coach to the mother of a 10-month-old child with Down syndrome who wants the child to sit in his high chair and join the family for meals. Then the role of the PT when she is using a coaching interaction style is to find out what the mother has tried with regard to having the child sit in the high chair and how those efforts have worked. Using this information as a starting point, the PT asks the mother to show how she puts the child in the high chair. The therapist and parent then analyze the child's positioning in the high chair and jointly brainstorm options for improvement. In this way, the PT is using and sharing her expertise (e.g., knowledge of muscle tone, positioning, movement, coordination necessary for self-feeding at meals) and, at the same time, is acknowledging and building on what the parent knows, is doing, and sees when the child is in the high chair. Together, they develop a joint plan to have the child in the high chair when the PT is not present at meals.

Similarly, an early literacy coach is an expert coach who has knowledge of classroom environmental arrangements, materials, teaching practices, and curricula that promote the early literacy development of children in the classroom. The early literacy coach shares his or her knowledge and skills by using a coaching interaction style with the classroom teacher. For example, the early literacy coach and teacher may analyze the learning centers in the classroom to determine opportunities for children's print awareness, starting with what the teacher knows about print awareness and strategies for promoting this understanding among the children. The early literacy coach and teacher then jointly generate alternatives to identify the most effective options and research-based strategies for promoting print awareness in the classroom, after which they develop a joint plan for implementing those strategies.

Reciprocal Peer Coaching

In a peer coaching situation, both individuals have similar knowledge and skills; therefore, they work together to determine and use what they know or are learning. For example, peer coaching may be implemented following two teachers' participation in an introductory early literacy workshop provided as a staff development opportunity at their school. Presumably, both teachers had general knowledge of the importance of early literacy learning opportunities for young children from their university training and from a few workshops at conferences they attended after graduation. The teachers were energized by the early literacy workshop and immediately wanted to implement some of what they had learned. They mutually decided to focus on print awareness, so they started by analyzing how their classroom learning centers promoted that skill. They shared their assessment of each other's classrooms. They used a coaching interaction style to generate ideas for improvement on the basis of what they had learned from the workshop and to develop action plans for implementation. In order to extend their learning beyond the content presented in the workshop, both had to explore other resources related to early literacy, share the new information with each other, and work together to apply the information to their classrooms.

The Coaching Approach Used in This Book

As described in this book, coaching uses an expert-based approach (Ackland, 1991) rather than a peer-to-peer approach. It also uses a contextual model (Stober & Grant, 2006) to guide the coaching process with elements of both goal-oriented (Ives, 2008) and adult-learning (Cox, 2006) coaching approaches. In this expert approach, whether coaching parents, other care providers, or colleagues, the coach is considered to be an expert because he or she has professional experience and specific knowledge and skills related to the discipline. In this approach, the recipient of coaching becomes involved in the coaching relationship because of a recognized need

Coaching as Defined in This Book

Approach: expert based

Model: Contextual with elements of goal-oriented and adult learning for the knowledge, skills, and experience of the coach. As part of the adult-learning approach to coaching, the person who will receive coaching support "is perceived to be a mature, motivated, and equal participant in a learning relationship with a facilitator (coach) whose role is to aid the learner in the achievement of his or her primarily self-determined learning objectives" (Cox, 2006, p. 195).

As defined by Stober and Grant (2006), the contextual model of coaching has seven thematic factors: 1) a specific outcome or goal toward which both the coach and coachee are working, 2) a rationale for how coaching fits the coachee's needs and particular situation, 3) a procedure that is based on the rationale and that requires the active participation of both the coach and coachee, 4) a meaningful relationship between the coach and coachee, 5) a collaborative working alliance that focuses specifically on the development of the coachee, 6) the coachee's ability and readiness to change, and 7) the coach's ability and readiness to help the coachee make the desired changes. Seven key principles facilitate the process of change and development within the contextual model: collaboration, accountability, awareness, responsibility, commitment, action, and results. In the contextual model of coaching that is described in this book, the interaction is based on a collaborative relationship between the coach and coachee in which the coachee maintains a certain degree of accountability to the coach. This accountability should be seen, not in a negative way, but rather as a means for the coach to support the coachee in fulfilling the joint action plans that are necessary to help the coachee achieve his or her desired outcome. As described in Chapter 5, a role of the coach is to help the coachee become aware of the current situation through reflective questioning, observation, and feedback, and then to develop alternatives for change (i.e., a plan). The responsibility for fully implementing the alternatives and action that will result in the desired changes lies with the coachee, with the level of support needed from the coach. The process requires the coachee to make an ongoing commitment to move forward. The entire process is focused on the results—that is, the intended outcome for the coachee.

Evidence-Based Definition of Coaching

The definition of coaching used in this book differs from previous descriptions found in the business and education literature. It focuses on the operationalization of the relationship between coaching practices and the intended consequences as well as on the processes used to produce the observed changes (Dunst, Trivette, & Cutspec, 2002). Based on a synthesis of research on coaching practices (see Chapter 2) and drawing from the theories and practices of the adult-learning, behavioral, and goal-focused approaches to coaching, the practice of coaching may be defined as follows:

> An adult learning strategy in which the coach promotes the learner's (coachee's) ability to reflect on his or her actions as a means to determine the effectiveness of an action or practice and develop a plan for refinement and use of the action in immediate and future situations.

In addition to simply knowing the definition, professionals in the field must understand the characteristics of a practice in order to know what to do to achieve the desired effect. The coaching research synthesis in Chapter 2 was guided by a process that focused on the extent to which the specific characteristics of the practices are related to differences in their outcomes or consequences (Dunst et al., 2002). More specifically, the research synthesis examined the characteristics of coaching that were related to variations in the use of newly learned practices or the improvement of existing skills. Although the steps in the coaching process vary (Doyle, 1999; Flaherty, 1999; Hanft et al., 2004; Kinlaw, 1999), the coaching research literature suggests that coaching has five practice characteristics that lead to intended outcomes: 1) joint planning, 2) observation, 3) action/practice, 4) reflection, and 5) feedback. The definitions in Box 1.3 are based on descriptions in the coaching research literature and highlight the characteristics that are used to improve the coachee's existing abilities, develop new skills, and deepen his or her understanding of evidence-based practices.

TEN KEY ELEMENTS OF COACHING IN EARLY CHILDHOOD

The key elements of coaching further elaborate on the theoretical and conceptual principles that serve as the foundation for the practice and for the approaches to coaching that are used. As defined, explained, and illustrated through the examples in this text, coaching is based on 10 key elements of the practice as used in early childhood education. Coaching should be

1. *Consistent with the principles of adult learning.* The National Research Council (NRC; Donovan, Bransford, & Pellegrino, 1999) published a research synthesis on human learning and its implications for teaching. The research included in the NRC report indicated that, in order for a learner to gain deep knowledge of a particular content area, he or she must develop an understanding of how the knowledge may be used in a specific context and how it may be generalized to other situations (Bransford, Brown, & Cocking, 2000).

Definitions of the Five Key Characteristics of Coaching

Joint planning	Agreement by the coach and coachee on the actions they will take or the opportunities to practice between coaching visits
Observation	Examination of another person's actions or practices to be used to develop new skills, strategies, or ideas
Action	Spontaneous or planned events that occur within the context of a real-life situation that provide the coachee with opportunities to practice, refine, or analyze new or existing skills
Reflection	Analysis of existing strategies to determine how the strategies are consistent with evidence-based practices and how they may need to be implemented without change or modified to obtain the intended outcome(s)
Feedback	Information provided by the coach that is based on his or her direct observations of the coachee, actions reported by the coachee, or information shared by the coachee and that is designed to expand the coachee's current level of understanding about a specific evidence-based practice or to affirm the coachee's thoughts or actions related to the intended outcomes

---

2. *Capacity building.* Coaching builds the knowledge, skills, and abilities (i.e., capacity) of the coachee to be able to function without the ongoing support of the coach. Rather than creating dependency, the coach helps the coachee discover what he or she already knows and thus can do, shares new information and ideas, assists the coachee with developing the tools that are necessary to achieve the desired outcomes, and helps the coachee generalize the reflections and resulting actions to new and different situations. Capacity building of the coachee by the coach also ensures that the coach can replicate the process

used to identify the actions to be taken and the means for evaluating their effectiveness. The benefits of a capacity-building process are acquisition and use of new knowledge and skills as well as self-attribution related to the coachee's role in realizing the intended effects (Wilson, Holbert, & Sexton, 2006).

3. *Nondirective.* Flaherty noted that coaching is "not telling people what to do, [but] giving them a chance to examine what they are doing in light of their intentions" (1999, p. xii). This notion of nondirectiveness can be quite controversial in the coaching literature (Stober & Grant, 2006) and sometimes is considered to be synonymous with self-discovery (Trivette, Dunst, Hamby, & O'Herin, 2009). In fact, the coaching literature includes a range of nondirectiveness, from total self-discovery by the coachee (i.e., "ask, don't tell"; Whitmore, 2002) to the provision of direct feedback to the coachee without asking him or her to reflect and consider possible reasons or options (Goldsmith, 2000). The approach to coaching described in this text puts the element of nondirectiveness on a continuum, with instruction on one end, self-discovery on the opposite end, and nondirective interaction in the middle. Effective coaching consists of asking the right questions at the right time (Berg & Karlsen, 2007) to promote thinking (i.e., reflection) so that the coachee will become aware of and analyze what he or she wants to have happen, what he or she is currently doing that is supporting or inhibiting that goal, and what possible alternatives will result in achieving the goal. As a nondirective approach (Ackland, 1991), coaching does not mean that the coach can never share information with the coachee and must wait for the coachee's self-discovery; rather, the key to effective coaching is knowing when, how, and why questions are asked, information or feedback is shared, and a form of more directive instruction is used.

An effective coach knows how and when to ask questions, when to allow for self-discovery on the part of the coachee, and when to share information and expertise without coming across as tendentious or controlling (Stober & Grant, 2006). Clearly, if the coachee does not have the most basic knowledge of the content area as a foundation on which to coach, then the coach may need to share information or provide more direct supports. If, however, the coachee has even the slightest amount of knowledge or skill, then the coach will use this knowledge as a basis for building self-awareness and confidence. Accordingly, the coach may scaffold additional information and use the amount of feedback and instruction that is required to build the level of competence necessary for the coachee to reach the desired outcomes and continue to develop. As the coachee becomes more competent and confident in the use of the tools and strategies that will aid in acquiring knowledge, building analytical skills, generating alternatives, planning actions, and evaluating the effectiveness of a plan, the coach can reduce his or her involvement. Individuals who have previous experience as teachers or instructors tend to rely on or fall back into a directive mode when they are challenged by a particular situation, when their coaching skills are not yet fully developed, when they feel the need to prove what they know, or when they are trying to reassure themselves that they are being helpful to the coachee (Stober & Grant, 2006).

4. *Goal oriented.* Coaching is an interaction style used to achieve individual goals or outcomes that are identified by the coachee and that are related to desired knowledge or skills (Ives, 2008; Reiss, 2007). The outcomes of the coaching interaction are not arbitrary; they are clearly stated from the beginning of the coaching relationship. Although goals may change over time, their achievement by the coachee is the purpose of the coaching relationship. The relationship between the coach and coachee is defined by the coachee's goals, which may be the factor that determines who serves as the coach. If, for example,

the coachee needs certain information or intends to develop specific skills in a given area, then he or she may identify a person who possesses the requisite knowledge and skills to serve as his or her coach.

5. *Solution focused.* Coaching is focused on determining the present and creating the future rather than on analyzing the past (Ives, 2008). If coaching is related to a specific problem or problem area, the purpose of using a coaching approach is to identify possible solutions that can be implemented immediately, instead of concentrating on the problem itself as in traditional counseling or psychotherapy (Ives, 2008). Within the context of coaching, the coach and coachee work together to identify strategies and options to reach the intended goals. As a result, coaching tends to be more short term than counseling or psychotherapy.

6. *Performance based.* Coaching is about developing people on purpose (Doyle, 1999). The focus of coaching is the coachee's performance, application of knowledge gained, and demonstration of skills resulting from the coaching process (Flaherty, 1999; Kinlaw, 1999; Reiss, 2007). Performance is measured in terms of growth, development, and learning over time, relative to the coachee's desired outcomes. Coaching that focuses on performance is action oriented rather than driven by emotions or feelings (Ives, 2008). Coaching requires the coachee to actively participate and be engaged in order for learning and behavioral change to occur.

7. *Reflective.* Coaching is a reflective process (Jackson, 2004). Reflection is looking back in order to look forward (Daniels, 2002). It is a means of reaching a deeper understanding of what a person already knows and is doing. It can also discover what modifications or new knowledge and skills might be necessary in current and future situations to obtain a desired outcome. Reflection, active participation, and engagement on the part of the person being coached are used both to strengthen that person's competence with regard to what he or she can do and to build on current knowledge or skills in order to acquire new ideas and actions. As a result, the person's confidence is enhanced, causing him or her to continue to do what works, to try new possibilities, and to evaluate the effectiveness of all these actions. Reflection is a valuable tool for adult learners and can easily be taught (Showers & Joyce, 1996).

8. *Collaborative.* Coaching is a partnership and a reciprocal process in which both the coach and coachee bring knowledge and abilities to the relationship (Hanft et al., 2004). The coach must learn what the coachee knows, understands, and is doing, including his or her preconceived knowledge about coaching and ideas for change, and how potential changes might be applied and might affect the coachee's current situation. The coachee may learn the coach's processes for reflecting upon and generating ideas, developing resources, solving problems, and planning actions, in addition to gaining any specialized knowledge that the coach provides in the form of feedback. Coaching cannot be based on the coach's power over the coachee; in other words, it cannot be a hierarchical relationship in which the coachee implements actions due to directives, intimidation, or a need to satisfy or please the coach.

9. *Context driven.* Coaching is a relationship that is built on the achievement of goals related to functional activities, beginning with the current situation experienced by the coachee. The content of coaching is never separated from the context in which targeted performance and/or jointly identified solutions are used. The act of coaching includes observations and

actions by the coach and the coachee in current situations related to the coaching goals, where the identified solutions may be tried and joint plans carried out. Coaching relates to immediate actions and adaptations within and across contexts, rather than conversations about "what ifs" or the future.

10. *As hands-on as it needs to be.* Some authors (Parsloe & Wray, 2000; Whitmore, 2002) suggest that coaching be "hands-off" and advise relying totally on a self-instruction approach. Especially in early coaching interactions, however, the role of the coach may need to be more hands-on. The coach may assist the coachee in identifying possible options or external resources, share information to build deep factual knowledge on the topic, model an action for the coachee, and provide feedback on the coachee's actions following the coachee's self-reflections (Berg & Karlsen, 2007). As the coachee becomes more confident and competent in his or her performance, the coach's role becomes more focused on process than content (Ives, 2008). That is, the coach continues to prompt the coachee to reflect on and analyze ideas, consider alternatives, and plan actions. Over time, feedback by the coach becomes more affirmative and less informational.

ORGANIZATION OF THIS BOOK

This book is intended to be a working guide for how to operationalize the practice of coaching in early childhood settings. Each chapter, therefore, features learning tools to assist the reader in applying the chapter's content to real-life contexts. *Coaching scenarios* are woven into chapters to illustrate and provide examples for how individual characteristics or elements of the practices described might look when implemented. Mirroring both the coaching characteristics explained in the text and the characteristics of adult learning provides opportunities throughout the book for readers to *reflect*, *observe*, and *practice*. Opportunities for reflection include thinking about current or future practices and applying or using the information learned within a particular chapter or section of a chapter to build on one's current knowledge and skills. Observation opportunities provide a time to observe one's own practices or the practices of others regarding a specific characteristic or element of coaching. The practice opportunities provided throughout each chapter include ideas for how to put information into action by applying what is being learned to a real-life context. *Remember* notations within each chapter or chapter section contain important elements of coaching practices that are necessary for adding to or building one's own conceptual and operational frameworks for coaching.

Terminology Used in This Book

The Early Childhood Coaching Handbook contains terminology that may not be familiar to the reader or may be defined by different readers in different ways. To ensure a common understanding of the terminology used, the authors have provided definitions of some of the terms used throughout the text.

Caregiver—Any individual who cares for and is important in the life of a child, including, but not limited to, a grandparent, aunt, uncle, family friend, baby sitter, and nanny.

Child care provider—An individual who works in a child care center or family child care home.

Coach—The person using the coaching characteristics to support the learning and development of another individual to achieve a desired or intended outcome.

Coachee—The individual who has a desired outcome and who receives the support of someone serving in a coaching role.

Early intervention practitioner—An individual who works in an early intervention program and who supports a coachee by using the coaching practices. Early intervention practitioners may include, but are not limited to, early childhood educators, early childhood special educators, nurses, nutritionists, OTs, PTs, psychologists, service coordinators, social workers, and SLPs.

Literacy coach—An individual who usually has a background in education, has specialized knowledge and experience in the area of literacy, and is responsible for providing support to teachers related to the classroom environment and teaching strategies that promote the literacy development of the students in the teachers' classrooms.

Parent—An individual who is directly responsible for the care of his or her biological, adopted, or foster children.

Teacher—In this book, an individual who teaches in an infant–toddler, preschool, kindergarten, or elementary school classroom.

CONCLUSION

The purpose of this book is to define coaching and assist the reader in applying the research-based characteristics of coaching practices in early childhood contexts. The text describes an expert-based, rather than a peer-to-peer, approach to coaching and a contextual coaching model that includes elements of both goal-oriented and adult-learning models. Ten key elements of coaching further elaborate on how it may be implemented in early childhood contexts: Coaching should be consistent with adult-learning and capacity-building research, as well as nondirective, goal oriented, solution focused, performance based, reflective, collaborative, context driven, and as hands-on as it needs to be. Coaching may be used across early childhood settings and with all the important people who support children's learning and development within those settings.

RESOURCES

Bransford, J.D., Brown, A.L., & Cocking, R.R. (Eds.). (2000). *How people learn: Brain, mind, experience, and school.* Washington, DC: National Academies Press.

This report provides the findings of a 2-year review of the research on how both children and adults learn and the implications of the findings for teachers and teaching.

Ives, Y. (2008). What is coaching? An exploration of conflicting paradigms. *International Journal of Evidence Based Coaching and Mentoring, 6*(2), 100–113.

This article describes various coaching approaches that differ in definition and purpose.

Reiss, K. (2007). *Leadership coaching for educators.* Thousand Oaks, CA: Corwin Press.

This text provides the background, competencies, tools, and techniques for developing and implementing a successful coaching program for teachers.

The International Coach Federation: http://www.coachfederation.org/

The International Coach Federation is an organization for professional coaches. The website provides core competencies for professional coaches as well as research, resources, and other pertinent information.

Chapter 2

Research Foundations of Coaching

Coaching is an adult learning strategy that is used to support the coachee in identifying, obtaining, and mobilizing the knowledge and skills necessary to achieve an intended outcome. In order for coaching to be effective, however, a person must move beyond the *term* and *definition* to determine the *characteristics* of the practice that when put into practice lead to the intended consequences. The characteristics of effective coaching that are described in this book were obtained from a review of available research. The research indicates that coaching for the purpose of learning and capacity building is based on five practice characteristics. The purpose of this chapter is to review previous syntheses and meta-analyses of the research on coaching. In addition, it will examine the research that documents the use of the practice-based characteristics of coaching and demonstrates the extent to which coaching is effective for promoting and supporting adult learners' use of new practices or improvement of existing skills.

OVERVIEW OF RESEARCH ON COACHING

The coaching models used in most of the programs that have been studied have focused on solving specific problems, learning new skills, and refining existing skills (Joyce & Showers, 1982). Research studies have documented the successful use of coaching by general educators and administrators (Bruce & Ross, 2008; Delany & Arredondo, 1998; Kohler, Crilley, Shearer, & Good, 1997; Kohler, McCullough, & Buchan, 1995; Munro & Elliott, 1987; Phillips & Glickman, 1991; Roberts, 1991; Sparks, 1986; Stichter, Lewis, Richter, Johnson, & Bradley, 2006; Zwart, Wubbels, Bohuis, & Bergen, 2008). Research has also documented coaching by special educators for various purposes (Kohler et al., 1997; Miller, 1994; Miller, Harris, & Watanabe, 1991) and as a strategy to promote collaboration between special and general educators (Gerston, Morvant, & Brengelman, 1995; Hasbrouck & Christen, 1997; Tschantz & Vail, 2000). Studies also indicate that coaching has been found effective in preservice preparation programs for special and general educators (Cegelka, Fitch, & Alvarado, 2001; Kurtts & Levin, 2000; Morgan, Gustafson, Hudson, & Salzberg, 1992). Coaching is an effective strategy for supporting the learning of parents of young children and teachers in early childhood programs (Hendrickson, Gardner, Kaiser, & Riley, 1993; Kohler et al., 1995; Marchant & Young, 2001; Miller, 1994; Peterson, Luze, Eshbaugh, Jeon, & Kantz, 2007; Shanley & Niec, 2010). Coaching has also been used successfully for professional development and program improvement with physicians (Homa et al., 2008; Sekerka & Chao, 2003).

RESEARCH REVIEWS, SYNTHESES, AND META-ANALYSES ON COACHING

Research on the effectiveness and use of coaching dates back over 2 decades. Due to the large number and varying type and focus of studies that have been completed over time, different authors have reviewed and/or synthesized the outcomes of previous research for various purposes. These purposes include determination of the effectiveness of coaching to support adult learning, facilitate transfer of new knowledge and skills to real-life settings, and identify the characteristics of effective coaching. Rather than providing detailed descriptions of coaching studies completed to date, the discussion that follows will present an overview of previously conducted reviews and syntheses of the research.

In 1991, Ackland reviewed 29 studies of peer and expert coaching conducted between 1982 and 1989. He found that three characteristics were common to all effective peer coaching programs in the studies he reviewed. The first characteristic is that peer coaching was nonevaluative. That is, coaching was not intended to evaluate the coachee's performance, but rather to create a safe learning environment. The second characteristic is that peer coaching included observation that was followed by feedback. Feedback was provided in one of three ways. Sometimes the coach gathered information and shared it with the coachee, sometimes the coach and coachee worked together to analyze the data and improve performance, and sometimes the coach shared specific ideas to support the coachee related to performance improvement. The third characteristic is that peer coaching was directed toward improving instructional techniques. Much of the research on coaching up to this time focused on helping teachers learn and apply new methods for promoting student learning.

Bruce Joyce and Beverly Showers synthesized the research on staff development that included training followed by coaching as a strategy for implementing newly learned knowledge and skills (Joyce & Showers, 2002; Showers, Joyce, & Bennett, 1987). Their findings indicated that when coaching was used to support another person's learning and when it was provided in the actual context in which the newly learned knowledge and skills were to be used, almost all of the individuals studied demonstrated strong knowledge, consistent demonstration of the skills, and appropriate transfer of the knowledge and skills to the real-life context (see Chapter 9). In addition, the individuals studied were much more likely to use new skills and ideas when they received coaching as they were trying the new skills in the real-life setting.

Fixen, Naoom, Blasé, Friedman, and Wallace (2005) synthesized the research in the area of practice implementation. Implementation is defined by these authors as the specific set of activities that is intended to be used in a program to ensure fidelity to an intervention. The intervention (i.e., the known practices used by a teacher, therapist, or other professional) must be well defined in order for it to have the intended effect on the child, family, or other recipient of the intervention. Of 1,054 studies reviewed by Fixen and colleagues, 22 contained the results of experimental analyses or meta-analyses of implementation variables and were included in the synthesis. They also examined the critical functions of implementation, including training and coaching. The conclusions indicate that evidence supports the use of coaching as a strategy for effective implementation of newly learned skills and practices as part of an intervention. That is, coaching is the most useful practice to support implementation of a well-defined intervention.

In 2009, Trivette, Dunst, Hamby, and O'Herin synthesized the research on the effectiveness of four adult learning methods (accelerated learning, coaching, guided design, and just-in-time training). The authors reviewed 79 studies that included either randomized controlled trials or comparison group designs. Instead of focusing on the adult learning method itself, Trivette and colleagues examined the extent to which the characteristics of the four methods may be attributed to the learner outcomes. Findings from the research synthesis on human learning by the National Research Council (NRC; Bransford, Brown, & Cocking, 2000) were used as the framework analysis.

The purpose of the NRC synthesis of available research on learning was to identify teaching practices and environments that promote successful learning. The NRC identified three key findings from the research synthesis on human learning. First, a learner enters a learning environment with preconceived ideas about a subject matter. Accordingly, the learner may not develop an understanding of new information and skills that are being taught if his or her current understanding is not recognized and made explicit. Second, in order to develop a deeper level of understanding in a particular area, the learner must 1) have a solid base of factual knowledge, 2) understand these facts within the context of a conceptual framework, and 3) organize the information to facilitate easy recall, use, and transfer to other situations of the new knowledge. Third, the learner must acquire a metacognitive approach in which the learner assesses his or her own level of understanding, establishes learning goals, and measures progress (Bransford et al., 2000; Donovan, Bransford, & Pellegrino, 1999).

For purposes of the synthesis, Trivette and colleagues (2009) used the NRC findings to identify six adult learning method characteristics. They conducted various analyses to determine which characteristics of the adult learning methods resulted in differences in learner outcomes. "Each of the four adult learning methods was associated with positive posttest outcome differences between the experimental and control or comparison groups" (Trivette et al., 2009, p. 6). Furthermore, "the more actively involved the learners were in judging the consequences of their learning experiences (evaluate, reflection, and mastery), the stronger the relationship between the adult learning method characteristics and the study outcomes" (p. 6). In other words, coaching requires active participation of the coachee. In order to maximize the desired outcome, the coach should engage the coachee in reflective conversations that analyze current practice or performance.

In sum, results of previously conducted research reviews, syntheses, and meta-analyses found coaching to be an effective practice for promoting the use of newly learned knowledge and skills. Coaching ensures improvement of existing skills and transfer of new abilities to the actual context in which the knowledge, skills, and abilities will be used. When the characteristics of coaching practices are consistent with the research findings on how people learn, the coachee can achieve positive outcomes.

RESEARCH ON COACHING AS AN EFFECTIVE HELPGIVING STRATEGY

The mission of early childhood intervention and the purpose of effective helpgiving practices are to build the capacity of parents and other care providers, support and enhance parent confidence and competence, and assist parents and other care providers in sustained achievement of desired outcomes (Dunst & Trivette, 2009; Hanft, Rush, & Shelden, 2004; Workgroup on Principles and Practices in Natural Environments, 2007). Studies have shown that the manner in which support is provided to families makes a substantial difference in the outcomes of intervention (i.e., in whether the intervention has positive or negative consequences). In other words, "how" practitioners provide intervention opportunities and experiences for parents that are intended to influence the behavior or present levels of functioning of family members is critical and actually determines the success of the interventions used (Bandura & Locke, 2003; Dunst, Hamby, & Brookfield, 2007; Dunst & Trivette, 2009; Dunst, Trivette, & Hamby, 2006). Coaching has been described in the early childhood intervention literature as a strategy that practitioners can use to build the capacity of parents to support children's learning and to identify and obtain desired resources and supports (Campbell, 1997;

Dinnebeil, McInerney, Roth, & Ramasway, 2001; Hanft & Pilkington, 2000; Hanft et al., 2004; Rush, 2000; Shelden & Rush, 2001). A capacity-building process involves three components: 1) practitioners' support of parents' strengths and abilities to achieve desired results (Dunst & Trivette, 1996), 2) parents' recognition and use of current and new abilities to achieve preferred outcomes, and 3) parents receiving opportunities and embracing responsibility for actively working toward their desired outcomes (Wilson, Holbert, & Sexton, 2006).

Coaching in early childhood can be conceptualized as a particular type of helpgiving practice within a capacity-building model to support parents and other care providers in using existing abilities and developing new skills to attain desired life circumstances (Dunst & Trivette, 1994, 1996; Dunst, Trivette, & LaPointe, 1994; Rappaport, 1981). For example, researchers have identified two clusters of help giving that have capacity-building influences (Dunst & Trivette, 2009; Trivette & Dunst, 2007): relational helpgiving and participatory helpgiving. Relational helpgiving includes practices and characteristics that promote positive relationships with the coachee (i.e., trust, effective communication, respect, empathy), whereas participatory helpgiving strategies demonstrate flexibility, responsiveness, and individualization. Research indicates that in order to achieve desired outcomes, both types of helpgiving need to be present in the interventions that are used to support family members of young children (Dunst & Trivette, 2009; Trivette & Dunst, 2007). Coaching is a strategy that supports both relational and participatory helpgiving. Coaches use relational helpgiving as they develop and sustain a partnership with the coachee. Participatory helpgiving characteristics are inherent in the coaching process: identifying parent and care provider priorities for support; actively engaging the parent in demonstrating, developing, and evaluating desired skills and/or resources; and promoting ongoing opportunities for continued growth and development (see Chapter 3 for more details).

RESEARCH DELINEATING THE COACHING CHARACTERISTICS

It is necessary to understand the characteristics of a practice or, as Fixen and colleagues (2005) described, a set of specific activities to implement a program, in order to inform a practitioner how to achieve the desired effect or outcome. The research reviews, syntheses, and meta-analyses that we have highlighted describe general characteristics of coaching (Ackland, 1991; Joyce & Showers, 2002; Showers et al., 1987), implementation research (Fixen et al., 2005), and adult learning methods (Trivette et al., 2009). None of these studies, however, examined the specific characteristics of coaching that were used to operationalize the practice and that can be attributed to positive learner outcomes related to variations in the use of newly learned practices or improvement of existing skills.

The authors conducted an extensive review of coaching research in order to identify the evidence-based characteristics of coaching across fields (i.e., education, medicine, business, professional development) and types of individuals (i.e., administrators, early intervention practitioners, general education teachers, special education teachers, parents, physicians, students) who engaged in coaching as a strategy for professional or personal growth. The review included relevant studies of coaching published between 1980 and 2010. It is not intended to serve as a comprehensive research synthesis on the efficacy of coaching. Rather, the intent was to examine the extent to which the characteristics of the practice of coaching were used for the purpose of learning new practices or improving the use of existing skills, resulting in positive learner outcomes as defined by research. The following search descriptors were used: peer coaching, expert coaching, reciprocal coaching, technical coaching, interactive coaching, collegial coaching, coaching and adult learning, coaching and training, coaching and research, coaching and staff development, and peer teaching. The primary databases searched for relevant studies were Psychological Abstracts (PsycINFO), Educational Resources Information Center (ERIC), Academic Search Elite, Business Search Elite, Info Trac Expanded, ABI/INFORM complete, CINAHL–Nursing and Allied Health, and Google. In addition, hand searches were completed for relevant journal articles, book chapters, and books in order to locate additional studies. The reference list of each newly identified study was reviewed to determine whether it contained studies that had not yet been identified. Studies were included in the analysis if coaching was identified as the implementation strategy used for skill development and if three or more of the characteristics of coaching (joint planning, observation, action/practice, reflection, feedback) were present. Studies were excluded if the study included only one or two of the characteristics of coaching or insufficient information was provided about the coaching procedures, or if the study was a single participant design.

A total of 39 studies were included in the analysis. Of those selected, 16 studies used a reciprocal peer coaching model, 13 used a peer coaching approach, and 10 used an expert-as-coach model. Reciprocal peer coaches are defined as individuals who are in the process of learning a new skill and who are supporting one another in doing so. Peer coaches are defined as individuals who have the same or similar role, but one has particular knowledge and skills that he or she uses to coach the other. Experts are people with specific content knowledge or skills who are generally from outside the organization and provide coaching to specific individuals as part of the program or project. Experts may be workshop trainers, researchers, higher education faculty members, or other individuals who have the content expertise and/or coaching expertise and who have received specific training on how to use coaching to facilitate knowledge transfer and utilization.

The 39 studies included 832 participants. Of these participants, 401 took part in studies of reciprocal peer coaching, 167 were involved in studies of peer coaching, and 264 participated in expert-as-coach studies. In the studies that used reciprocal peer coaching, 187 of the participants were undergraduate students and 214 were experienced teachers and building administrators. The studies using peer coaching included 12 undergraduate students, 105 experienced teachers and building administrators, 4 parents, and 26 physicians. The coaching studies that used an expert-based coaching model involved 42 experienced teachers and building administrators, 9 graduate students, 205 parents, and 8 physicians. Thirteen of the studies were conducted with students in university training and 22 of them were conducted with individuals who were in the work force.

The research settings included 6 studies of individuals who were involved with early intervention and preschool programs, 21 studies of teachers at the kindergarten and elementary levels, 11 teachers at the junior or mid-high level, and 7 teachers at the high school level. Three of the studies were conducted with teachers in special education classrooms, 26 studies involved teachers in general education classrooms, and 4 studies were of teachers working in an integrated setting that included both students in general education and students who received special education support. Five of the studies in the analysis assessed the impact of the coaching on students of coached teachers. The children ranged in age from preschool to adolescence. All of the children studied were either working below their grade level or eligible for special education services. Four studies involved parents as members of the coaching dyad. Two studies focused on physicians receiving coaching.

Although the steps in the coaching process varied across studies (Doyle, 1999; Flaherty, 1999; Hanft et al., 2004; Kinlaw, 1999), the research on coaching delineates five practice characteristics that lead to the intended outcomes: 1) joint planning, 2) observation, 3) action/practice, 4) reflection, and 5) feedback (see Table 2.1). The definition of each characteristic is based on

Table 2.1. Coaching practice characteristics

Study	Joint planning	Observation	Action/practice	Reflection	Feedback
Anderson & Radencich (2001)	Y	Y	Y	N	Y
Bowman & McCormick (2000)	Y	Y	Y	Y	Y
Bruce & Ross (2008)	Y	Y	Y	Y	Y
Delany & Arredondo (1998)	N	Y	Y	Y	Y
Gordon, Nolan, & Forlenza (1995)	Y	Y	Y	Y	Y
Hasbrouck (1997)	Y	Y	Y	Y	Y
Hendrickson, Gardner, Kaiser, & Riley (1993)	Y	Y	Y	Y	Y
Homa et al. (2008)	Y	Y	Y	Y	Y
Horowitz et al. (2001)	N	Y	Y	Y	Y
Hosack-Curlin (1988)	Y	Y	Y	N	Y
Huntington, Anderson, & Vail (1994)	N	Y	Y	N	Y
Kohler, Ezell, & Paluselli (1999)	Y	Y	Y	Y	N
Kohler, Crilley, Shearer, & Good (1997)	Y	Y	Y	Y	Y
Kohler, McCullough, & Buchan (1995)	Y	Y	Y	Y	Y
Kurts & Levine (2000)	Y	Y	Y	Y	Y
Mallette, Maheady, & Harper (1999)	Y	Y	Y	N	Y
Marchant & Young (2001)	N	Y	Y	Y	Y
Miller (1994)	Y	Y	Y	Y	Y
Miller, Harris, & Watanabe (1991)	Y	Y	Y	Y	Y
Morgan, Menlove, Salzberg, & Hudson (1994)	Y	Y	Y	N	Y
Morgan, Gustafson, Hudson, & Salzberg (1992)	N	Y	Y	N	Y
Munroe & Elliot (1987)	Y	Y	Y	N	Y
Nolan & Hillkirk (1991)	Y	Y	Y	Y	Y
Phillips & Glickman (1991)	Y	Y	Y	Y	Y
Peterson & Hudson (1989)	Y	Y	Y	Y	Y
Peterson, Luze, Eshbaugh, Jeon, & Kantz (2007)	N	Y	Y	Y	Y
Ross (1992)	Y	N	Y	N	Y
Sekerka & Chao (2003)	N	Y	Y	Y	Y
Shanley & Niec (2001)	N	Y	N	Y	Y
Showers (1984)	Y	Y	Y	Y	Y
Showers (1982)	Y	Y	Y	Y	Y
Slater & Simmons (2001)	Y	Y	Y	Y	Y
Sparks (1986)	N	Y	Y	N	Y
Stichter, Lewis, Richter, Johnson, & Bradley (2006)	N	Y	Y	N	Y
Tschantz & Vail (2000)	Y	Y	Y	N	Y
Williamson & Russell (1990)	Y	Y	Y	N	Y
Wineburg (1995)	Y	Y	Y	Y	Y
Wynn & Kromrey (1999)	Y	Y	Y	Y	Y
Zwart, Wubbels, Bohuis, & Bergen (2008)	N	Y	Y	Y	Y

N = 39 studies

Key: Y, yes; N, no

descriptions from the coaching research literature and on the way in which the characteristic is used to improve existing abilities, develop new skills, and deepen the understanding of evidence-based practices of the coachee.

Joint Planning

One definition of joint planning as delineated in the research studies that were reviewed is agreement by both the coach and learner on the actions to be taken by both or the opportunities for the coachee to practice between coaching visits. Joint planning ensures that the parent actively participates in the use of new knowledge and skills between coaching sessions. It occurs as a part of all coaching conversations and typically involves discussion of what the parent agrees to do between coaching interactions to use the information that has been discussed or the skills that were practiced. For example, as a result of the coaching conversation with the practitioner, a parent may offer her child choices during each meal.

Observation

In the research studies that were reviewed, observation involved the examination of another person's actions or practices (either the coach or coachee) in order to develop new skills, strategies, or ideas. Observation did not necessarily occur during every coaching conversation, but it was used over the course of several coaching visits. Observation may occur when the coach directly observes an action taken by the coachee that provides an opportunity for later reflection and discussion. Conversely, the coachee may observe the coach model a particular strategy or technique, after which the coachee may reflect on, discuss, or perhaps practice the strategy. An example of observation would be a practitioner observing the parent reading a book to his child. Observation may also involve modeling by the practitioner for the parent. In such a case, the practitioner may build on what the parent is already doing, demonstrate additional strategies (e.g., allowing the child to choose a book), and reflect with the parent on how the example matches the parent's intent and/or what research informs us about child learning.

Action/Practice

Action or practice opportunities for the coachee occurred during the research studies in the course of spontaneous or planned events. These events happened within the context of a real-life situation that provided the coachee with opportunities to practice, refine, or analyze new or existing skills. The characteristic of action provides opportunities for the coachee to use the information that has been discussed with the coach or to practice newly learned skills. Action may occur during or between coaching interactions. For example, when a parent reads a book with the child before bedtime, the parent encourages the child to select the book, describes the pictures as she reads, and then pauses to give her child a chance to take a turn. All of these actions are based on previous discussion and practice with the coach.

Reflection

Reflection as demonstrated in the research studies was the analysis of existing strategies to determine how the strategies are consistent with evidence-based practices and how they may need to be implemented without change or modified to obtain the intended outcome(s).

Reflection follows an observation or action and provides the parent with an opportunity to analyze current strategies and refine her knowledge and skills. During reflection, the practitioner may ask the parent to describe what worked or did not work during observation and/or action and to generate alternatives and actions to continually improve her knowledge and skills.

Feedback

Feedback that took place as part of the research studies is defined as information that is provided by the coach and that is based on the coach's direct observations of the coachee, actions reported by the coachee, or information shared by the coachee to expand his or her current level of understanding about a specific evidence-based practice. Feedback occurs after the coachee has had the opportunity to reflect on his or her observations or actions, or after the coachee has practiced new skills. Feedback includes statements by the coach that affirm the coachee's reflections (i.e., "I understand what you are saying") or add information to deepen the coachee's understanding of the topic being discussed and jointly develop new ideas and actions. An example of informative feedback is the coach listening to the parent's reflection on what she has tried in order to potty train her child and what the parent has found to be either successful or unsuccessful, then sharing additional ideas. An example of affirmative feedback is the coach describing what he or she observed the parent do to successfully support his child's continued interest in shared book reading.

> ### *Remember*
>
> The five research-based characteristics of coaching that should be present within and across coaching interactions are the following:
>
> Joint planning
> Observation
> Action/practice
> Reflection
> Feedback

A review of 39 studies of coaching revealed five characteristics of the practice: joint planning, observation, action/practice, reflection, and feedback (see Table 2.1). When used in combination, these characteristics led to the coachee's achievement of the intended outcomes or purposes for entering into a coaching relationship. When coaching is used to support a coachee in identifying and using existing abilities, or obtaining and mobilizing new knowledge and skills to achieve a desired outcome, these five characteristics should be present.

CONCLUSION

Clearly, coaching is an evidence-based practice that can be used effectively to support adults who are involved in the lives of young children. Positive outcomes have been demonstrated across contexts (e.g., home, community, classrooms) and settings (e,g., early intervention; early childhood; elementary, middle, and high schools; universities), and with a variety of adult learners (e.g., parents, care providers, teachers, physicians, students) related to knowledge and skill acquisition and use. Furthermore, conceptualizing coaching as a helpgiving practice that is used intentionally to partner with parents in order to build their capacity to identify priorities and achieve their desired outcomes provides additional evidence for the use of coaching in early childhood contexts where parent or teacher-implemented practices, techniques, and strategies are the recommended approach.

Although research is plentiful on the effectiveness of coaching in a variety of contexts and with different types of adult learners, some questions remain unanswered. Further research is needed to determine how frequently each of the five characteristics of coaching must be present in a given interaction or across a series of interactions in order to achieve desired outcomes (see Chapter 10). Although questions remain about the nuances of implementation of the evidence-based characteristics of coaching, the presence of the five characteristics we have described (i.e., joint planning, observation, action/practice, reflection, and feedback) promotes positive outcomes for people who are important in the lives of young children. Coaching is an evidence-based strategy that practitioners can use to assist them in moving from primary use of child-focused interventions to evidence-based interventions that promote growth and developmental progress for young children and that enhance the confidence and competence of their family members and other care providers.

RESOURCES

Stober, D.R., & Grant, A.M. (Eds.). (2006). *Evidence-based coaching handbook: Putting best practices to work for your clients.* Hoboken, NJ: John Wiley & Sons.

This edited text provides in-depth descriptions of different types of conceptual and theoretical frameworks for coaching and the research base that supports each framework.

Trivette, C.M., Dunst, C.J., Hamby, D.W., & O'Herin, C.E. (2009). Characteristics and consequences of adult learning methods and strategies. *Practical Evaluation Reports, 2*(1), 1–32.

This report is a research synthesis of the effectiveness of four adult-learning methods (accelerated learning, coaching, guided design, and just-in-time training) compared with six adult-learning method characteristics from *How People Learn* (Bransford, Brown, & Cocking, 2000). This report includes specific recommendations for training and technical assistance.

Chapter 3

Characteristics of Effective Coaches

What does it take to be an effective coach? Do specific characteristics exist that affect or predict an individual's ability to serve in the role of coach? How does a coach's personality influence his or her effectiveness? These are a few questions that might come to mind for a practitioner who is considering implementing a coaching style of interaction.

In her chapter "Talking to Families," P.J. McWilliam (2010) noted that there are many challenges to developing effective family–professional partnerships and that interpersonal factors play a substantial role in the quality of such relationships. In their seminal work, Dunst and Trivette (2009) researched characteristics of effective helpgiving that relate to the field of early childhood. These key principles must be employed in order to provide "help" that is indeed helpful and meaningful rather than being detrimental and creating dependency. In their text *Using Skilled Dialogue to Transform Challenging Interactions*, Barrera and Kramer (2009) provide valuable information on how two people who are very different from each other can effectively engage in a nonhierarchical and nonjudgmental partnership. This chapter is intended to compile the information from such sources in order to help both experienced and novice coaches develop a deeper understanding of what characterizes an effective coach and to promote self-reflection among coaches to ensure that they take a research-based approach to helpgiving.

FAMILY-CENTERED PRACTITIONERS

Understanding and implementing family-centered practices is a key principle in early childhood intervention (Brewer, McPherson, Magrab, & Hutchins, 1989; Hanson, Johnson, Jeppson, Thomas, & Hall, 1994; Johnson, 1990; McBride, Brotherson, Joanning, Whiddon, & Demmitt, 1993; Shelton, Jeppson, & Johnson, 1987; Shelton & Stepanek, 1994, 1995; Turnbull, Turbiville, & Turnbull, 2000; Workgroup on Principles and Practices in Natural Environments, 2007). Although key elements of family-centered care have been delineated, infusing the approach into the day-to-day implementation in early childhood systems, programs, and individual teacher and therapist practices is easier said than done.

At the core of the provision of family-centered care lies the premise that practitioners believe that all families are capable and competent. In addition, when a coach is using a family-centered approach, he or she enters into the process of developing a relationship with the family. The coach pays particular attention to "leveling the playing field" and supporting parents and other care providers, recognizing what they have to offer and contribute in the partnership. McWilliam (2010) provided a checklist for implementing principles of family-centered care by effectively communicating with families in ways that 1) create opportunities for informal dialogue, 2) acknowledge family strengths and competencies, 3) solicit parents' opinions and ideas, 4) seek understanding, 5) demonstrate caring for the entire family, and 6) acknowledge and respond to the feelings and emotions of the family.

When a coach is implementing family-centered care, his or her ability to effectively communicate with family members is an essential skill. Characteristics of an effective communicator include but are not limited to demonstrating attributes of being caring, empathetic, and engaging. Use of active listening and being mindful of and responsive to nonverbal communication also are behaviors and strategies that, when implemented, lead to expanded opportunities for nonhierarchical coach–coachee interactions (Burley-Allen, 1995). In the literature about family-centered practices, interpersonal qualities of practitioners are considered to be vital factors for promoting positive outcomes for families (Blue-Banning, Summers, Frankland, Nelson, & Beegle, 2004; Dunst & Trivette, 2009; McWilliam, Tocci, & Harbin, 1998; Park & Turnbull, 2003). Trust, honesty, respect, and behaviors that promote equitable relationships are repeatedly mentioned as characteristics of effective practitioners who are implementing family-centered care.

Reflect

Think about a family that you are currently supporting or have worked with in the recent past. Take time to answer the following questions about specific ways that you implement components of family-centered care when you are talking with this family.

1. How do you create opportunities for informal dialogue with family members?
2. What are some ways that you acknowledge family strengths and competencies?
3. How can you do more to solicit parents' opinions and ideas?
4. What are specific strategies that you use to seek understanding?
5. How do you demonstrate that you care about the entire family?
6. When have you acknowledged and responded to feelings and emotions of the family? (McWilliam, 2010, pp. 144–146)

Remember

Characteristics of an effective communicator include but are not limited to being caring, empathetic, and engaging.

RELATIONAL AND PARTICIPATORY HELPGIVERS

As we mentioned in Chapter 2, over the past several decades, the work of Dunst and Trivette (see Dunst & Trivette, 2009, for summary and review) informs the field of early childhood intervention in many ways, but particularly important are their in-depth contributions related to effective helpgiving practices. Helpgiving that promotes positive outcomes for all family members and is family centered has two components: 1) relational helpgiving practices and 2) participatory helpgiving practices.

Relational helpgiving practices focus on the relationship between the helpgiver and the help receiver, particularly the help receiver's appraisal of the presumed beliefs of the helpgiver toward the help receiver. More specifically, relational helpgiving includes both helpgiver interpersonal skills with help receivers and the attitudes of the helpgiver about the help receiver's capability to become more competent. For example, consider a situation in which an early intervention coach is supporting a young, first-time mother and her newborn infant who was prenatally exposed to cocaine. If through his actions, comments, or behavior the coach appears to the mother to be negative or judgmental, their partnership will be compromised and the outcomes for that parent and child will probably not be optimized. Relational helpgiving practices include behaviors such as compassion, empathy, active listening, openness, honesty, and trustworthiness. The help receiver must feel supported and must know and believe that the helpgiver cares about him or her on a personal level, as well as caring about the outcomes for the help receiver and his or her family (Dunst & Trivette, 2009).

The second component of effective helpgiving practices is participatory helpgiving. Participatory helpgiving includes both choice and action on the part of the help receiver and responsiveness and flexibility on the part of the helpgiver. It emphasizes support of the action and participation of the help receiver and focuses on strengthening existing help receiver capabilities and promoting new help receiver competencies. Participatory helpgiving practices meaningfully involve help receivers in the choices and decisions that they make and the actions that they take to achieve their desired goals and outcomes. The focus of participatory helpgiving is to implement strategies that support the help receiver to attribute accomplishments, new skills and capabilities, and achievement of desired outcomes to his or her actions and decisions. Research indicates that in order for positive outcomes to be achieved, both relational and participatory helpgiving practices must be present (Dunst & Trivette, 2009).

Consider a practitioner who observes that one of the children she supports through home visiting does not have any nice toys. The coach is concerned about this situation. She knows that her program has an abundance of nice toys that are no longer used because they have stopped taking toy bags with them to home visits and instead use what children and families have readily available in their environments. The coach decides to give a few of the former toy bag toys to the family. On her next visit, the coach is surprised by the parent's reaction to her gift. The mother expresses thanks, but the coach notices that she becomes quiet and more withdrawn. Although the coach had good intentions, she violated a primary premise of effective helpgiving practices. Yes, the coach demonstrated relational helpgiving; a caring and generous attitude toward the child and family. She did not, however, implement participatory helpgiving practices in this situation. In addition, a significant finding in this area of research is that provision of supports in the absence of an identified family priority or need results in negative outcomes regarding the capacity of family members (Dunst & Trivette, 2009).

Consider an alternative response on the part of the coach that demonstrates both relational and participatory helpgiving practices. As the coach was getting to know the family, she began identifying the interests of the child. The mother mentioned that her young son loved a particular toy that they had seen at the grocery store, but indicated that she could not afford to buy it and that she felt bad about the situation. The coach then asked the mother how she might support her in feeling better about the situation. The mother responded eagerly that she was very interested in identifying some options for toys for her child. A discussion ensued between the coach and coachee about what the mother thought the child liked about particular toys at the store. They also explored past strategies that the mother had used to identify and obtain needed resources, such as shopping at yard sales, the thrift store, and the flea market. As the conversation continued, the mother considered additional options—for example, trading toys with a neighbor or family member and visiting the local library. Then she developed a plan for when and how she would accomplish her goal of obtaining toys for her child.

In the second version of the scenario, the coach demonstrated both relational and participatory helpgiving practices. She showed that she was listening to the parent and displayed care and concern for the mother's feelings and priorities. In addition, the coach engaged in participatory helpgiving practices by implementing a resource-based conversation that engaged the mother in identifying previous strategies, analyzing past successes, and developing a plan of action to achieve her desired outcome.

In light of the evidence about relational and participatory helpgiving practices, particularly with regard to empowerment of family members, practitioners must be aware of and develop skills which ensure that families know and believe the practitioners care about them. In addition, a practitioner must implement strategies and demonstrate behaviors that promote choice and action on the part of the coachee. The coach must support the coachee to readily attribute achievement of desired outcomes to his or her actions. Parents' attribution of the importance and success of their participation, decisions, and actions is a critical factor in building their own capacity to care for their children.

> **Remember**
>
> The two components of effective helpgiving practices, relational and participatory helpgiving, *both* must be present in order to achieve positive outcomes for help receivers. Use of *only* relational helpgiving behaviors (e.g., compassion, empathy, openness) will not promote and enhance the help receiver's capacity (Dunst & Trivette, 2009).

CHOOSING RELATIONSHIP OVER CONTROL

As we will discuss later in this book (in Chapters 7 and 10 specifically), working closely with people from diverse backgrounds can be a new and challenging experience for many early childhood practitioners. Diversity can be expressed in many ways, such as through cultural beliefs and traditions, types and variety of life experiences, and socioeconomic challenges. When they are working with family members and other care providers, practitioners who are using coaching are immediately faced with many of these issues, as the need to communicate effectively is critical for every early childhood coach. Being open to coaching relationships with people who are different from oneself is an essential element of becoming an effective coach.

The literature that we reviewed about characteristics of coaches that depict use of family-centered care and effective helpgiving describes the behaviors and traits that a coach should possess. The attitudes and beliefs of a coach are also important. Hanson and Lynch (2010) and Lynch and Hanson (2004) provided insights that early childhood coaches can consider when developing a new partnership. A coach might think about how his or her own beliefs, past experiences, and traditions are different from the coachee. Barrera and Kramer (2009) have written extensively about how to approach and improve interactions with others, particularly when they have different backgrounds and life experiences. Barrera and Kramer refer to their approach as Skilled Dialogue, and their writings contain helpful information and specific strategies for coaches in a variety of challenging situations, particularly when the coach is inexperienced or has difficulty finding success.

Understanding and embracing diversity is a complex challenge for most early childhood coaches. The concept of "choosing relationship over control" (Barrera & Kramer, 2009, p. 51) seems particularly useful from a coaching perspective. Specifically, a coach who chooses to value the relationship with the coachee, rather than controlling the interaction, places an "implicit and explicit focus" on developing mutual understanding, respect, and acknowledgment of the other person's perspective in connection with one's own (Barrera & Kramer, 2009, p. 52):

> Skilled Dialogue calls for a disposition toward choosing relationship over control . . . 1) as a counterbalance to the tendency to choose control; 2) as a direct expression of another's dignity and worth as equal to one's own; and 3) as a more effective means of establishing truly collaborative partnerships.

The coaching relationship is not about agreeing 100% of the time with the coachee or condoning his or her particular behaviors or actions. Developing a true partnership, however, does require constant reflection on the part of the coach and active consideration of the other person's ideas and viewpoint. The coach may find himself or herself in situations in which it is difficult to remain open to understanding how the coachee views the world, his or her possible options and choices, and his or her responses to the decisions that have been made. When a coach feels uncomfortable or judgmental, seeking to understand the coachee's view will certainly afford extended opportunities for the coaching relationship to grow, unlike what might happen in situations in which a coachee feels that his or her coach does not approve of the choices or decisions he or she has made.

Context is a key feature involved in choosing relationship over control (Barrera & Kramer, 2009). Specifically, the coach should strive to create an interpersonal context in which the knowledge and experiences of the coach are tied to a real person (the coachee) who has real thoughts and feelings and about whom the coach actually cares. When a coach steps outside the context and considers a choice or decision made by the coachee based on what he or she (the coach) would have done or what he or she feels the coachee "should" have done, then the relationship is at risk due to the imbalance created by the hierarchical nature of the coach's thoughts. Instead, when a coach is faced with a lack of understanding he or she should seek to view the situation from the coachee's perspective and gather more information that will support the coach in maintaining an open, honest, and caring perspective.

For example, consider a situation in which a coach has supported a parent in her priority to maintain a budget so that she will be able to keep the electricity on in her apartment. The parent has been making progress for the last several months in achieving her desired outcome. Then the coach receives a phone call from a practitioner at another agency asking if he knew that the family's electricity had been shut off for several days. When faced with this information, the coach has two choices: relationship or control. If the coach chooses control, he may have a plethora of responses, including but not limited to 1) judgment ("I'll bet she spent all her money on beer and cigarettes."), 2) anger ("I can't believe she spent the money on something besides the electricity!"), and/or 3) disappointment ("I'm so disappointed . . . why does she always make such poor decisions?") In this same scenario, if the coach chooses relationship over control, here are a few of the thoughts that might come to mind: 1) "Hmmm . . . I wonder what happened?" 2) "I'd better call to share what I've heard and learn more about what happened," and 3) "This wasn't her

Reflect

The concept of choosing relationship over control is described by Barrera and Kramer (2009). It is critical for coaches to embrace this notion, which places strong emphasis on acknowledging and understanding another person's perspective, especially when it differs from that of the coach. Consider a situation in the past when you were faced with a challenging situation because you had a different opinion, belief, or understanding of the situation than the person you were supporting. Carefully reflect on how you responded to the situation. How did you react when the person made a choice that you felt was "wrong" or would result in negative consequences? What were your options? What came to mind in terms of how the conversation should proceed? Did you choose relationship over control, or did you choose control over relationship? How would it have looked if you had made the opposite choice? For a coach, choosing relationship over control is all about shifting to a focus of really trying to understand the coachee's perspective instead of attempting to convince him or her to make a different decision or choice.

plan. I need to learn more about what happened." Each of the thoughts that occur to the coach when he chooses relationship over control depicts a situation in which the coach immediately knows he needs to learn more about what happened in order to support the mother in her current situation. Partnering with people who share opinions, views, and beliefs that contrast with one's own is not easy. It does, however, afford the opportunity for continued learning experiences that further develop a coach's skills and abilities to provide support to a wider range of people with varying priorities. Coaches who choose relationship over control will continue to experience learning opportunities that prepare them to be better at their jobs every day. Recognizing these experiences as valuable and meaningful—even experiences that could never have been imagined or planned for—can help coaches enjoy all of their coaching relationships.

"BIG FIVE" PRACTITIONERS

Personality attributes clearly are an important factor for any early childhood practitioner, but they must be considered critical for practitioners who serve as coaches. Due to the significance of the relationship component in a coach–coachee partnership, practitioners' abilities to self-reflect on the presence or absence of personality traits is instrumental in developing their coaching skills (Passmore, 2008). Considerations of personality dimensions can assist the coach in understanding and preparing to approach certain situations, or deciding what his or her response might be to a challenge. Measures of personality have explored personality traits and an accepted premise exists that all personality attributes are represented in five core areas: 1) conscientiousness, 2) extroversion, 3) agreeableness, 4) openness to experience, and 5) emotional stability (Barrick & Mount, 1991; Goldberg, 1990; Judge, Higgins, Thoresen, & Barrick, 1999; McCrae & Costa, 1987; Morgeson, Reider, & Campion, 2005). McCrae and Costa further noted that it was important for a coach to consider these personality factors, which are referred to in the literature as the "Big Five."

Remember

A "Big Five" coach is

1. Conscientious
2. Warm and friendly
3. Agreeable
4. Open to experience
5. Emotionally stable

Reflect

Consider the "Big Five" personality characteristics of an effective coach. Think about yourself and how people describe you. Make a list of specific examples of how these personality characteristics do or do not match you in your role as an early childhood coach.

Conscientiousness

A *conscientious* person is responsible, punctual, well organized, reliable, dependable, predictable, hardworking, and careful and pays attention to detail. In studies of early childhood intervention, this characteristic is repeatedly recognized as a critical trait for practitioners to possess (Bell, 2004; DeGangi, Wietlisbach, Poisson, Stein, & Royeen, 1994; Dinnebeil, Hale, & Rule, 1996, 1999; Dunst, Trivette, & Johanson, 1994; Lowenthal, 1992; O'Connor, 1995; Park & Turnbull, 2003; Soodak & Erwin, 2000). For example, an early childhood coach must understand the importance of and recall many details on a regular basis. Specific details about particular children and complex family situations must be part of a coach's daily working knowledge in order for the coach to support every family to which he or she is assigned.

In addition, individual coaching conversations are usually limited by time. In other words, a specific time is scheduled for the visit to occur. For any coach, planning for meaningful conversations within a set period of time can be challenging, especially in natural settings in which a coach needs to be prepared for just about anything. Also consider the fairly concrete aspect of a coach's role in maintaining a busy and punctual home-visiting schedule. Visits are planned to begin and end at a specific time and to allow adequate time for travel between locations. For example, an Early Head Start home visitor must see families on his or her caseload for 90-minute visits on a weekly basis, at a minimum. It is essential to show up on time for every scheduled visit. Being prepared, organized, and mindful of the topics to be discussed at the home visit are clear ways of demonstrating conscientious behavior so that scheduled conversations and visits do not exceed the planned time for the visit and thus do not negatively affect the timeliness of subsequent visits throughout the day. Of course, situations do arise that impede a coach's ability to arrive on time. In these situations, a conscientious coach will make every effort to contact a family to alert them that he or she may be tardy and to confirm that an altered time of arrival is acceptable.

Extroversion

Extroverts often are described as being sociable, friendly, talkative, outgoing, and warm. The specific term *extroversion* does not readily surface in studies of early childhood intervention; however, the words warm, caring, friendly, able to engage in informal sharing, comfortable with self-disclosure, and sense of humor do appear frequently across a variety of studies (Dinnebeil et al., 1996; Harrison, Lynch, Rosander, & Borton, 1990; Lowenthal, 1992; O'Connor, 1995). The nature of the work really requires an early childhood coach to be outgoing in new and differing situations and contexts.

Consider an early literacy coach working in a small town. Her roles and responsibilities include working with families from a variety of cultures as well as with teachers in child care settings and local preschools. She also spends time with the local children's librarian for a few hours each month. She has opportunities to meet families of all sizes and configurations. She visits some homes in which the members of the household change frequently and she meets someone new on almost every visit. She also works with interpreters when families do not speak English. The agency for which the early literacy coach works uses an interpreting service from a larger city a few hours away, and they often send different interpreters to support her. It is essential for the coach to be comfortable meeting new people and working in these or similar circumstances in order for her to successfully support the parents and teachers with whom she works. Knowing how to comfortably initiate conversations with new people, being at ease sharing personal experiences as a means for building relationships, and using a sense of humor appropriately when circumstances become intense are all examples of extroversion that benefit an early childhood coach.

Agreeableness

The words courteous, flexible, trusting, generous, selfless, respectful, and acquiescent are often used to describe a person who is *agreeable*. Being agreeable is an important trait in promoting practitioner–family partnerships according to a variety of studies. The specific terms respectful or demonstrating mutual respect were mentioned in every study reviewed (Bell, 2004; DeGangi et al., 1994; Dinnebeil et al., 1996, 1999; Dunst & Trivette, 2009; Dunst et al., 1994; Harrison et al., 1990; Lowenthal, 1992; O'Connor, 1995; Park & Turnbull, 2003; Soodak & Erwin, 2000).

On a recent visit to a family child care home, a home visitor had an unplanned opportunity to demonstrate his agreeable and flexible demeanor. The child care provider greeted him at the door and invited him inside. Their plan for that day was to take the three children in her care out to the backyard and to discuss safety and the children's interest in exploring outside. When the home visitor walked into the living room, the children were happily playing with toys and looking at books. The television was on (quite loud) and the child care provider immediately sat down on the sofa with her eyes fixed on the television. The early childhood practitioner greeted the children and stated to the child care provider, "Our plan from last time was to go out back today. How would you like to proceed?"

The child care provider replied, "Oh, I forgot. I got so tied up in this news report on CNN. They think they've found those guys that tried to rob that bank. I just love this reporting. It's like you're right there with them. Is it OK if we stay inside? I don't want to miss this. My sister will call me tonight and I don't want her to know more about it than I do."

The home visitor replied, "Sure. Would you like to reschedule our appointment? I know how it is when things come up."

She stated, "No, no . . . I don't want you to go. I can keep my eye on this while we do our stuff. I can show you how I've been reading books to them if you want to see."

As the home visitor thought about his options, he tried to figure out how to conduct a home visit that was different from the one that had been planned and that required the television to be loudly playing in the room. Although he was struggling a bit, he knew that this was what the child care provider and children would be doing if he had not been there. He thought about how he could be courteous and respectful, yet be helpful during the visit. "OK, that sounds good. First, let me ask, would you be reading books while this news report is on?"

She replied, "Honestly, no. I'd probably wait a bit to catch the details and then get back to the kids."

"OK. What do you think about me just watching what you would be doing if I wasn't here, and then we can talk about ways that you're being responsive to the children, even during times like this, when you need to attend to something that's important to you?"

She quickly stated, "Is that all right with you? It's OK with me."

During the next few minutes while she watched the report on CNN, he observed the children going up to the child care provider and interacting with her: showing her a toy or asking her for a drink. One of the children climbed up beside her on the sofa with a book. In each instance, she responded in a kind, gentle, and responsive way. She even stopped watching the television to read a few pages of the book to the child beside her. The home visitor then shared his observations with her and more discussion ensued.

In this scenario, the home visitor demonstrated an agreeable and adaptable attitude toward trying something completely different from what he had been expecting. He was quite concerned initially that focusing a visit on watching television did not really fall under the realm of good practice in early childhood. Because his priority was to be respectful and courteous regarding the child care provider's request, he reflected on how to make the most of the new situation. He was agreeable to the situation and shifted his priorities to be supportive of the person he was coaching.

Openness to Experience

A person who is *open to experience* might be described as objective, flexible, adaptable, innovative, independent, someone who prefers variety, open-minded, and imaginative. Being open to experiences is a critical factor for a coach in early childhood intervention who is supporting families, teachers, and other care providers. As early childhood coaches spend most of their time in settings that are different from their own (i.e., families' homes, community settings, preschool teachers' classrooms), demonstrating a flexible "go-with-the-flow" attitude can assist in helping everyone involved to feel comfortable and more relaxed. Flexibility and openness to viewing new experiences as learning opportunities is often mentioned as an effective characteristic of early childhood practitioners (Bell, 2004; DeGangi et al., 1994; Dinnebeil et al., 1996; Dunst & Trivette, 2009; Dunst et al., 1994; Lowenthal, 1992; O'Connor, 1995; Park & Turnbull, 2003; Soodak & Erwin, 2000).

For a coach in an early childhood setting, being open-minded, flexible, and creative are requisite traits. Working with children and their family members and care providers in their natural environments provides endless opportunities for a coach to be innovative and adaptable. A speech-language pathologist (SLP) who was new to home visiting was faced with a surprise on a recent home visit with a family that she had been supporting for a short while. The previous plan for the home visit was to support the family around the noon meal. The SLP came prepared with ideas for assisting the parents and the child to communicate more effectively during their family meal at the kitchen table. When she arrived at the home, she heard the father calling out to her, "Hey . . . we're back here. Come on around!" The SLP followed the voice and saw the father and some of the child's teenage siblings down by the creek at the far end of their property. The father then said, "I hope it's okay, we're playing down at the creek. I know we were going to eat lunch together, but we've been having so much fun catching crawdads that we aren't ready to head to the house. I just came up to the house to get more bacon to use as bait and decided to bring some snacks down to the creek for us to eat."

The SLP replied, "Oh! OK, I've never caught crawdads. Will it be all right to leave my shoes and calendar up here on the porch?"

The father stated, "Sure. Good thing you wore a skirt . . . you won't get your britches wet. Come on! Be careful of the stickers in the yard." He bounded back down to the creek with the rest of the children and the family dog while the SLP placed her shoes and paperwork on a chair on the back porch.

On her way down to the creek, the SLP quickly thought about what she needed to do to be supportive of the family. Although she had planned (and prepared) for a meal in the kitchen with the child in his high chair, she was flexible and open to meeting the family where they were on that day and at the particular time of her scheduled visit. She thought that a snack time by the creek would probably happen, so observing the family as they included the youngest child in having a snack would provide great opportunities for shared communication. She also mused that catching crawdads was jam-packed with opportunities for all kinds of learning, including communication. She readjusted her perspective and hurried down the hill to the creek. As she met the family knee deep in creek water, she said, "Where shall we begin? How can I help?"

This scenario depicts a situation in which an early childhood practitioner, although she had been prepared for another circumstance, was able to shift her plans and be open to a new experience. Her response was adaptable to what was important to the family at the time of her visit. Although she was not prepared or dressed for catching crawdads at the creek, she was able to view the new opportunity with interest and excitement. She was flexible in adjusting her mental plan and demonstrated an open and eager attitude to join the family in an important natural learning opportunity.

Emotional Stability

Calm, at ease, relaxed, secure, trustworthy, and even-tempered are descriptors of a person who demonstrates *emotional stability*. Bell (2004) examined the effects of individual characteristics of team members on the overall effectiveness of teams. In this meta-analysis, effective team members were considered to be agreeable, conscientious, and competent in their area of expertise, and to have high general mental ability, openness to experience, and mental stability, as well as generally liking teamwork. In studies of early childhood intervention, factors that were related to emotional stability were reported across a number of studies, which examined effective practitioner–parent interactions (DeGangi et al., 1994; Dinnebeil et al., 1996; Dunst & Trivette, 2009; Dunst et al., 1994; Lowenthal, 1992; O'Connor, 1995; Park & Turnbull, 2003; Soodak & Erwin, 2000).

Think about a situation in which a home visitor has parked her personal vehicle on the street outside a family's home. During the visit that day, they were focusing on ideas for supporting the family in coming out to the front yard to get into the car without their young child bolting out the front door and running toward the street. After reviewing how their week had played out, they discussed some ideas and the practitioner went out to the front yard ahead of the family. As she stationed herself strategically in the yard for the family to try opening the front door, the neighbor across the street backed his car out of his driveway and crashed into her parked car. The family observed the situation and safely secured the child before opening the door and joining her out on the front lawn. Of course, the practitioner was shocked, upset, and concerned about the status of her vehicle. The neighbor jumped out of his car, obviously upset, and shouted, "Why did you park there? You never park there. Oh, man . . . this is bad."

She replied in a calm voice, "I parked there because we thought we might take a car ride today and I wanted my car to be out of the way. Do you want me to call the police or do you want to make the call? I'll also need to call my office to let them know what has happened."

The neighbor stated, "Why do we have to call the police? I've got insurance. I'll take care of it. I'm not a jerk!"

The home visitor replied, "Sir, I wasn't implying anything about your character when I brought up contacting the police. I'm required to contact the police. It is the policy of my agency. I will make the call." In this situation, although she was faced with a very emotional and upsetting circumstance, the coach was able to demonstrate a calm, composed demeanor. When the neighbor demonstrated hostility and a confrontational attitude, she remained even tempered and relied on her knowledge of policy and procedure for this situation.

Although the trait of competence is not included as one of the "Big Five" core personality traits, it is mentioned in a number of studies as a critically important characteristic of a coach (Bell, 2004; DeGangi et al., 1994; Dinnebeil et al., 1996, 1999; Dunst & Trivette, 2009; Dunst et al., 1994; Harrison et al., 1990; Lowenthal, 1992; O'Connor, 1995; Park & Turnbull, 2003; Soodak & Erwin, 2000). For an early childhood coach who is working in the areas of early intervention, early literacy, or early childhood special education, competence is often a prerequisite. Coaches in these settings are in the role because they have specialized training and often have licensing or credentialing in a particular area of expertise or knowledge.

For example, a teacher with 35 years of experience takes pride in staying current with evidence-based practices. She finds herself in a role teaching children with disabilities more often. She is open to including children with unique needs in her preschool classroom, but does not feel that she is at her best when asked to teach children with significant disabilities. She is eager to receive support for including a child with cerebral palsy in her classroom. In this situation, a coach *must* have knowledge, skills, and experience that will benefit the classroom teacher.

Consider another situation in which a parent home schools her children. The mother uses an academic approach with her children. She has never felt so perplexed about how to engage one of her children in learning as when she started trying to teach her sixth and youngest child. This mother has conducted a bit of Internet research and has come to the realization that her youngest child is going to need a different approach because of his learning style. She desires a coach to assist her in learning new ideas and strategies—one who will build on what she already knows, yet challenge her to think differently about how best to support her child. The coach for this mother must be knowledgeable in many areas, but he certainly must have a strong understanding of evidence-based approaches to early learning.

In recent years, the educational system has emphasized an increased accountability for practitioner competence related to evidence-based practice, not only to ensure the highest probability of achievement of desired outcomes, but also to provide protection for consumers. Families enroll in early childhood programs and partner with practitioners because they trust them and presume that they have the needed or desired experiences and knowledge. Teachers and child care providers agree to participate in a coaching relationship for similar reasons. They believe that the coach has expertise, knowledge, experience, and/or skills which will benefit them in ways that enhance their success in supporting the young children in their care. Competence and knowledge of early childhood development, family support, and adult learning are critical components for coaches from every discipline who are associated with the field. Monitoring of required competencies is necessary at every level by individual practitioners, programs, agencies, and oversight systems to ensure that parents have not misplaced their trust or made false presumptions about the type of support that is available.

Practice

Think about the early childhood program or agency where you work. How does the program evaluate and ensure that positive outcomes are happening for children and families? What do you think about the current process? What ideas do you have for improving or expanding the current system to ensure that families and young children are receiving evidence-based supports and services from competent practitioners?

Now think about yourself. How do you monitor your own competencies related to evidence-based practices in early childhood intervention? What do you do on a daily, weekly, and monthly basis to stay current with emerging evidence in early childhood intervention and your particular area of expertise? Develop a plan or reevaluate your existing plan to ensure that you make time to consider your own competencies as an early childhood practitioner. Invite a colleague to observe you as you implement actual practice. Make time to discuss the observation and develop a plan for using the information to challenge yourself to continually improve the quality of your skills and practices.

CONCLUSION

For a coach to be effective, he or she must have a set of key characteristics or traits that is evident to the coachee. Research also informs early childhood practitioners that using family-centered practices, relational and participatory helpgiving, and skilled dialogue inherently require a coach to possess certain characteristics. The coaching literature describes the "Big Five" personality traits that define a quality coach: conscientiousness; extroversion; agreeableness; open to experience; and emotional stability. Coaches who are competent, open to experiences, adaptable to a variety of situations and circumstances, able to demonstrate a caring, empathetic demeanor, and honest and trustworthy will be effective.

Remember

Here is an easy way to remember the five characteristics of an effective coach:

Competent (skilled, knowledgeable, helpful)
Open (objective, respectful)
Adaptable (flexible, open, agreeable)
Caring (empathetic, able to be an active listener, encouraging)
Honest (trustworthy)
C-O-A-C-H!

RESOURCES

Barrera, I., & Kramer, L. (2009). *Using skilled dialogue to transform challenging interactions: Honoring identity, voice, and connection.* Baltimore: Paul H. Brookes Publishing Co.

This text provides in-depth descriptions of ways to respond to interactions and ideas to help practitioners consider and better understand the perspectives of others, especially when they are working with individuals who have diverse backgrounds.

Dunst, C.J., Trivette, C.M., & Hamby, D.W. (2008). *Research synthesis and meta-analysis of studies of family-centered practices.* Asheville, NC: Winterberry Press.

This document includes a synthesis and meta-analysis of research that is related to family-centered practices, including in-depth information related to participatory and relational helpgiving.

Chapter 4

Coaching Compared with Other Approaches to Adult Interaction

Coaching practices are consistent with research evidence about how people learn (Bransford, Brown, & Cocking, 2000; Donovan, Bransford, & Pellegrino, 1999) and they are a reasonable means for interacting with the important adults in young children's lives. The field has yet to agree, however, on a common definition for these practices or to select research-based characteristics that clearly define how coaching practices should be implemented for optimal outcomes. As a result, coaching is often confused with other approaches for interacting with adults for the purposes of support, learning, and personal growth. Some of the most common strategies for adult learning and interaction that people struggle to differentiate from coaching are *consultation*, *mentoring*, *supervision*, *counseling*, and *direct teaching*. The intent of this chapter is to briefly describe each of these strategies as it is defined in early childhood literature, compare the strategy with coaching, and provide an example to illustrate the difference between coaching and the other adult learning strategy or interaction style.

CONSULTATION

Perhaps the interaction style that is most frequently confused with coaching is *consultation*. Like coaching in early childhood, consultation lacks a commonly agreed on definition. Consultation is often characterized by the consultant gathering information, identifying and analyzing problems, and then making recommendations to resolve the problems (Reiss, 2007). In their book *Consultation in Early Childhood Settings*, Buysse and Wesley (2005, p. 10) define consultation in early education and intervention as "an indirect, triadic service delivery model in which a consultant and consultee work together to address an area of concern or a common goal for change." These authors further indicate that the purpose of consultation is not only to focus on the present concern, but also to avoid related issues in the future. In their consultation model, the consultant, consultee, and client form a triad. Within this triad, the consultant is an early childhood special educator or a therapist, the consultee may be a parent or early childhood professional, and the client could be a single child, a group of children, or an early childhood program. This consultation model has eight stages that include setting goals, selecting strategies, and implementing and evaluating the plan.

In contrast, coaching in early childhood may be referred to as a direct or indirect service delivery or an adult learning approach in which the coach is a teacher or therapist; the coachee is a parent, other care provider, or colleague; and the benefactor of the coaching may be a single child, group of children, parent, or teacher. Although the goals of the coaching relationship are owned by the coachee, the coach and coachee work together in a nonhierarchical manner to define the goals further and participate in an interactive process of observation, reflection, and actions that both take. This process does not rely solely on the coachee to develop alternatives or solve the problem after questioning by the coach, nor does the coach gather just enough information from the coachee to determine what elements of the coach's expertise need to be shared with the coachee. Rather, the coach works with the coachee to identify what he or she already knows and is doing, shares information and ideas as needed by the coachee, assists the coachee in identifying and selecting alternatives, and then, as in consultation, develops a formal plan for action by the coachee with support of the coach, if necessary. Coaching in early childhood is based on and defined by the characteristics of the practice (described in Chapter 5) that are used as appropriate within a coaching interaction rather than through sequential stages or steps.

The primary tasks of consultation are suggesting a new strategy (problem solving), encouraging the consultee to implement a strategy (social influence), and providing training or coaching to assist the coachee to learn a new strategy (professional support) (Wesley & Buysse, 2004). The primary tasks of coaching are reflective discussion, action-oriented conversations that include observation and modeling, feedback, and joint planning. Coaching is used to promote the coachee's capacity to generate solutions or results to questions, problems, or situations that arise for the coachee. Through discussion, observation, action, feedback, and planning the coach assists the coachee in reflecting on what is currently happening and whether the current circumstances match what the coachee would like to have take place. The conversations between the coach and coachee are intended to promote awareness and reflection on the part of the coachee. Observation and modeling are used to further assist the coachee in actualizing possible ideas or practicing new strategies with the support of the coach. Providing feedback is an essential task of coaching. Feedback is information that the coach shares with the coachee to promote growth and learning. The coach shares new information in a way that matches the coachee's priorities and plans specifically to enable immediate implementation of the information by the coachee. This process encourages ongoing evaluation on the part of the coachee to assess whether the coaching relationship is effectively promoting independent reflection and action on the part of the coachee. The primary difference between coaching and consultation is the use of reflective questioning to assist the coachee in generating new ideas, evaluating the effectiveness of the new ideas and strategies, and implementing a jointly developed action-oriented plan that will serve as the topic of conversation in the next meeting between the coach and coachee.

Consultation versus Coaching Scenario

The following examples will help demonstrate the difference between consultation and coaching in early childhood intervention.

Consultation Example

Justin is a 2½-year-old boy with cerebral palsy. His family recently moved to the area and enrolled him in the Happy Hearts Child Care program. Although the staff members at Happy Hearts are glad to have Justin in their program, he is the first child with such significant motor issues to be served by the center. Justin's teacher, Katie, is a bit nervous about having him in her class. Since Justin is also enrolled in the local early intervention program, his therapist, Lyn, visits the child care program to consult with Katie about how to include Justin in the classroom activities. The early intervention program and Justin's parents arranged for the individualized family service plan (IFSP) meeting to occur at Happy Hearts in order for Katie and her assistant teacher to be able to participate and contribute to the development of the plan. At that time, the purpose of Lyn's consultative role was discussed and Katie agreed to work with Lyn to support Justin's participation in the classroom activities along with the other children. During Lyn's visit, Katie expressed her concerns that in her classroom children have a lot of freedom to select the activities they wish to do. As part of the assessment process prior to the development of the IFSP, Lyn had observed Justin and Katie in the classroom, so she had seen all the different centers that Katie had created for the children to suit their varied interests. During her assessment visit, Lyn had noted that because Justin is in a wheelchair and has difficulty communicating, Katie or her assistant teacher always determined the center or activity in which he would participate. Katie had shared with Lyn that this just did not "feel right" to her. These concerns were noted as part of the IFSP development process. Katie and Lyn agreed that one goal of their consultation would be that Katie and her assistant teacher would create strategies that would allow Justin to choose a center or activity. Justin's parents agreed and developed a similar goal related to activities at home. Katie and Lyn then agreed on a time for Lyn's next visit to the classroom. The following dialogue represents how the conversation between Lyn and Katie might proceed during Lyn's next visit:

Lyn: Hi, Katie. Based on my observation of your classroom the other day and then our discussion during the IFSP meeting, I have a couple of ideas about how we can help Justin pick which center or activity he wants to participate in.

Katie: Great. I'm anxious to hear your ideas. I really want this to work.

Lyn: Well, I'll share my ideas, but then we'll need to agree which idea you think will work best for both you and Justin.

Katie: Sure.

Lyn: Okay, my first suggestion would be . . . [Lyn reaches into her bag and pulls out a switch device that has three slots for pictures and is operated by the child tapping the picture, which causes a voice recording of the name of the picture to play.] . . . this really simple electronic device. This will allow Justin to pick the center he wants and also associates the picture with the recorded name of the picture.

Katie: He seems to like pictures, so I like that part. It's a little big, though.

Lyn: Right. It has its advantages and disadvantages. He's a bright little boy and he's able to pick from more than three choices. The switch device has the sound element, so you wouldn't have to be right with him all the time.

Katie: It's pretty bulky and we may have to change out the pictures and recordings pretty frequently.

Lyn: This would just be something to start with to see how this strategy for allowing him to pick his activity would go.

Katie: What's your other idea?

Lyn: My other suggestion would be to use a picture board that would include pictures of the different centers. The way it works is that you present the board to him and then you allow him to choose which center he wants by eye gaze, pointing, or tapping on the picture. We would teach him how to use it and determine the method that would work best for him right now. If you think this idea would work better, I brought some materials that we could use to make it. What do you think?

Katie: I like that idea better than the other one because it's simpler and I think will be easier for us to use. Could you help me make it?

Lyn: I'd be happy to help you and then we can try it out to see how it works.

Katie: All right.

Lyn: I brought some pictures of items that you have in the different centers. See how they are large enough that we will be able to see which one he is looking at or trying to point to or touch. We can stick them onto this file folder. Let's be sure to put them far enough apart so that it will be clear which one he is trying to indicate.

Katie: All right. Let's pick the pictures of the centers and put it together.

[Katie and Lyn assemble the picture board, and then they try it out with Justin.]

Lyn: That seemed to work pretty well. What do you think?

Katie: I like it. Of course, we all are going to need more practice, but it is much better than us just assuming which center he wants and moving him over to it.

Lyn: Absolutely. One thing I noticed though was that since we determined that we need to start by having him select the center by using eye gaze, you might want to give him just a little more time to make his selection.

Katie: Okay, sure. I think I anticipated what he wanted and maybe went a little too fast. I see how when you tried it you waited a little longer to be sure.

Lyn: Well, this is just a start. It is going to take some practice and patience, but I know you can do it. It fits more with your program philosophy. So, our plan will be for you and your assistant teacher to use the picture board between now and when I come back next week.

Katie: That sounds good. I'll look forward to seeing you next week.

During the next visit, Katie and Lyn evaluated their previous plan to determine how successful Katie and the assistant teacher had been. They determined that the picture board worked when the teachers were near Justin and could hold it up for him, but they needed a strategy to use when they were not close to him and he wanted to select a new center. During the follow-up visit, Lyn shared other ideas with Katie and they modified their plan, tried the new strategies, and developed a specific plan for what would happen in the interim before Lyn's next visit.

Coaching Example

During the assessment visit at Happy Hearts prior to the IFSP meeting, Lyn observed what Katie and the assistant teacher were doing to help Justin select which activity he wanted. They seemed to be watching where he tried to look, and then they would move him over to that area. Lyn also noted that the teachers had large pictures of each center with the name of that center written beneath the picture. As part of the assessment visit, Katie had explained to Lyn that the program philosophy was for the children to be able to choose their activities of interest, so they wanted Justin to be able to choose his favorite activities as well. Katie explained the other strategies they had tried in addition to the one Lyn had observed.

During the IFSP meeting, Katie, Lyn, and Justin's parents determined that one of the outcomes they wanted on the IFSP was for Katie and the assistant teacher to know which activity Justin wanted during free play time, so they could move him to that area and help him engage with the other children and materials. Lyn explained that she would continue to observe Katie and Justin in the classroom and would ask some questions so that she and Katie could reflect on what was working or not working and how they could get closer to the goal. Then together they would come up with some ideas to figure out how Justin could let them know what he wanted.

Lyn: Well, Katie, this is our first visit following the IFSP. When I was out here prior to the IFSP meeting, I learned a lot from my observation and assessment, so I'm ready to get started. How about you?

Katie: Definitely.

Lyn: How do you currently go about having the children select which activities they want to start with at free play time?

Katie: Well, at our morning circle time, we talk about our day and the children pick the activities where they would like to start.

Lyn: How do they pick?

Katie: I have pictures of each center here on this board, and I point to each child in turn as they sit in the circle and ask them which activity he or she wants. As each child tells me, I move the child's picture over by the picture of their activity. I have the same pictures of the centers over by the actual centers as well, with the name of the center written beneath it.

Lyn: I noticed that when I was here for my earlier visit. How do you go about having Justin pick?

Katie: Well, since he can't really tell us where he wants to go or even point at it, we just kind of guess and then move him over to the center.

Lyn: It seemed to me like you were even trying to see where he tried to turn his head to look at a center.

Katie: Yeah, we do that, too.

Lyn: How could you use the system that you are already using with the other children with Justin as well?

Katie: I'm not sure, since he can't tell us or even point to the pictures. I do think he recognizes the pictures, though.

Lyn: What seem to be his favorite activities?

Katie: I think he likes the sand table, the blocks, and the housekeeping area the best.

Lyn: How do you know?

Katie: He makes lots of happy sounds and watches what the other children are doing when he's in those areas. He tries to lift up his arms to get to the toys, so we help him grab the cups and shovels to fill and dump at the sand table or build with the blocks. You know, things like that.

Lyn: Sounds like those might be the places to start. So, how could you help him pick between those activities?

Katie: Do you think we could use the pictures that we already are using with the other children? How could he pick?

Lyn: Yes, you can absolutely use the pictures. He seems to do quite well with pictures. From what I observed and am hearing you say, he also looks at what he wants—he uses eye gaze—and makes what you called "happy sounds."

Katie: But we can't carry our big board with pictures of all the centers on it around or keep taking him over to it every time we think he wants to change activities.

Lyn: I agree. So, what are some other options if pictures seem to work?

Katie: I'm not sure.

Lyn: How did you make the pictures that you are using now?

Katie: We used our digital camera to take the pictures, and then we just printed them out.

Lyn: One strategy that we use for some children who don't use words yet is called a picture board. We use pictures of objects or people, put them on something with stiff backing, and then teach the child to, in Justin's case, look at the picture of what he wants. Later, he might be able to point to it or tap the picture of what he wants.

Katie: Then I could just print out smaller versions of the pictures we already use?

Lyn: Sure. They need to be big enough for you to be able to tell what he is looking at, but small enough so that you could put several on the picture board.

Katie: Okay, we can do that.

Lyn: What could we put the pictures on so all of the pictures of the activities will be in one place?

Katie: Hmmmm . . . [Katie looks around the work area.] What about the cardboard backing off this packet of construction paper?

Lyn: That'll work.

[Katie and Lyn print out the pictures of Justin's favorite centers and attach them to the cardboard. Lyn shows Katie how to use the picture board during free play time and they teach Justin how to use eye gaze to select the desired activity.]

Lyn: How do you think that worked?

Katie: I like it, and more importantly, I think he liked it. It's just going to take a little practice for us to get the hang of it.

Lyn: At first, you might find yourself anticipating his desire rather than getting him to communicate his request, but he will soon start getting the hang of it.

Katie: He was starting to get the hang of it in just the few times we tried this morning.

Lyn: I think so, too! How could you use this idea to help Justin do other things here in the classroom?

Katie: I was just thinking that same thing! Meal and snack times seem like no-brainers for using this strategy. We could put some pictures of juice, milk, and water on another board. We could also put what we are having for snack or lunch and he could pick what he wants a bite of next.

Lyn: Want to try it?

Katie: Later today I will take some pictures of drinks and snacks. We'll start there.

Lyn: Okay. Well, you are really busy, so I don't want to take up a lot more of your time, but based on what we've done today, what's your plan for what you are going to do until the next time we get together?

Katie: I am going to keep using the picture board of the centers to have Justin pick what activity he wants to do and when he wants to change activities. I am also going to make a picture board for snack and lunch.

Lyn: How will you keep Justin's mom and dad in the loop?

Katie: I will show them the picture board that we made this morning and the one I am going to make this afternoon. We both can talk with them about how these ideas might fit at home, don't you think?

Lyn: Well, we know that meals and snack happen at home, so we can talk about that. We'll also be exploring other activities they do at home and how he can have some control in communicating about parts of those activities as well. Now, when do you think it would make sense for me to come back based on the plan that we've made today, and what should be our focus during that visit?

Katie: I need some time to try this and to teach Justin how to use the picture board like we tried today, and next time let's focus on some other activities where we can use the picture board. Since this is really new for all of us, I sure don't want too much time to pass before we evaluate how things are going. Today is Wednesday. Could you come by sometime on Monday?

Lyn: My Monday morning is packed, but I do have about 30 minutes in between some other visits in the afternoon. Would that work?

Katie: I think so. I'll look forward to seeing you then.

Lyn: See you then.

During the next visit, Lyn had Katie reflect on and evaluate their previous plan to determine how successful Katie and the assistant teacher had been. Lyn asked Katie what ideas she had to modify the plan. They determined that the picture board worked when the teachers were near Justin and could hold it up for him, but they needed a strategy to use when they were not close to him and he wanted to select a new center. During the follow-up visit, Lyn had Katie generate all the possible alternatives for making this happen that she could think of, then Lyn shared some of her ideas, and together they modified their plan. They tried the new strategies during outdoor play, reflected on how successful they were, made further modifications, and then developed a specific plan for what would happen until Lyn's next visit and for the focus of the that visit.

In the example illustrating consultation, Lyn started with her own ideas and had even planned ahead by bringing a device that she thought might be helpful. Lyn was the problem solver. In the coaching example, Lyn started the visit by asking Katie what she was already doing. Lyn then built on Katie's experience and knowledge of Justin to jointly develop a strategy that fit well within Katie's classroom. In the coaching example, Katie took the lead in solving the problem, with support as needed from Lyn. In this way, Lyn builds Katie's capacity to problem solve when she is not present.

MENTORING

Like consultation, *mentoring* lacks a commonly agreed on definition (Ives, 2008). Most definitions or descriptions of mentoring, however, describe it as an informal (Davis, Middaugh, & Davis, 2008), long-term (Davis et al., 2008; Mink, Owen, & Mink, 1993), instructional (Ives, 2008) process in which the mentor shares his or her personal experiences (Reiss, 2007), usually to enhance career growth (Mink et al., 1993). Black, Suarez, and Medina define mentoring as

> a nurturing, complex, long-term, developmental process in which a more skilled and experienced person serves as a role model, teacher, sponsor, and coach who encourages, counsels, befriends a less skilled person for the purpose of promoting the latter's professional and/or personal growth. (2004, p. 46)

This definition suggests that a mentor may use coaching with the mentee. The purpose of coaching within the mentoring relationship is to promote the mentee's development and learning.

When coaching is used as an interaction style with adults, however, it can be formal or informal and short term to intermediate in length, and it builds on the coachee's prior knowledge, experiences, and actions. Mentoring is based entirely on the personal experiences of the coach, but in coaching the coach and coachee also examine other resources for information, including but not limited to current research and literature that is directly related to what the coachee wants and needs to know in order to analyze current knowledge and actions, develop alternatives, and create a plan of action to achieve his or her intended goals. The topic of mentoring is focused solely on career growth, discipline-specific knowledge and skills, or learning the culture of an organization, but coaching content includes a much broader range of potential questions, issues, problems, skills, and outcomes.

Mentoring versus Coaching Scenario

The following examples will help demonstrate the difference between mentoring and coaching in early childhood intervention.

Mentoring Example

When Joy came to work for the Mindquest Preschool as a teacher, Karen was assigned by the school's director to serve as Joy's mentor during her first year. Karen had served as a teacher at Mindquest for the past 15 years. Karen's role would be to orient Joy to the program's philosophy, curriculum, paperwork, and culture. When Joy had questions, Karen would be her first point of contact. Karen's classroom was located next door to Joy's. Karen would use her 15 years of experience as a teacher and Mindquest employee to support Joy in her new position.

During the week prior to the start of school, both Karen and Joy were in the process of setting up their rooms in preparation for the children's arrival. Joy knew from her orientation with Karen that the program had heavy emphasis on early literacy development. Because Joy was a recent graduate, this would be her first experience in setting up a classroom, so she sought the advice of her mentor. Karen was more than happy to help. She had Joy come next door to her classroom where she showed her each of the learning centers she had created, labels that she had made for different objects within each center and around the classroom, and books with relevant topics that she had selected and strategically placed within each center. Karen also shared the letter that she gives to parents on the first day of school to explain the school's philosophy of learning and her own classroom philosophy. She invited Joy to make a copy of the letter to give to the parents of children in her classroom.

This brief scenario described how Karen used her role as Joy's mentor to orient her to the preschool, provide guidance about the classroom environment, and teach her how to inform parents about the program's and her own philosophy. In contrast, the scenario that follows demonstrates how Karen could use a coaching approach to adult learning and support while still serving as Joy's mentor.

Coaching Example

When Joy asked Karen for advice about how to set up her classroom, Karen told Joy that she would be happy to help her. She asked Joy to share what she had learned in school about creating classroom environments for preschoolers, particularly literacy-rich environments. Then Karen built on Joy's knowledge by explaining more about Mindquest Preschool's philosophy on learning and early literacy development. The two then discussed how that philosophy matched current research about child learning. Karen asked Joy how the school's approach complemented what she had learned and what she was thinking in relation to her own classroom environment. Then Karen asked Joy if she would like to learn more about putting the philosophy into action by analyzing Karen's classroom. The two began by looking at Karen's classroom as a whole and then further investigated how Karen had thoughtfully designed each center to be consistent with the program philosophy, which includes promoting early literacy development. As they finished their tour of Karen's classroom, they sat down at a table and Karen asked Joy to reflect on how her classroom compared with Joy's current vision for structuring structure her own classroom. Joy shared the many ideas that were now filling her mind based on what she had seen, what they had discussed, and what Joy had learned from her educational program. Karen asked Joy what supports she needed from her or the director to get started and they sketched out a plan.

Karen also asked Joy how she planned to ensure that the parents of children in her classroom understood both the program's and Joy's own philosophy about child learning and development. Joy said that she had considered having a brief parent meeting one evening during the first week of school, calling each parent and explaining it to them individually, or sending each parent a letter or email. Karen asked Joy to elaborate on the advantages and disadvantages of each option. After carefully considering the possibilities, Joy decided that she would send an email to each parent because email was one of the methods that she wanted to use on an ongoing basis to remain in close contact with the parents of children in her classroom.

In this scenario, Karen, the mentor, still used her years of experience and knowledge of the program and its practices to assist Joy. Rather than basing everything on Karen's experience and own classroom model, however, she used a coaching interaction style and a set of criteria that used Joy's education, current research, and program philosophy to guide Joy's thinking. As a result, she helped Joy discover what she already knew and helped her explore how both of them could build on that knowledge to meet program priorities and create an appropriate classroom environment and communication method with parents. This experience built Joy's capacity to use the program philosophy as a framework and developed her competence and confidence as a new teacher at Mindquest.

SUPERVISION

The role of a supervisor is to ensure that the employee's job duties are fulfilled and that work meets a certain criteria (Hanft, Rush, & Shelden, 2004). *Supervision* inherently is a hierarchical, power-over relationship in which the supervisor directs the employee's actions and evaluates the employee's performance. Clearly, coaching is its antithesis. Coaching is a partnership between the coach and coachee, who work together to ensure that the coachee achieves his or her goals. The coachee evaluates both the progress that he or she has made toward achievement of the goals and the success of the coaching process and relationship.

An increasingly common method of supervision in early childhood is reflective supervision. Reflective supervision involves a relationship that promotes ongoing opportunities for learning, teaching, and professional growth to ensure quality services. Reflective supervision allows the supervisee to broaden and deepen his or her knowledge through the investigation of theories, practices, and policies; participate in ongoing reflection on his or her practices in a safe environment; engage in critical thinking and practice; and determine personal goals and monitor progress (Dinnebeil, Buysse, Rush, & Eggbeer, 2008). The three key features of reflective supervision are reflection, collaboration, and regularity and consistency (Fenichel, 1992).

Of the approaches to adult interaction and learning that are described in this chapter, reflective supervision is most consistent with the characteristics and elements of coaching. Both reflective supervision and coaching involve an ongoing, collaborative relationship that helps the supervisee or coachee reflect on his or her practices in light of theories and approaches within and across disciplines in early childhood and early intervention for the purposes of learning and development. In reflective supervision, the coach is always the coachee's supervisor and is responsible for the coachee's professional development. In coaching, the coach could be, but is not limited to being, the coachee's supervisor, and coaching topics and outcomes may extend to other content in addition to quality of services for young children.

Supervision versus Coaching Scenario

The following examples will help demonstrate the difference between supervision and coaching in early childhood intervention.

Supervision Example

Stephanie, the director of a large preschool program affiliated with one of the prominent churches in town, noticed that one of the school's teachers, Liz, had not taken her mixed-age class outside to play in the last 3 days. The center had just recently completed a renovation of the outdoor play area, which includes all-natural play elements with both an open and covered play area. The money for the project had been provided by several private donors, and Stephanie felt that these individuals and their families should see the space in use on a regular basis. But rather than using the outdoor space, Liz and Kristi, her coteacher, had opted to either remain in their classroom or use the indoor play space that was set up in the church's gymnasium. As Liz was getting ready to walk out the door to the staff parking area on the third afternoon, Stephanie asked to see her in the office for a few minutes.

Stephanie: Liz, I know you are on your way home, but I need to talk with you about something.

Liz: Yeah, I have an errand to run and then I need to get home as early as possible tonight.

Stephanie: Well, this won't take but a minute. I couldn't help noticing that 3 days this week, you have kept the children inside rather than giving them time outdoors. I reviewed your lesson plans and you had clearly indicated that you would be taking the children outside.

Liz: Oh, I know, but it's been kind of chilly out, so Kristi and I thought it would be better to stay inside and go to the gym instead. They have plenty of room to run in there and it's warmer.

Stephanie: Our program standards indicate that we will provide time during the day for outdoor play. Only in situations of extreme weather conditions would we keep the children inside. "Kind of chilly" would not be considered to be an extreme weather condition. I have already checked the weather forecast for tomorrow and the temperature is expected to be in the low 50s with light winds. I will expect you to have your class outside tomorrow.

Liz: But . . .

Stephanie: The donors to our program have been very generous, so I want to be sure they and others in our community see how much we use and appreciate our beautiful, new outdoor space. Will you explain this to Kristi or would you prefer me to talk with her?

Liz: I guess I can talk with her.

Stephanie: Thanks, Liz. I won't keep you any longer. See you tomorrow.

In this scenario, Stephanie observed that Liz's practices were inconsistent with the program standards. She informed Liz of the standard and told her to comply. The scenario is an example of supervision in its purest sense. The following example illustrates the same situation, using a coaching approach.

Coaching Example

Stephanie: Hi Liz, I see you are on your way out the door. As soon as it is convenient for you, I'd like to talk with you about something. I'd really like Kristi to be part of the conversation, too.

Liz: Oh, well, I was on my way to run an errand and then I need to get home as soon as I can tonight, but if it won't take too long, we can talk now. Kristi is still in our room.

Stephanie: Okay, would you like to meet in my office or back in your room? This should take only a few minutes.

Liz: Let's head back to the room and Kristi can join us.

[Back in the classroom] Stephanie: I wanted to touch base with the two of you because I would like to talk with you about something I noticed.

Kristi: What's that?

Liz: Yeah, is there a problem?

Stephanie: You know how I always review your lesson plans for the week and I also check in periodically just to see how things are going. Well, I observed the last 3 days this week, you have been taking the children to the gym rather than going outside. Tell me how you came to this decision.

Liz: Well, it's been a little chilly, so we decided that we would rather keep the children inside than go out in the cold.

Kristi: . . . and it's just easier than trying to bundle them up and get them outside and no sooner do we get their coats on then it's time to come back in. Besides, they really like the stuff in the gym. They can run and play in there, too.

Stephanie: How is that consistent with our program standards related to outdoor play?

Kristi: I don't know.

Liz: Well, we are supposed to have outdoor play on a daily basis unless the weather is too bad.

Stephanie: The program standard says "extreme weather conditions." How would you define that?

Liz: I guess maybe if it was raining.

Kristi: Blowing snow, sleet, or temperatures below freezing?

Stephanie: How does that compare to the weather this week?

Liz: I think it's been in the low 50s or upper 40s most of the week, but some of the parents don't send hats and gloves for their children, so I don't want them to get too cold.

Stephanie: That is important, too. What ideas do you have to resolve that?

Kristi: We could tell the parents they need to make sure they tuck hats and gloves in their children's coat pockets, so that we will have them if we need them.

Stephanie: That's one idea. What else can we think of?

Kristi: We could check the "lost and found" box in the office for hats and gloves that might fit the children in our class. I wouldn't mind taking them home and washing them, and then we could keep them in our room in case the parents forget.

Liz: I could include the reminder about warm clothes in a note that I was preparing to send home to the parents this week. I could remind the parents about our program standard of having the children experience outdoor play on a daily basis and tell them how important it is for the children's learning and development. Then I could ask that they be sure to always dress their child in layers, so we can always plan to go outside unless the weather is too bad.

Kristi: And you could give them examples of times when we wouldn't take them outside.

Liz: Sure.

Stephanie: That sounds like a plan for upcoming days. What is your plan for tomorrow?

Kristi: I don't mind checking the "lost and found" box before I leave tonight and taking what I find home to wash.

Liz: That would be great, Kristi. Thanks. I can bring some of the hats and gloves my children have outgrown. Our outdoor play space is so great, I certainly want to be able to use it. Many programs don't have anything near as nice.

Kristi: I know it was expensive. I want to make sure we can use it, but at the same time, I want to make sure the children are warm and stay healthy.

Stephanie: I appreciate your concerns. I think we have developed a very workable plan that will be consistent with your planning as well as our program standards. Above all, the children will be warm and can have fun in the new outdoor space. Thanks for taking the time to talk with me about this.

Liz: No problem.

Kristi: Thanks for bringing it to our attention.

The revised scenario using a coaching approach involved both of the teachers who were responsible for the classroom. Stephanie demonstrated respect for the teachers' time by asking Liz to choose a good time to meet. Stephanie shared her observation that the children had been kept indoors and then asked the teachers for their viewpoint. Rather than telling them that their behavior was inconsistent with the program's standard, she asked them to reflect on their knowledge of the standard, define the wording of the standard, and compare it with the justification for the decision they had made. The information and the rationale the teachers provided to justify their decision gave Stephanie further insight into their decision. The information sharing session provided an opportunity for the supervisor to engage the teachers in generating potential alternatives and actions to resolve the present situation, which in turn would assist them with meeting the program standard. Stephanie continued asking questions about the actions that the teachers would take until a concrete and immediate plan was developed. The plan that they developed achieved all of Stephanie's possible objectives for bringing this situation to the teachers' attention.

COUNSELING

Counseling focuses on a therapeutic relationship between the counselor and client or patient. The purpose of counseling is to remediate a particular dysfunction, solve a problem, or heal emotional pain. The role of the coach, in contrast, is to promote future learning, growth, and development (Ives, 2008; Mink et al., 1993; Reiss, 2007). Counseling focuses on the other person's feelings, whereas coaching focuses on changing actions (Ives, 2008).

Counseling versus Coaching Scenario

The following examples will help demonstrate the difference between counseling and coaching in early childhood intervention.

Counseling Example

The following scenario involves Teresa, a nurse with the early intervention program, and Carla, a mother whose child, Angel, was born 7 weeks prematurely. Due to her premature birth, Angel had serious medical complications and was not expected to live. Angel remained in the hospital for 3 months. She is now doing better than her doctors had expected. Angel is Carla's second child. Her first child was also born prematurely and died 2 days after birth. Teresa has been working with Carla for the past few weeks. The visits have focused on Angel's continued weight gain and growth as well as mother–child attachment issues. Carla has expressed that she is still afraid Angel might die, so she feels like she is "holding back" to protect herself from another heartbreak. Carla saw a psychologist while Angel was still in the hospital to help her cope with her feelings about Angel, her previous pregnancy, and the loss of her first child. When Angel was discharged from the hospital, however, Carla was no longer able to keep appointments with the psychologist because she did not want to take Angel out of the house due to concerns about her health and she did not trust anyone else to take care of her.

On this day when Teresa arrives at Carla's home, she notices that the window shades are closed and the house is very dark. Although it is the middle of the afternoon, Carla is still in her pajamas. She is holding Angel, who is cooing and appears clean, content, and well fed. When Teresa asks Carla how things are going, she says that she is having a "down day," but that she will be all right. Teresa then asks how she is feeling and what a "down day" means, and Carla indicates that she is overwhelmed by taking care of Angel. She is still afraid that Angel might die, so she always keeps Angel with her and when she puts her down in her crib, she sits beside it just to make sure that Angel keeps breathing. Carla shares that her husband is working double shifts at the plant in order to pay for the large portion of the medical bills that were not covered by their insurance, so he cannot really help care for Angel. Besides, he is a heavy sleeper and she's afraid that if he were responsible for caring for Angel while Carla sleeps, he might not hear Angel's cries. Teresa shares her observations of Angel and additional information that is based on her extensive experience working with infants who were born prematurely. Teresa then prompts Carla to talk further about her feelings of being overwhelmed and her fear that Angel might die. She also prompts Carla to talk about any good feelings that she has about Angel and to compare how her experience with Angel has differed from the situation with her first infant that died. Teresa tries to help Carla talk about how the death of her first child is affecting her ability to bond with Angel and how her fears about Angel are hurting her ability to function.

Clearly, Carla has some strong emotions tied to the situation with Angel, probably as a result of the similar situation in which her first child died. Using her observations and prior knowledge of the situation, Teresa starts trying to get Carla to talk about her feelings and to identify some solutions that might improve the present situation. The intent of this conversation appears to be to address Carla's emotional state and identify potential solutions.

This conversation represents a type of counseling in that it focuses on feelings and solutions rather than on Carla's goals for Angel and the support she needs to address these goals. The content and process of this conversation are also beyond the expertise and scope of practice of many early intervention practitioners. The following scenario is based on the same situation and illustrates how an early intervention practitioner would use a coaching interaction style.

Coaching Example

When Teresa enters Carla's home, she sees that the window shades are closed, the room is dark, and Carla is still in her pajamas. Carla is holding Angel and Teresa can see that Angel is clean, her coloring is good, and she is softly vocalizing. Teresa reminds Carla that their plan had been to weigh and measure Angel as well as focus on her feeding and nutritional intake during this visit. Before moving to those topics, however, Teresa explains to Carla that she is concerned about her because the last time she came to visit, she found Carla and Angel in a similar situation (staying indoors in a darkened house). Carla told Teresa about feeling overwhelmed, worrying that Angel might die, and feeling stressed about her lack of support from her husband and the financial strain that the hospital bills have placed on her family. Teresa shared the goals for Carla that they had written on Angel's IFSP related to promoting Angel's continued growth and new learning. Teresa asked Carla if these were still her goals for Angel, and Carla nodded to indicate that they were. Teresa then asked Carla how her current situation was helping her support Angel's growth and development. Carla expressed that it was not helping, but that her feelings about Angel's health were all that she could think about.

Teresa prompted Carla to think about her options for getting the help she needed to address these feelings. Carla indicated that the psychologist at the hospital had been very helpful and had offered to continue seeing her, but she did not feel comfortable leaving Angel with anyone to go to the appointments, nor did she want to take Angel with her because of the potential risk to Angel's health. Because Carla was adamant that she did not want to take Angel out of the house right now except to doctor's visits, Teresa and Carla then brainstormed alternatives for someone that she would trust to care for Angel so she could talk with the psychologist. Carla decided that her mother was probably the best option. In order for Carla to become comfortable with her mother taking care of Angel while she was at her appointment, they decided to start by having her mother spend time with Angel while Carla was home. Carla's plan was to talk to her mother and have her mother come over sometime in the next week, and to contact the psychologist's office to schedule an appointment. They also agreed that during their next visit, Carla's mother would be present so Teresa and Carla could talk with her mother about Angel's IFSP and what they were doing to help Angel specifically with her feeding and nutritional intake. Carla felt that it would help ease her mind if her mother knew what Teresa and Carla had been working on together regarding feeding.

In this scenario, Teresa recognized that Carla needed supports that she was not trained to provide. Rather than ignoring the red flags that she was seeing in order to carry on with the original plan for her visit, Teresa used her coaching skills to assist Carla in 1) analyzing the current situation and evaluating whether it enabled Carla to achieve the outcomes on Angel's IFSP, 2) generating alternatives to help with the present situation so that Carla could work toward the goals on the IFSP, and 3) developing a joint plan of action that would assist Carla in obtaining the specialized help that she wanted and needed. At her next visit, Teresa planned to follow up with Carla about her implementation of the joint plan and return to working on the outcomes related to Angel's growth and development on the IFSP.

DIRECT TEACHING

Direct teaching involves the transfer of knowledge from a person with expertise, knowledge, and skills in a particular content area to an individual or group. Teaching usually is linear, based on specific learning objectives that are developed by the instructor, and guided by or based on a written curriculum (Reiss, 2007). Students follow the pace that is set by the instructor. The instructor typically employs some type of testing to determine the extent to which the student has mastered the content.

Consistent with the research on adult learning, a coaching process begins with the coachee examining what he or she already knows or is doing (Bransford et al., 2000). The coach uses his or her knowledge and expertise to supplement or further the coachee's knowledge. Coaching does not follow a linear trajectory that is based on an explicit curriculum. Instead, coaching is based on the coach and coachee's reflection and analysis of a present situation or previous actions, followed by generation of alternatives or strategies to support the coachee in achieving the goals and objectives that he or she has identified. The coach and coachee sometimes need to go beyond their own knowledge to explore other resources for information. Coaching is individualized and proceeds at the pace set by the coachee. With the coach's support, the coachee continually assesses the effectiveness of the ideas and strategies that he or she jointly develops with the coach to determine whether they apply to the current situation. The coach and coachee also go beyond the present to examine how the coachee might apply the knowledge, information, and/or skills in future situations.

Direct Teaching versus Coaching Scenario

The following examples will help demonstrate the difference between direct teaching and coaching in early childhood intervention.

Direct Teaching Example

In the following scenario, Kathy, a home visitor for an Early Head Start program, uses direct teaching to instruct Heather, the mother of 2½-year-old Manuel, how to read a book to him. Kathy and Heather have been working together for the past 6 months.

Kathy: Heather, today I thought we could talk about reading books. It's important for parents and their children to read together. It's really never too early to start reading with your child.

Heather: Okay.

Kathy: I brought several books with me today to show you how you can read to Manuel. First, let's get him up here on the couch with us. Here, he can sit right between us. [Kathy picks Manuel up and puts him on the couch between herself and Heather.] Wow, big boy, you are getting heavy. Let's look at this book together, okay?

Heather: I'm always afraid he's going to rip the pages out of the books.

Kathy: Well, that is a common concern of many parents. To solve that problem, see how the books I brought with me today have thicker pages? Some of them are even made from cardboard, which makes it harder for him to tear up.

Heather: Oh, good idea.

Kathy: Now, let's see if he wants to help us hold the book. He can even help us turn the pages. When you are reading together, you can go by the story, you can make up a story to go with the pictures, or you can even just talk about the book. We want to follow his lead, so if he wants to move ahead in the story, that is okay. We don't want to force him to stay on a particular page longer than he can attend to it because that might cause him to lose interest in the book and reading together. We want to make it fun for him. Let me show you.

[Kathy proceeds to read the book to Manuel while Heather observes. Kathy uses a playful voice while reading the story. She changes her voice to sound like different characters in the story. When Manuel wants to turn the page, they go ahead and move forward. As she finishes reading the sentence on the page, Kathy asks Manuel short "what" questions. Sometimes Manuel responds to the question and sometimes he does not. When he does not answer the question, she provides the answer. When Manuel says something about a picture in the book, Kathy paraphrases back what he says.]

Kathy: Before he gets tired of this and doesn't want to read with us anymore, I want to have you try it. Here's what you need to do. Start by reading the sentence on the page and point to the words with your index finger as you read them. This shows him what you are reading. Use a playful, interesting voice when you're reading to capture and hold his attention. When you finish the page, then ask him a "what" question, like "What is that, Manuel?" or "What do you see?" or "What are they doing?" When he says something, then you say it back to him. A good way to remember this technique is "read, ask, repeat." That means read or tell some of the story to him, ask him a "what" question about the pictures on the page, and then repeat what he says about the picture. Okay? You try it.

[Heather reads the next few pages to Manuel while Kathy observes. When Manuel starts to become a little restless, he closes the book. Heather tries to reopen the book and return to the page they had been reading. Manuel squirms out from between Kathy and Heather, gets off the couch, and goes to get his toy bear. He brings it over to his mother.]

Heather: That didn't go too good. I don't think he liked it. I don't think I did as good as you, but I was trying to remember—read, ask, repeat.

Kathy: You did great! Don't be so hard on yourself. He was just getting tired. Let's talk about your book reading to him.

Heather: Okay.

Kathy: You read five pages together before he wanted to stop. That's really good to start. Whenever he gets tired and closes the book, don't try to force him to keep reading. That might make him not want to do it with you anymore. Also, you don't have to try to get him to repeat the words you say or the names of things pictured in the book. If he does, repeat him, but if he doesn't, you can just move on. You used a nice playful voice when you were reading and he seemed to like it a lot. That helped to hold his attention. You asked some "what" questions.

Heather: Yeah, I forgot to ask them after every page, but I did it on most of the pages.

Kathy: That's okay. You don't have to ask them after every page. Sometimes he was starting to tell you what the pictures were, so you could just repeat him. Like when he said "bear," you could say, "yes, big bear" and you could even growl like a bear and tickle him like you were a bear trying to get his belly.

Heather: Yeah, I think he might like that and think it's funny.

Kathy: So, this week the two of you could read books together. Do you have any books you could read?

Heather: Yeah, we have some books around. I'll check out some of the books in his sister's room that maybe she's outgrown.

Kathy: That would be good. What I'd like for you to do this week is to try reading a story or at least a few lines from each page, and then talk about the pictures. Remember to use the read, ask, repeat technique. Use "what" questions. Help him answer the questions if you need to and then repeat back what he says. Be sure to tell him what a good job he is doing. Just have fun with it. When he gets tired, then stop. Does that sound like a plan?

Heather: Okay, I guess we can try that.

In this scenario, Kathy brought some books for Heather and Manuel to learn to read together. Kathy demonstrated what she wanted Heather to do, instructed her regarding how to read the book to Manuel, and then had Heather try it. After Heather tried reading part of the book to Manuel, Kathy gave her feedback about what worked as well as what she should do differently. To conclude the session, Kathy gave Heather instructions about what to do during the week related to reading until their next visit.

Coaching Example

The following scenario illustrates the use of a coaching approach to the same topic with the same participants. Notice how Kathy begins this portion of the visit and how she uses reflective questions to build Heather's capacity around the book-reading activity. Note, too, the manner in which Kathy provides feedback to Heather after she reads the book to Manuel.

Kathy: Heather, the last time I visited, you mentioned that you really want Manuel to be ready for the Head Start classroom when he turns 3 years old. You also said that you want him to be able to read and write as soon as he can.

Heather: I want him to do good in school. I know he is still too little to really know how to read and write, but I think he's really smart, so I want to help him as much as I can.

Kathy: Manuel is a smart little boy! It's never too early to start thinking about these things and how we can help our children learn. How do you think young children learn to read?

Heather: I guess when their teacher or their mom or dad teaches them their letters and how to sound them out and put them together.

Kathy: One thing that we know from research that works with children Manuel's age to help them start learning about reading is parents and children reading together.

Heather: Well, I did that with my daughter, but Manuel just wants to tear up magazines or books whenever he gets his hands on them.

Kathy: What ideas do you have to help him learn to read books with you?

Heather: Well, I guess I need to be with him when he is looking at books for one thing.

Kathy: That's certainly a place to start. Then, you can show him how to look at books and read them. What else?

Heather: I've seen some of those books that have thick pages made of cardboard or plastic or something so it's harder for the kid to tear them up.

Kathy: So, starting him with books that are harder to tear would enable him to use the book and turn the pages himself without tearing them.

Heather: I don't have any of those books with thick pages, but I like to go to garage sales and yard sales, so I could look for some.

Kathy: Remember how we have also been using and talking about things that Manuel likes and is interested in as a way to help him learn. How would that approach apply to the books?

Heather: You mean like the trains and animals? He really likes those.

Kathy: Yes. Finding books that are about things that Manuel likes will help to hold his attention longer.

Heather: His sister has a story book about a brown bear, but it doesn't have those thick pages.

Kathy: Would you like to try reading that book with him? We could show him how to treat the book with gentle hands.

Heather: Sure, I think his sister has outgrown that book anyway. [Heather goes to her daughter's room to find the book and returns with it in a couple of minutes.]

Kathy: Heather, how did you read this book with Manuel's sister?

Heather: Oh, I'd just read the story to her. When she was littler she wanted to hear it over and over and over again. It just about drove me crazy.

Kathy: That can just about drive us crazy, can't it? But, you know what? Telling a story over and over helps a child learn to tell the story himself and can help him learn to read the story eventually. The child learns that the book has a beginning, middle, and an end. He will come to know that the words on the page tell what is happening in the picture. He will also know if you try to skip a page, too!

Heather: [laughing] Well, that's for sure. I had to read every word the same way every time with Manuel's sister or she would tell me, "No mommy, that's not right," or "You missed a part!"

Kathy: Actually reading the story together and talking about it helps children learn more about reading. How else did you read together with your daughter?

Heather: Sometimes we just looked at the pictures in a book and would talk about them.

Kathy: That's another way to do it. One more way to read together is for you just to make a story up as you go.

Heather: Now, I'm not sure I could do that. I'm not very creative.

Kathy: That's okay. You can just read the story or talk about the pictures. Would you like to try reading this book about the brown bear with Manuel?

Heather: Okay. I guess so.

Kathy: Where could Manuel be when you are reading with him?

Heather: I think he might like to sit in my lap.

Kathy: Okay. You know a lot about reading from what you told me you did with your daughter, so would you like to read the story to him while I watch, or would you like me to read the book while you watch?

Heather: I think I'd really like to see you do it first. I could learn from how you do it.

Kathy: Sounds to me like you know quite a bit, but I'm happy to go first. Another thing we know from research about parents reading to their children and what seems to help children learn is that parents should read the story or talk about the pictures, then ask the child some "what" questions, then repeat back to the child what he says. It is also helpful to make it fun, which it sounds like you also did with your daughter. [Heather shows Manuel the book and asks him if he wants to read it. He indicates *yes*, so she puts him in her lap. Kathy sits beside Heather so that both everyone can see the book.] Heather, while I am reading to Manuel, I would like you to watch how I ask him "what" questions, and how I repeat back what he says when he answers my question.

Heather: Okay. I can do that.

[Kathy reads about five pages of the book. Manuel acts like he wants to get down, so Kathy asks Heather if it is okay for him to get down and run around for a few minutes while they talk.]

Kathy: Heather, what did you see me do that we had discussed?

Heather: After you read a couple of sentences, you asked him a question like, "What is that?" or you asked, "What is brown bear doing?" When he answered, you said, "Yes, brown bear is sleeping." A couple of times he didn't say anything, so you just went on to the next page. You let him help you turn the page, too, and he didn't tear it. When he wanted to get down, you let him go. Why were you running your finger underneath the words when you read them?

Kathy: That shows him that the words have meaning and relate to what is happening in the picture on that page.

Heather: Oh. Okay.

Kathy: How does the way I read to him match how you might do it?

Heather: We don't really read together because I didn't think he would like it, but I think he likes this story because he likes bears and animals so much. He stayed with it longer than I expected. I could ask him to tell me about the pictures, too.

Kathy: Here he comes and, look, he's bringing his toy bear. You wanna try it?

Heather: Okay. [Heather puts Manuel back in his lap and reads the rest of the book to him. Then Manuel closes the book and jumps down off his mother's lap.]

Heather: Well, I can't believe that! He let me read the rest of the book to him!

Kathy: What caused that?

Heather: He liked it and toward the end he would tell me the pictures on the page and I didn't even ask! Sometimes I forgot to say the name of the picture back to him, though.

Kathy: That's okay. He learned that fast how to share the story with you! You asked some *what* questions and I noticed you also asked, "Where is brown bear?"

Heather: Was that okay?

Kathy: Sure! Asking other types of questions that require him to answer without just saying "yes" or "no" are great. You also had to wait a little longer for him to answer you a few times, and your waiting paid off.

Heather: It did. He came up with an answer!

Kathy: That's the way to read with Manuel. What other ideas do you have for how you could read together?

Heather: I could try changing my voice so it sounds like the different animals talking. I saw somebody on television do that once. Is that too silly?

Kathy: No, not at all. That would be fun and probably hold his attention. How do you think you might use reading books together this week?

Heather: I'm going to look through my daughter's room for some other books he might like and I can look at some garage and yard sales this week. I don't think she has any books about trains. He loves trains.

Kathy: What are you going to remember from how you read to him today that you'll do this week?

Heather: I'm going to read the story to him and maybe use different voices. I can ask him to tell me what he sees in the picture. When he tells me what he sees, then I can say it back to him like, "Yeah, you see brown bear!"

Kathy: How will you remember how you read it today that worked so well?

Heather: I don't know.

Kathy: A way that might help you remember is to think *read, ask, repeat.* You read the story, ask him a question that he will understand, and then repeat back what he says to encourage him to talk more about the pictures. Read, ask, repeat.

Heather: Read, ask, repeat. Yeah, that sounds easy enough.

Kathy: It may be a way to help remember how to do it, or you can just think back to what you did today that made it go so well and be so much fun for Manuel. Well, it sounds to me like you have a good plan for what you are going to try between now and the next time I come back?

Heather: I think so. It was fun! I'm excited about this. Next time when you are here, let's practice it again!

Kathy: That sounds great! I'm excited, too!

Using a coaching approach to adult interaction rather than only direct teaching, Kathy first built on something that was important to Heather (i.e., helping Manuel develop reading and writing skills), and then linked it to the early literacy activity of shared reading. Kathy asked what Heather knew about reading to children, shared information from research about how young children learn, and then asked Heather to share her ideas. Kathy tied this topic back to what they had discussed in previous conversations. Kathy then asked Heather if she wanted to try what they had been discussing about book reading or whether she wanted Kathy to model the concepts. Heather asked Kathy to model, so Kathy carefully explained what she wanted Heather to pay particular attention to during the model. When they debriefed Kathy's book reading, Kathy asked Heather to compare it with what they had previously discussed as well as with the way that Heather might do it herself. Consistent with a coaching interaction style, Kathy invited Heather to try it, and then the two reflected on what Heather did that was consistent with both Kathy's model and their previous discussion of some of the characteristics of shared reading.

To conclude their coaching conversation, Kathy asked Heather about her plan to use what they had discussed. The use of coaching in this scenario was consistent with adult learning, built on what Heather knew and wanted to have happen, and included additional pieces of information from Kathy in order to support Heather's use of the research-based characteristics of shared reading. Rather than just telling Heather what to do, showing her how to do it, giving her feedback about her attempt, and then giving her an assignment to do before the next visit, in the coaching scenario, Kathy systematically built Heather's competence and confidence around shared reading to enable her to use the technique with Manuel in order to achieve her desired outcomes.

CONCLUSION

Coaching is often compared with consultation, mentoring, supervision, counseling, and direct teaching. Coaching can be used by someone who is functioning in a consultant, mentor, supervisor, counselor, or teacher role, but the process of coaching and the characteristics of the practice used differ from the interaction styles that traditionally are used within those roles. Coaching is unique because the characteristics of the practice may be used across roles and settings, but coaching also may be self-contained and may be used by someone who is functioning solely in the role of a coach.

RESOURCES

Buysse, V., & Wesley, P. (2005). *Consultation in early childhood settings.* Baltimore: Paul H. Brookes Publishing Co.

This text provides the theoretical framework and stages of consultation and tools for implementation.

Dinnebeil, L.A., Buysse, V., Rush, D., & Eggbeer, L. (2008). Skills for effective collaboration. In P. Winton, J. McCollum, & C. Catlett (Eds.), *Effective professionals: Evidence and application in early childhood and early intervention* (pp. 227–245). Washington, DC: Zero to Three Press.

This chapter compares and contrasts consultation, coaching, and reflective supervision as methods for collaboration in early childhood settings.

Gallacher, K. (1996). Supervision, mentoring, and coaching: Methods for supporting personnel development. In P.J. Winton, J.A. McCollum, & C. Catlett (Eds.), *Reforming personnel preparation in early intervention* (pp. 191–214). Baltimore: Paul H. Brookes Publishing Co.

This chapter provides descriptions of supervision, mentoring, and coaching as used in early childhood intervention.

Chapter 5

How to Use a Coaching Style of Interaction

Coaching is a predictable process that both parties in the coaching relationship understand (Kinlaw, 1999). Although the person who receives support from a coach may not initially know the characteristics that eventually lead to the intended results, the coach's efforts to consistently operationalize the characteristics make the process much clearer. Over time, the process becomes so familiar to the coachee that he or she anticipates the questions the coach might ask and begins the coaching conversation by sharing these reflections with the coach. Ultimately, the coachee uses the process with such regularity that the role of the coach becomes to affirm the coachee's reflections and plan, at which point the coachee needs far less support from the coach. In this way, the interaction builds the coachee's capacity and helps him or her achieve the intended outcomes. The coachee can then apply the knowledge and skills that he or she learned through the process to current and future situations.

GETTING STARTED

A coaching relationship may be formal or informal, long term or short term, and regular or intermittent. The two parties mutually agree to enter into a formal coaching relationship and create a written plan that delineates the goals or outcomes to be achieved. Formal coaching relationships often originate when one member of the coaching dyad seeks support or a service offered by an agency whose staff members use coaching as a primary interaction style. Formal coaching relationships may also be established when a person is assigned to a coach as a follow-up to a training event.

One example of a formal coaching relationship is a parent obtaining the support of an early childhood intervention program. Suppose the parent's child has an individualized family service plan (IFSP) that includes the parent's desired outcomes related to his child's development. The early intervention practitioner as coach would then work to support the parent in reaching the IFSP outcomes and could use coaching as a formal mechanism for building the parent's capacity to promote his child's learning and development.

Another example of a formal coaching relationship might be the assignment of an early literacy coach to a classroom teacher who is learning how to organize her classroom and implement a new curriculum that is designed to provide increased literacy learning experiences. The coach and the teacher would assess the current classroom environment and the teacher's understanding of the new curriculum; then they would develop a written plan that included the outcomes they intended to result from the coaching process.

In informal coaching, both parties also mutually agree on the relationship and identify the outcomes that they wish to result from the coaching process. Rather than writing the outcomes and a coaching plan, however, the parties simply agree on them. Informal coaching relationships generally occur between colleagues or peers.

For example, a physical therapist who is new to an organization might ask a more experienced therapist in the organization how to share information at team meetings most effectively. The therapists enter into an informal arrangement in which, prior to each meeting, the more experienced therapist assists the new therapist in reflecting on the most important information that she wishes to share during the team meeting. After the meeting, they debrief together. The debriefing involves the new therapist reflecting on how her presentation matched what they had planned and how she might need to revise her sharing of information at future team meetings.

Whereas the relationship between a mentor and mentee may last for a lifetime, the length of a professional career, or the period of time that both are employed by the same organization, a coaching relationship lasts for the jointly agreed on period that is necessary to achieve the intended outcomes and build the capacity of the coachee. Long-term coaching relationships tend to focus on multiple and/or complex outcomes over time.

Examples of long-term coaching relationships are a parent and practitioner working together within an early intervention program, an early literacy coach working with a teacher for a school year, or a therapist working with a preschool teacher for a year as the teacher includes a child with disabilities in her classroom for the first time. Short-term coaching relationships may be established to address singular or very specific goals of the coachee. The previous example of the physical therapists working together on presentation of information in team meetings might be a short-term coaching relationship that extends across a period of two or three team meetings. Another type of short-term coaching relationship could involve two peers who agree to support each other to implement a new teaching strategy after they both attend a training at the beginning of the school year. They may plan to observe one another using the new strategy three times, meet after school to reflect and share feedback, and develop a plan to continue refining their use of the practice.

Parties in a coaching relationship may meet regularly or intermittently. Regular coaching meetings or opportunities occur on a specified frequency, such as weekly, every other week, or four times within the next 3 weeks. The next meeting in a series of regular coaching opportunities is scheduled in the course of developing the joint plan at the end of a coaching conversation. Intermittent coaching meetings occur as needed by the coachee. If a speech-language pathologist (SLP) is learning how to administer a new assessment procedure, it may not make sense for her to schedule regular meetings with her coach. Instead, she might schedule intermittent meetings after she has had the opportunity to use the new assessment procedure.

A person who is knowledgeable about the use of coaching practices may also use those skills in a one-time conversation, depending on the circumstance. For example, consider a situation in which a person asks a colleague about respite care resources for families with young children with disabilities. Rather than merely handing the person a list, the colleague uses a coaching approach by finding out what the person and families already know about respite services and what they have previously tried. The colleague in the coaching role shares information about the use of formal and informal supports. They then review the coaching colleague's list of formal resources and brainstorm alternatives together. As a result, the coachee discovers that it might be a good idea to discuss with the families informal resources of extended family members and friends. No further coaching conversations with the colleague are necessarily warranted.

A coaching relationship may be initiated in a number of ways. A person may approach another individual who has specialized knowledge or skills that may be useful. For example, a less experienced practitioner might approach a more experienced colleague or supervisor for assistance, or a parent might seek the services of an agency to meet a specific need. A coaching relationship may also be initiated when one person offers to support another person by using coaching as an adult learning, capacity-building, or goal-attainment process. In this situation, the relationship is generally colleague to colleague or supervisor to supervisee. A third type of coaching relationship may be established between two peers who bring the same or similar sets of skills and knowledge to the partnership, who are willing to learn together and support one another through reflection, observation, practice, feedback, and planning, and who will hold each other mutually accountable in this effort. Finally, a coaching relationship may be initiated when a coach is assigned to or selected for a coachee by matching the coach's specialized knowledge or expertise with the personal characteristics and/or desired outcomes of the coachee. For example, a literacy coach might be assigned to a preschool teacher to implement an early literacy curriculum, an early intervention practitioner might be assigned to a family on the basis of the child's IFSP outcomes, and an early childhood special educator might be assigned to a preschool teacher to support the full inclusion of a child with disabilities in the regular preschool classroom.

The concept of coaching as a capacity-building process may be new to some individuals. In order for those individuals to begin to understand the coaching process and the roles of the coach and coachee, the coach should take the time at the beginning of the formal coaching relationship to explain the process.

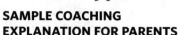

Practice opportunity

SAMPLE COACHING EXPLANATION FOR PARENTS

I'd like to take a few minutes to talk with you about what our visits will look like. In order to best support you in your everyday interactions and care of your child, I'll be asking you questions and also observing you doing what you usually do in situations that relate to the priorities you have for your child. I'll ask these questions and make these observations for several reasons. First, I want to make sure that I understand what you already know and what you've already tried and explore any ideas you've been thinking about. I'll ask these questions to gain information and also to help you think about what's been working and what hasn't. I expect that you might have lots of questions for me, too. I'll answer your questions openly, honestly, and to the best of my ability. As we share information with one another, sometimes you'll be teaching me things about your child and family, and sometimes I'll be sharing new information and ideas with you. We'll practice new ideas together, I'll try things, you'll try things, and during each visit, we'll come up with a plan together. During our planning, we'll decide what we will be responsible for doing between visits. You'll choose what strategies you will practice as part of your daily activities and think about what worked and what you might do differently as a result of your practice. We will also plan activities that need to happen or decide what information we need to gather between visits. Our plan will help us decide when our next visit needs to occur. My intent is that by interacting with you in this way I can support you in recognizing all of the effective strategies you are already using and we may come up with new ideas together to support your child as part of your everyday activities.

PLANNING THE COACHING PROCESS

Regardless of the type of coaching relationship or the way in which coaching is initiated, in order for the coaching experience to result in the coachee's learning and/or achievement of a goal or outcome, the process must begin with an initial coaching plan. The plan should be simple and include descriptions of the current state or situation, the desired future state (i.e., goals or outcomes that should result from the coaching process), and initial plans for how to actualize the future state. The Coaching Plan document appears at the end of this chapter.

The Coaching Plan document or a similar coach-developed document may be used to develop the initial coaching plan and the joint plan that should be created at the end of each coaching conversation. To create the joint plan, the coach and coachee may decide to use and update the initial coaching plan, or they may start a new Coaching Plan sheet for each joint plan.

For both the initial plan and the series of ongoing joint plans, the first step is to describe what is happening currently. In the initial coaching plan this is a description of the current state. In subsequent joint plans, this is a brief description of the progress or what the coach and coachee were able to achieve during the coaching visit. Examples include "Parent reads to the child every night," "Teacher reads a book to the children every morning during circle time," and "Parent models correct use of word without asking child to say the word every time."

This current state is followed by the coachee's description of what he or she would like to have happen. In the initial coaching plan, this description is the coachee's vision for what will occur as a result of the coaching process. In the joint plan that follows a single coaching conversation, it may be the coachee's description of the progress that he or she expects based on what the coachee agrees to do between coaching sessions. Examples include "Andre will tell his mother what he wants to eat at meals using a word or gesture" and "The children will help retell the story at circle time."

The third box on the Coaching Plan includes the specific action plan for what the coach and/or coachee will do to realize the coachee's vision in the initial plan and the coachee's desired outcomes between each coaching conversations as part of the joint plan. This box on the Coaching Plan lists the specific actions to be taken, who will be responsible for the action, and when the action will be completed. The coach and coachee can document progress and follow up on this action plan at the beginning of the next coaching conversation.

Informal coaching relationships generally do not include a written coaching plan. The coach should ensure, however, that both parties in the coaching relationship clearly understand the intended outcome(s) of the partnership. In order to accomplish this understanding in an informal relationship, the coach may ask the coachee some initial reflective questions for clarification and initial planning purposes, such as 1) What is happening now? 2) What would you like to have happen, what needs to happen, what would you like to see, or what would the ideal situation look like? 3) What are your ideas about what we can do to make this happen? After the coach has this information, the coaching partners can begin moving forward in the coaching process.

APPLYING COACHING CHARACTERISTICS TO COACHING SITUATIONS

Teaching and learning experiences and problem-solving processes often follow specific steps or a linear process. Coaching, however, is not a step-by-step process. A coach must apply research-based characteristics in a fluid manner while following the lead of the coachee. Coaching uses the five coaching characteristics (i.e., joint planning, observation, action/practice, reflection, feedback) over time rather than involving a prescribed sequence of the characteristics. For example, a coach observed a parent reading to her child (observation). After the book reading, the coach asked the parent how allowing the child to turn the pages of the book when she was ready to move on promoted the child's sustained attention to the activity (reflection). The parent and coach generated some additional strategies to help promote the child's participation in this activity, and then the parent tried the new ideas (action/practice). After reflection on how the new ideas worked, the parent and coach discussed which strategies the parent was going to keep doing during book reading time over the next week (joint plan).

In another example featuring the same situation, the parent asked the coach for ideas about helping the child attend to book reading for longer periods of time. The coach asked the parent what she was currently doing (reflection). The coach shared information about ways to use the child's interests and follow the child's lead during the book reading activity (informative feedback). The coach then asked the parent how the activity would look if the parent tried it and how she might modify the ideas to make them her own (reflection). The coach asked the parent if she wanted to try it and she agreed (action/practice on the part of the parent; observation on the part of the coach). The coach asked the parent how she felt it matched her expectations (reflection). The coach let the parent know that what she did matched what they had discussed and appeared to help the child interact for a longer period with the parent and the book (affirmative feedback). The parent and coach discussed what the parent would do until the next visit with regard to what they had discussed and what the parent had tried (joint plan).

Observation

Observation is the examination of another person's actions or practices with the aim of developing new skills, strategies, or ideas. Initially, the coach observes what the coachee would typically do in a given situation. Over time, the coach or coachee may observe the use of new skills, strategies, or ideas, still within the actual context. Observation may not necessarily occur during every coaching opportunity, but it is minimally used over the course of several coaching visits. Observation of the coachee practicing or using recently discussed ideas and strategies is a critical characteristic of the coaching process and provides an opportunity to promote further reflection and provide feedback.

Types of Observation

Observation may involve the coach watching the coachee perform an action or vice versa.

Observation of the Coachee by the Coach   Observation typically involves the coach directly observing an action on the part of the coachee that provides an opportunity for later reflection and discussion. Examples of observation are an early literacy coach observing a classroom teacher reading a book to the children, an early intervention practitioner watching a parent feeding her child, or an early childhood special education teacher viewing a preschool teacher use a hand-over-hand technique with a child with cerebral palsy.

Observation of the Coach by the Coachee (i.e., modeling by the coach)   The coach may model a behavior or activity to determine how an idea or strategy that the coach and coachee developed together might work or to help the coachee see what the coach is talking about. Modeling is intentional, direct, and specific. That is, the coachee knows that he or she is observing the coach do something that relates to the intended outcomes of the coaching process. The coach never merely models an action hoping that the coachee will see what works and assuming that the coachee will then repeat the action when the coach is not present. Modeling can be a planned observation of the coach by the coachee or it may occur spontaneously when an opportunity serendipitously presents itself within the context of the coaching meeting. Planned modeling follows a seven-step process.

First, prior to modeling, the coach should explain to the coachee what he or she is going to do and why. For example, if the coach and parent want to figure out some strategies for supporting the child's participation during meals by teaching the child how to communicate what he wants to eat, the coach and parent may start by giving the child a choice between two items. The coach and parent decide that the coach will try this technique with the child first and they determine that the two choices will be milk or juice because those options are the child's favorite drinks. The coach explains to the parent that she is going to hold both drink options at the child's eye level, ask him which one he wants, hold up each drink as it is named, and wait expectantly for the child to either gesture toward the desired drink or attempt to say "milk" or "juice."

The second step of planned modeling is to give the coachee something specific to observe or do. In the previous example, the coach may ask the parent to observe how long the coach waits before repeating the choices if the child does not respond clearly by gesture or vocalization to indicate what he wants. In that way, the parent knows the particular aspect of the coach's modeling that he or she is supposed to be analyzing.

Third, the coach models while the coachee observes. During the modeling demonstration, the coach implements what the coach and coachee planned. If the plan is unsuccessful, the coach may alter the plan during the model and try something differ-ent, explaining the change of plan either

Remember

Coaching can be as hands-on as it needs to be.

during the modeling or immediately afterward. Depending on the circumstance, the coach may narrate what he or she is doing to help the coachee understand what he or she is observ-ing or "think out loud" in order for the coachee to learn how the coach decides what to do in the moment, such as implementing the plan as discussed, adding to the plan, or deviating from the plan. If the coach is modeling actions with a child, the coach may be as "hands on" as nec-essary in order to show the coachee what he or she might ultimately do when the coach is not present. Sometimes the coach must figure out during the modeling opportunity what works or does not work while analyzing this activity with the coachee.

Fourth, the coach debriefs with the coachee what happened during the modeling. The debriefing includes a discussion of what worked, what did not work, what the coach could have done differently, how this scenario might look the same as or different from what the parent ordinarily does, and what ideas the parent obtained that he or she might try. In the sce-nario about giving choices during meals, the parent might indicate that she will increase her wait time and will use the word for the drink (i.e., "milk" or "juice") immediately after the child attempts to say the word and then will give the child the requested drink quickly.

Fifth, the coach invites the coachee to try what the coach modeled. Depending on the situation and the comfort level of the coachee, he or she may agree to try what the coach just modeled. The coach should work to create an environment in which the coachee feels safe trying new ideas and allowing the coach to observe, but the coachee should never be pressured to try something that he or she does not want to do at that time.

Sixth, the coach and coachee reflect on how the activity that the coach modeled might work when the coachee tries it or what happened when the coachee tried what the coach had modeled and the coach observed. The discussion might cover what worked or did not work, what might or might not work, what would the coachee do differently, how would the coachee continue to do the activity, and in what other ways or at what other times could the coachee try the activity.

The seventh and final step of modeling is to develop a plan for how the strategy or activity will happen when the coach is not present. Using the results of their observa-

tions, debriefing, and reflection, the coach and coachee determine very specifically when, what, where, and how the coachee can use what he or she observed. For the meal example, the parent may decide that she is going to give the child a choice between two items to drink and two items to eat at breakfast and snack times. Furthermore, during their bath routine each evening, she is going to give the child a choice between two toys that he can play with during this time.

Example of Modeling by the Coach

Phyllis, a SLP, is visiting Rebecca, a mother, and Tony, who is 2 years and 10 months old, in their home. Tony loves cars and trains. During the past couple of visits, Phyllis and Rebecca talked about and tried ways both to promote Tony's participation in play and to provide many opportunities to expand Tony's one-word utterances into two-word combinations. The joint plan was for Rebecca to follow Tony's lead when he was playing with his cars and, each time he used a one-word utterance, to expand it into a two-word phrase. Rebecca shares with Phyllis that she tried to do this but felt that she was not having much success. While Phyllis and Rebecca talk, Tony is busily playing with his toy cars and pushing them from the living room floor into the kitchen. Phyllis asks Rebecca if she wants to enter into Tony's play right now while Phyllis watches and then they can talk about what was working or not working. Rebecca says that she would feel a little uncomfortable with Phyllis watching her do this. Phyllis asks if Rebecca wants her to try it first. Rebecca indicates that she would prefer that.

Phyllis then explains that she is going to try to provide lots of examples of two-word phrases for Tony while they are playing and that any time Tony says one word, she is going to expand it in to a two-word phrase such as "push car" and "car go" (Step 1). Phyllis asks Rebecca to watch how she expands his one-word utterances and how she waits expectantly for him to take a turn (Step 2). Phyllis then proceeds to join Tony's play. Tony makes some car sounds and Phyllis says, "go car." Tony continues to play, and then Phyllis says again, "go car," as she pushes one of Tony's cars. Tony then shouts, "go!" Phyllis says, "go car." Without looking at Phyllis or his mother, Tony pushes his car hard into the kitchen cabinet and says, "go car!" Phyllis repeats him (Step 3).

After a little more play and expansion with Tony, Phyllis turns to Rebecca and asks her how what she and Tony did matched what Rebecca and Tony do (Step 4). Rebecca says that it looked pretty much the same as when she tried that technique with Tony, but that Phyllis waited longer for Tony to say the words and Phyllis used more of a "kid voice." Phyllis invites Rebecca to try what Phyllis had just done with Tony (Step 5). Rebecca declines the offer and says she'll do it later when they are playing together. Phyllis says that is certainly fine and asks Rebecca what she might try differently now that she has watched what Phyllis and Tony did (Step 6). Rebecca says that she is going to give him more time to respond and that even if he does not respond, she will keep building on his words and she will keep saying more two-word phrases. Rebecca also says that she needs to use some of the phrases over and over again and be patient for Tony to pick up on them.

Phyllis agrees with what Rebecca says and asks her specifically when she is going to try these new ideas as part of their joint plan between visits (Step 7). Rebecca says that she definitely is going to try this whenever she and Tony are playing with his cars, which usually happens several times a day. She says that she might also try it whenever he plays with his train set. Rebecca shared some examples of two-word combinations she could use when they play with the train. Phyllis asks how, if at all, Rebecca might use the "kid voice" that Phyllis used with Tony. Rebecca says that when no one else is around, she might try that because it really seemed to catch his attention. Phyllis again affirmed the plan that Rebecca had outlined describing what Rebecca would be doing in between their visits, and they also planned where they would focus for their next visit.

Not all opportunities for the coachee to observe the coach allow the coach to plan prior to modeling. Often during coaching interactions, an event occurs that could be a potential learning opportunity for the coachee, but if the coach does not seize the moment, the learning opportunity will be lost. For example, suppose that a coach and a teacher are having a coaching conversation in his classroom about positive behavioral supports when they observe one child kick another child. The coach sees this situation as an opportunity for observation by the teacher and modeling by the coach, so she demonstrates one way to address the situation. After the intervention by the coach, the coach and coachee debrief the observation and model, and then they develop a plan for options that the teacher might implement in a similar situation when the coach is or is not present.

> ### Practice opportunity
>
> Use the following questions and comments to prompt an opportunity for observation.
>
> - "Let's try it."
> - "Can we try that now?"
> - "Would you mind showing me how you do that?"
> - "How would that look/how does that look when you do it?"
> - "How about you try?"
> - "How about you take a turn?"
> - "Let's see the two of you do it."
> - "Would you be comfortable trying this while I watch?"

Action/Practice

Action or practice consists of spontaneous or planned events that occur within the context of a real-life situation that provide the coachee with opportunities to practice, refine, and/or analyze new or existing skills. If the action occurs when the coach is present, it provides an opportunity for reflection, feedback, and joint planning. Action should also occur outside the coaching interaction; the joint plan from the previous coaching conversation should promote active participation on the part of the coachee to try new ideas and strategies between visits.

Types of Action

Action may involve practice by the coachee or active participation by the coachee in an activity.

Practice by the Coachee   Practice while the coach is present allows the coachee to try the new skill, strategy, or idea while the coach observes. The coach then has an opportunity to prompt the coachee to reflect on what worked or did not work and why. After the coachee has reflected, the coach can provide immediate feedback related to the coachee's reflections and the coach's direct observations. Typically, the coachee practices an activity after he or she has observed the coach modeling an idea or strategy, or the coachee may try something that they have just discussed that does not require the coach to model it.

Active Participation by the Coachee   Active participation involves an individual accepting responsibility for and readily engaging in experiences and opportunities that are intended to achieve a particular outcome (Wilson, Holbert, & Sexton, 2006). Active participation happens *between* coaching conversations and demonstrates that the coachee is trying to use the knowledge, skills, strategies, and ideas that were identified or learned during the coaching meeting. Opportunities for active participation are included in the joint plan that is developed at the conclusion of the coaching conversation and are then revisited at the beginning of each new coaching conversation.

Reflection

The coaching characteristic of reflection differentiates the coaching process from other approaches, including basic problem solving that individuals often use, consultative models in which the consultant asks questions to learn and decide what information to share with the consultee, and teaching models in which the teacher uses questioning to assess learning. Reflection is the coachee's review and analysis of what he or she already knows or is doing to determine what modifications or new knowledge and/or skills the coachee needs in order to achieve the desired outcome in both the current situation and the future. Daniels described coaching as the process of "looking back with the goal of looking forward" (2002, p. 54). The coach's purpose for using reflection is to build the capacity of the coachee in a way that will promote ongoing self-assessment, planning, and acquisition of knowledge or skills by teaching the coachee to be aware of, continually examine, and refine his or her current knowledge and behavior (Gallacher, 1996; Gilkerson, 2004). In essence, the process of reflection assists an individual to build on what he or she currently knows or is doing to develop new knowledge and actions when they are needed. Initially, the coach encourages the coachee to reflect by asking reflective questions; however, over time the coachee is able to reflect without the assistance of the coach.

The coach's use of reflection follows an observation or action by the coach or coachee, and it precedes the giving of feedback to the coachee. The observation or action provides context on which the coachee may reflect. Allowing the coachee to reflect on the observation or action first often decreases the need for the coach to provide some types of feedback. When reflection relates to the coachee's knowledge, the coach asks about what is known, what may need to be known, how the coachee might acquire the knowledge, and what plan the coachee wishes to make for knowledge acquisition. When reflection relates to the coachee's actions, the coach prompts the coachee to reflect on what is or is not happening with regard to the intended outcome, ideas for actions that could occur, and a plan for implementing the intended actions.

Schon (1983, 1987) defines three types of reflection: reflection *on* action, reflection *in* action, and reflection *for* action.

Reflection *on* action involves thinking about what the coachee has done. It is often the most commonly used type of reflection by a coach and allows the coachee an opportunity to analyze his or her actions with regard to the desired outcome. Examples of questions that are used to promote reflection *on* action include "What just happened?" "What did you do?" and "How did that compare to what you wanted to have happen?"

Reflection *in* action is "just-in-time coaching" or "coaching-on-the-fly"—the coach is in the midst of the action with the coachee and prompts the coachee to consider how what is happening and which of the coachee's options in the present moment will yield the desired outcome. Some examples of this type of reflection are "What is happening right now?" "What are you doing right now that is going to get you to your goal?" "What are your options?" "What could you be doing right now?" and "What can you try right now?"

Reflection *for* action prompts the coachee to develop a plan to reach the intended outcome. Examples of reflection *for* action are "What are you going to do next time?" "Considering what we just learned or discussed, what do you plan to do similarly or differently in the future?"

When a coach–coachee partnership is applying the coaching characteristic of reflection to real-life situations, the type of reflection that they use and the type and content of the coach's questions are key in helping the coachee to build on what he or she already knows, is doing, has tried, and thinks, both in a specific situation and in other circumstances. The process of reflective questioning, whether it is initiated by the coach or the coachee, promotes the coachee's ability to analyze existing strategies and develop alternatives to build on current strengths, address identified priorities, and lead to a plan for action.

The Framework for Reflective Questioning

The Framework for Reflective Questioning is a tool that may be used by a coach or coachee to become aware of, analyze, and establish plans that are related to the coachee's knowledge, actions, and results. The Framework was developed using the capacity-building model that is described in Chapter 2 and the concept of reflection as a characteristic of a coaching interaction style for supporting families and colleagues as part of early childhood intervention (Hanft, Rush, & Shelden, 2004; Rush, Shelden, & Hanft, 2003; Wilson et al., 2006). The four types of reflective questions and types of content were developed from a review of the literature on capacity building, coaching, and reflection (Costa & Garmston, 1994; Kinlaw, 1999; Schon, 1987; Whitmore, 2002). A task group of individuals at the Family, Infant and Preschool Program in Morganton, North Carolina, identified a pool of questions that examined how coaching could be used to support parents and practitioners in the use of natural learning environment practices. The task group reviewed each question to ensure that it was relevant and was stated broadly enough to be used in multiple coaching contexts. Next, the task group organized the questions by type and content. Once the framework was in a draft format, it was used by the task group members in coaching interactions with families. Their feedback was used to make changes and additions to questions on the framework. The Framework for Reflective Questioning is presented in Appendix B at the end of this chapter.

Types of Reflective Questions

The Framework consists of four different types of open-ended reflective questions: awareness, analysis, alternatives, and action.

Awareness questions promote the coachee's understanding of what he or she already knows or is doing (e.g., "What have you tried?"). The coach may use them initially to clarify the situation or issue for both the coach and coachee. Awareness questions are similar to typical assessment questions; therefore, they are familiar to most coaches and are already part of their repertoire. Awareness questions typically are *who*, *what*, *when*, and *where* questions. New coaches tend to use awareness questions primarily; however, these types of questions should be used sparingly to avoid making the coachee feel like he or she is being interrogated by the coach.

Analysis questions are used to support the coachee in comparing the current state (i.e., knowledge, skills, actions, or outcomes) to the desired future state (e.g., "How does what just happened compare to what you would like to have happen?"). Analysis questions often answer *how* and *why*. The answers to analysis questions are not readily apparent to the coach or coachee. These types of questions cause the coachee to examine his or her thoughts, feelings, actions, intentions, and knowledge.

Alternatives questions are used to provide the coachee with an opportunity to consider a variety of possible options to obtain the desired results (e.g., "What are all the possible ideas to consider?"). Alternatives questions provide an opportunity for both the coachee and coach to brainstorm and consider all of the possibilities without deciding on an option or committing to a joint plan. Alternatives questions are often the least used type of question, yet they provide both the coachee and coach with opportunities to share and explore their knowledge and ideas. After all of the possible alternatives are presented, the coach and coachee can decide which option or combination of options they will include on the joint plan.

Action questions assist in developing the joint plan of what the coachee is going to do as a result of the current conversation (e.g., "Who is going to do what before the next time we meet?" "What will we focus on during our next visit?"). Action questions confirm exactly which topics of all the ones that were discussed will be used, including specific steps for implementation. Action questions also allow the coach and coachee to create a backup plan in case the idea that they considered to be the best one does not work as planned.

Remember

The four types of reflective questions are

- Awareness
- Analysis
- Alternatives
- Action

Content of Reflective Questions

Reflective questions contain four different types of content: knowledge/understanding, practice, outcomes, and evaluation. Reflective questions that are related to *knowledge* and *understanding* help the coachee identify what he or she currently knows about a particular topic. Questions that focus on *practice* help the coachee explore what he or she is actually doing or has done in a particular situation. Questions about *outcomes* cause the coachee to think about current or intended results. Reflective questions that are based on *evaluation* ask the coachee to make judgments about the usefulness of opportunities in order to recognize what he or she already knows or is doing and to recognize new skills and knowledge that he or she desires to learn.

Remember

The types of reflective questions may include

- Knowledge and understanding
- Practice
- Outcomes
- Evaluation

How to Use the Framework for Reflective Questioning

The Framework for Reflective Questioning is not designed for use in a linear method in which the coach or coachee begins on the left side of the framework with awareness questions and then moves through analysis, alternative, and action questions. Nor should the coach or coachee move down the framework from knowledge through practice, outcome, and evaluation questions. Rather, the coach should use questions as they would naturally occur in a conversation, choosing them in response to questions or comments that are made by the coachee. During a coaching conversation, the coach generally uses knowledge, practice, and outcome questions as part of the variety of reflective questions that a given conversation may contain. One of the coach's goals is always to assist the other person in developing a plan for action before the coaching conversation concludes. Whereas the framework can guide the coach to select questions to promote the coachee's reflection, the coach may also ask questions during a coaching interaction that are not in the framework. Additional questions during a coaching conversation may be modeled after questions on the framework according to the intent (type) and content of the question.

The majority of questions asked should be analysis and action. Questions should be open ended rather than requiring only a yes or no response. Closed questions requiring a yes or no response typically are appropriate only in situations when the coach needs to ask the coachee's permission for something or to avoid making an assumption. An example of a closed question to ask permission would be, "Do you mind if I watch you feed him?"

Sometimes, a coach may have a good idea and want to offer a suggestion. Rather than trying to frame the suggestion in the form of a question (e.g., "What would happen if . . . ?" "What about . . . ?" "How about trying . . . ?" "What do you think about trying . . . ?" "How would you feel about . . . ?"), the coach may join the coachee in reflecting on the options that result from an alternatives question. Some coaches mistakenly ask questions in order to get the coachee to arrive at a predetermined answer or to agree with what the coach is thinking. Instead, the coach should ask reflective questions and should be open to the possibilities that the coachee generates. If the alternatives generated by the coachee are contrary to research evidence on the topic or have known negative consequences, however, then the coach should follow the alternatives question with analysis questions to identify the positive and negative features of the alternative. In this way, the coachee will also learn the process for making decisions. The coach may also share what he or she knows about the alternative generated by the coachee so that the coachee may make an informed decision about the options that he or she selects as a plan of action.

Remember

Primarily use open-ended questions (e.g., who, what, when, where, why, how) rather than closed-ended questions (i.e., questions that can be answered with a *yes* or *no* response).

Practice opportunity

Become comfortable with a few question stems from the Framework for Reflective Questioning that fit your style or personality. Write these question stems on a notepad that is easily visible to you during your coaching conversation. If you get stuck during your conversation, you can quickly refer to your notepad for a few questions that you know work. This strategy will help you avoid asking too many awareness questions and assist you in moving to analysis, alternatives, and the joint plan (action questions).

Occasionally, a coachee may respond to a question by saying, "Just tell me what I need to do" or "Don't coach me, just tell me." In these instances, the coach should respond by letting the coachee know that in order to be most helpful, the coach needs to have an idea of what the coachee already knows or is doing. Only then can the coach provide information that matches the coachee's interests, needs, or lifestyle. People are more likely to act on information if they play a part in identifying it and it is tailored to their specific situations.

Another response that coachees may give to a reflective question is "I don't know." In this circumstance, if the coach thinks the coachee does know the answer to the question because of previous information the person has shared or an action on his or her part that the coach observed, then the coach should rephrase the question to ensure that the coachee understands. Alternatively, the coach can point out the information that the coachee previously shared or the action that the coach observed. If the coach does not know the coachee's level of knowledge related to the question being asked, then the coach should share information and then ask the person how the information matches his or her current understanding, priorities, or ideas.

Practice opportunity

Give the coachee time to think and respond to the question that you have asked. Learn to be comfortable with silence. When you are faced with silence, do not feel compelled to repeat the question, clarify the question, fill the quiet with talking, finish the coachee's sentences, or immediately jump to making suggestions or sharing ideas. Instead, count to 10 before asking another question or moving to sharing information.

Observation opportunity

Read the nonverbal cues of the coachee. When you are asking reflective questions, be aware of how the coachee is reacting to the process. If you sense or perceive that the person is uncomfortable or even annoyed, reflect on your coaching skills. For example, are you drilling the person you are coaching, coaxing him or her to answer in the way that you want, not allowing the person to have enough thinking time, not listening to the person's answers, or thinking about what you are going to say next rather than paying attention to his or her answers?

Example of Use of Reflective Questions   Allison has been working with Chris and his grandson Isaac for the past 3 weeks. Chris is the temporary guardian of Isaac after he was removed from his mother because of neglect. Isaac is a very active 3½-year-old. When Allison first asked Chris to describe Isaac, Chris said that he gets in trouble a lot, he will not listen, he is mean, he has tantrums if he does not get his way, and he will run out the door of the trailer and into the road if Chris does not watch him closely. During the past few weeks, Allison has been talking with the grandfather about what Isaac likes and what types of things hold his interest as a means of supporting his positive behavior rather than only reacting to the behaviors that Chris does not want Isaac to do.

Remember

When you are asking reflective questions, be open to the possibilities of what the other person could say rather than trying to lead the person to your predetermined answer or idea. Trying to "coach someone into" something is coaxing, not coaching.

Allison: Last time when I was here, we talked about how Isaac really likes to draw, so tell me how you have used drawing as a way for the two of you to spend some good time together. [awareness question]

Chris: Well . . . last night he went to his room and came out with his Magna Doodle. He brought it over to me and wanted me to draw around his hand.

Allison: How does that fit with his interest in drawing? [analysis question]

Chris: He had me draw his hand, and then I asked him to draw my hand and he did it. He sure likes to draw and he did it for a long time. You know, he doesn't usually stick with anything for very long.

Allison: What was it that you did that made the difference here? [analysis question]

Chris: I guess I just paid attention to what he was wanting to do with the drawing. Then, I drew a happy face and he drew one, too.

Allison: [smiling] Wow, you kept the activity going with the happy face and drawing, which he likes. What are other ways you could keep an activity like this going for awhile? [alternatives question]

Chris: I don't know . . . maybe I could ask him to draw something for me or I could draw something else and see if he wanted to try and draw it.

Allison: And how could you do this with other things besides the Magna Doodle? [alternatives question]

Chris: I keep paper and pens around the house, so he can write or draw whenever he wants.

Allison: Based on the interaction with the Magna Doodle, what will you do differently? [analysis question]

Chris: Well, I'm going to take time to pay more attention to what he is drawing.

Allison: Chris, how does this match what you want to have happen with Isaac? [analysis question]

Chris: When I pay attention, then he doesn't hit at me or do some of the stuff I don't want him to do.

Allison: So, what are you going to try this week, and what should our plan be for our next visit? [action questions]

Chris: I'm going to spend more time being interested in what he is interested in and I'm going to use drawing as a time we can be with each other and not be yelling and trying to get him just to do what I want him to do. I'm pretty busy, but I think I can find time to do that. Next time, I'd like to talk with you about more ideas for how he can learn from drawing. He's not dumb, is he? I think he can learn and this shows it.

Allison: [smiling and nodding] I think so, too.

Feedback

Feedback is an important part of human learning that helps an individual build on what he or she already knows and is doing and can improve that person's use of the knowledge and skills that he or she is in the process of learning (Bransford, Brown, & Cocking, 2000). Feedback is information provided by the coach that is based on direct observations of the coachee by the coach, actions reported by the coachee, or information shared by the coachee to expand his or her current level of understanding about a specific evidence-based practice or resource. Feedback occurs after the coachee has had the opportunity to reflect on his or her observations, actions, or practice of new skills. The purpose of feedback should be to affirm the coachee's reflections (e.g., "I understand what you are saying") or actions (e.g., "Your child really seems to like the way you are holding her") or to add information to deepen the coachee's understanding of the topic being discussed in order to jointly develop new ideas and actions.

Types of Feedback

Although informative and affirmative feedback are the two types of feedback that should be used most often by a coach, coaches often use at least four different types of feedback. The four types of feedback are informative, affirmative, evaluative, and directive.

A common misperception about the use of a coaching interaction style is that the coach cannot share knowledge or expertise with the coachee. Informative feedback is the opportunity for the coach to share this type of information. The key to *informative* feedback is choosing the right time and way in which to provide the feedback. Informative feedback is sharing knowledge and information with the coachee that is directly related to an observation, action, reflection, or direct question from the coachee. Sharing information prior to reflection may be necessary when the coach knows without a doubt that the coachee has no previous knowledge of the content or situation and therefore has no foundation on which to be coached. In most cases, however, informative feedback follows reflection. Informative feedback should be provided in a way that is respectful of what the coachee already knows or is doing and that is compatible with the coachee's desired outcomes for the coaching process. The type of information shared may include research-based practices that are related to the content of the coaching conversation or ideas that result from the expertise and experiences of the coach.

When the coachee has no existing skills on which the coach may build, the coach may need to do some direct teaching of skills or strategies. Direct teaching as a form of informative feedback should always start with the least intrusive method for the coachee. Modeling by the coach is a minimally intrusive form of teaching and is followed by reflection on the part of the coachee, as prompted by the coach. A slightly more intrusive method of direct teaching would be to engage in side-by-side use of the skill or strategy with the coach verbally guiding the coachee in the use of the skill. Direct teaching could also take the form of "hand-over-hand" trials as the coach physically assists the coachee to use the skill or strategy. This most intrusive type of direct teaching may be necessary in some situations depending on the type of skill or strategy being taught and the learning style or preferences of the coachee.

At times, the content of informative feedback may be difficult to share because it may be contrary to the coachee's beliefs, actions, or ideas. The informative feedback should be based not on opinions or beliefs of the coach but on current research; program policies or procedures; or local, state, or federal law. The coach should provide this type of feedback empathetically, respectfully, and in a way that allows the coachee to make an informed decision, even if it is not the preferred decision of the coach. Nonetheless, the feedback has been provided.

Consider, for example, a parent who says that he believes spanking is an effective form of punishment and that he does not mind using it when it is needed. The coach may respond by providing informative feedback, such as the following:

> "Spanking is a form of discipline that some parents choose to use. What we know about spanking from research is that it might work in the moment to get the child to stop the behavior, but in the long term, it may not change the behavior. What we also find is that it teaches children that hitting is okay, so children who are spanked tend to hit their parents or other children. Another concern we have about a parent who uses spanking is that if

someone sees you spank your child and believes that it is abuse, that person could report you to the authorities. I just want to share this information with you, so that you are aware of all your options. I also have information about other ways of supporting your child that both research and other parents have found to be more effective than spanking. I would be happy to share this information with you if you are interested."

Affirmative feedback results from active listening and provides noncommittal acknowledgement to let the coachee know that the coach hears and understands what he or she is saying without agreeing, disagreeing, or making any other type of judgment. Examples of affirmative feedback may include objective "I" statements by the coach, such as "I see," "I understand," "I know what you mean," "I hear what you are saying," or "What I am hearing you say is _____." Affirmative feedback may also be based on the coach's perceptions of the coachee (e.g., "You seem really happy about that," "You don't like it when that happens," "You know what you want," "You read the story just like we discussed"). Comments by the coach on his or her perceptions or observations of others may also be affirmative feedback. Examples might include, "He really calms down when you talk to him in a soft voice," or "When you turned on the music, the children all put away what they were doing and came over for circle time without any protest."

Coaches often intend to provide affirmative feedback but actually provide feedback that includes a judgment of what the coach sees the coachee doing or hears the coachee report. This type of response by the coach is called *evaluative* feedback. Examples of evaluative feedback may include but are not limited to "Great," "Good job," "That's a good idea," "You're really smart to think of that," "Excellent thinking," "Way to go," "That's just super," "I like the way you did that," "I would agree with that," "That's how I would do it," or "You are really a good dad." Evaluative feedback is not wrong and should not be withheld. In fact, coachees report that they appreciate hearing the coach's assessment of how well the coachee's actions match the target skill or behavior. Coaches need to be aware of the frequency with which they provide evaluative feedback to guard against overuse. When evaluative feedback is overused, it becomes meaningless.

Directive feedback, which involves telling the coachee what to do, generally is inconsistent with the use of coaching practices. Telling may work in the short-term or immediate situation, but it does not build the capacity of a person to know what to do in future situations. For this reason, directive feedback should be used only in coaching situations where clear and present danger exists and the coach does not have time to engage the other person in a coaching conversation. For example, if a child is about to put his hand on a hot stove, someone in a coaching role would certainly intervene. If a coach sees opened prescription bottles within easy reach of the child, the coach would immediately ask the parent to close the medication and put it out of the child's reach. Then the coach could engage the parent in a coaching conversation by reflecting on how often medication is within the child's reach, what the consequences could be, and how the parent could ensure that the child will not have access to the medications.

Occasionally, people confuse directive feedback with direct instruction. Sometimes a coachee needs information about a particular topic before the coach can ask the coachee to reflect. For example, a parent might not have any previous knowledge about different types of nipples for bottles that would slow the flow of the formula and help prevent the child from choking. In that situation, the coach would need to provide instruction about different options for nipples. The instruction would not be considered directive feedback; it would be informative feedback, and its sharing would be followed by the coach and coachee reflecting on how the use of such nipples might be useful and on other possible ideas related to feeding.

Joint Planning

Joint planning is the agreement by both the coach and coachee on the actions that one or both will take or the opportunities that the coachee will use to practice between coaching visits and prepare for the next visit. The purpose of joint planning is to ensure that the coachee actively participates in the use of new knowledge and skills between coaching sessions. Joint planning occurs as a part of all coaching conversations and typically involves discussion of what the coachee agrees to do between coaching interactions regarding use of the information that was discussed or the skills that were practiced when the coach was present. A joint plan should also include planning for the next visit so that the coach and coachee can schedule the visit at a time which coincides with the activity that will be the focus of their interaction (e.g., bath time or when the siblings come home from school).

Opportunities to Use Joint Planning

Joint planning occurs at the beginning and end of the coaching discussion.

Beginning of the Conversation   The starting point for all follow-up coaching conversations is revisitation of the previous joint plan. In this way, the coaching conversation follows a predictable process: The coachee knows the explicit expectation that he or she will implement the joint plan between coaching conversations and then report on his or her reflections regarding the implementation of the joint plan the next time the coach and coachee meet. Initiating all follow-up conversations by referring to the previous joint plan also provides focus to the conversation. For example, suppose a coach and parent make a joint plan that the family will have the child at the table during family meals and will offer him a choice of a drink or a bite of food while modeling the appropriate word. At the next visit, the coach and parent revisit this joint plan and the parent reports that the child says "bite" when he wants a bite of food. The coach and parent continue to talk about what prompted this progress, what happened when he chose his food, what else the parent tried, how the siblings supported the child's participation during meal, and so on. Had the coach asked simply "How are things going?" rather than starting with the previous joint plan, the parent might have answered that the child is only using one word without further explaining the context. Starting with the previous joint plan provides context and a better opportunity for reflection by the coachee.

Revisitation of the joint plan should be as specific as possible rather than being general questions such as, "How are things going?" "How have you been doing since our last visit?" "What's new with Janie?" or "What have you done related to our plan from last time?" More specific ways of revisiting the joint plan include the following examples: "Last time I was here, you were going to provide Abraham with many opportunities to play while standing alongside the couch, so tell me what you did and how it worked." "You were going to use the ideas we talked about last time to help Sienna climb the steps and go down the slide at the park. Tell me about that." "You had planned to let LeBron dress himself. I'm eager to hear how that went."

> **Remember**
>
> Always begin a coaching conversation by reviewing the joint plan from the previous visit.

Conclusion of the Conversation The joint plan regarding what will occur between coaching visits and at the next visit can be developed either as the coach and coachee proceed through the coaching conversation by noting what each agrees to do as a result of a conversation item or at the end of the conversation when they review all of the actions, observations, and topics they discussed and determine together what could occur between coaching conversations. If the joint plan is developed at the conclusion of the coaching conversation, the coach may summarize his or her understanding of the joint plan or ask the coachee, "What would you like to focus on between now and our next visit?" or "Considering all that we've discussed today, what is your plan and when should we meet again?" or "What would you like to accomplish between now and the next time we talk?" "What would you like to focus on during our next visit?" Having the coachee summarize the joint plan allows the coach to learn what factor appeared to be most important for the coachee during the conversation and to check for the coachee's understanding of the actions or strategies that could result in the joint plan.

If the coachee summarizes the joint plan at the end of the visit but the coach believes that a critical strategy they discussed was left out, the coach may remind the coachee of the strategy and ask whether it also should be part of the joint plan. In most instances, the coachee will agree to include the strategy. If the coachee decides not to include the idea or strategy, the coach may need to ask the coachee about the decision in order to gain a better understanding of why the idea was not a higher priority for the coachee (it could be, e.g., too complicated, require too much time, be something that the coachee did not really understand). The coach may also reflect on why the coachee did not find the idea or strategy useful (the idea could be, e.g., impractical for the coachee, not directly related to the coachee's priorities, a strategy that ignored relevant information about the situation). Coaches should always ensure that time remains at the end of the coaching conversation for either review or development of the joint plan. The "jointness" of the plan may be compromised if the coach must hurry to complete the plan and begins to recommend or tell the coachee what to accomplish between coaching visits.

The Coaching Plan or a similar document may be used to capture the ideas and actions discussed during the coaching conversation and that the coachee intends to implement between meetings. The type of planning

> **Remember**
>
> At the beginning of the coaching conversation, after you have reviewed the joint plan from the previous conversation, jointly determine the time constraints of the current conversation and prioritize how best to spend the time.

> **Reflection opportunity**
>
> When the coachee does not complete the joint plan from the previous session before your next visit, you should ask yourself whether the plan was truly a joint plan or whether it was really your suggestion or recommendation. If it was the former, then you may ask the person at some point during the conversation whether the previous plan is still a priority and if it is, when and how the coachee will go about implementing it. If the joint plan never seems to be a priority for the person being coached, you may need to have an upfronting conversation similar to: "I've noticed that we have developed a joint plan every week for the past 3 weeks, but so far you haven't been able to implement the plan. Is this plan still a priority for you? If so, how can we modify the plan so that it will be useful for you?"

tool may vary depending on the learning style of the coachee and his or her preferred memory system. Some plans may be integrated so well into the coachee's everyday life activities that nothing in writing may be necessary. Some coachees may prefer to write the plan on a calendar or "to do" list. Others may want a checklist that can be put on the refrigerator. Whatever type of planning tool is used should lay out very specifically who will do what by when and in what context.

CONCLUDING THE COACHING RELATIONSHIP/PROCESS

The coaching process concludes when the coachee has determined that the outcomes on the initial coaching plan and any additional goals resulting from the coaching experience have been achieved. In essence, the coachee's competence and confidence have been built to the point that he or she can move forward in current and future situations without the immediate need of the coach. Before they end the coaching relationship, the coach and coachee develop a final joint plan that outlines how the coachee will continue to evolve his or her knowledge and skills. The plan will also delineate the point at which the coachee might consider reinitiating the coaching relationship with the current coach or another individual in a coaching role, depending on the circumstance and type of coaching support and perhaps expertise needed by the coachee.

CONCLUSION

This chapter has described the types of coaching relationships and how to initiate the coaching relationship and explain the coaching process. The chapter also provided a basic plan to identify the intended outcomes of the coaching relationship. The majority of the chapter focused on how to put into operation the five research-based characteristics of coaching practices: observation, action, reflection, feedback, and joint planning. This information is summarized in The Coaching Quick Reference Guide located at the end of this chapter.

RESOURCES

Rush, D.D., & Shelden, M.L. (2005a). Characteristics and consequences of coaching practices. *CASEmakers 1*(9), 1–3. Retrieved from http://www.fippcase.org/casemakers/casemakers_vol1_no9.pdf

This document is a bibliography of selected references related to the operational characteristics of coaching practices.

Rush, D.D., & Shelden, M.L. (2005b). Evidence-based definition of coaching practices. *CASEinPoint 1*(6), 1–6. Retrieved from http://www.fippcase.org/caseinpoint/caseinpoint_vol1_no6.pdf

This brief article describes the research behind the operational definition of coaching in early childhood intervention as well as the research-based characteristics of the practice.

Rush, D.D., & Shelden, M.L. (2008). Common misperceptions about coaching in early intervention. *CASEinPoint 4*(1), 1–4. Retrieved from http://www.fippcase.org/caseinpoint/caseinpoint_vol4_no1.pdf

This article lists responses to the 10 most common misperceptions about the use of coaching as an interaction style in early childhood intervention.

THE COACHING QUICK REFERENCE GUIDE

Characteristic: Observation

What the Coach Does
The coach observes the coachee within the context of his or her everyday activities.

What the Coachee Does
The coachee observes the coach model a behavior or activity in the context of an everyday activity with an explicit understanding of what and why he or she is watching.

Characteristic: Action

What the Coach Does
The coach supports the coachee in practicing, refining, and/or analyzing new or existing skills during real-life situations that occur during coaching interactions and between coaching visits.

What the Coachee Does
The coachee tries new ideas or actions that either were previously discussed and planned with the coach or resulted from a previous coaching conversation.

Characteristic: Reflection

What the Coach Does
The coach uses reflective questions to assist the coachee in analyzing the current situation, then encourages the coachee to generate alternatives and actions for continually improving his or her knowledge and skills, thereby achieving the desired outcomes.

What the Coachee Does
The coachee determines what worked or did not work and why it did or did not during the observation and/or action, as well as generates ideas for next steps.

Characteristic: Feedback

What the Coach Does
The coach uses noncommittal acknowledgment when it is appropriate to affirm what the parent or care provider says or does. He or she provides positive feedback when it is necessary. He or she shares information to build on the coachee's knowledge and skills.

Characteristic: Joint Planning

What the Coach Does
The coach begins every coaching conversation by reviewing the previous joint plan and asking what the coachee did between conversations to implement the plan.

What the Coachee Does
The coachee shares what he or she has tried or accomplished between coaching conversations.

What the Coach Does
The coach ends every coaching conversation with a plan of who is going to do what by when, based on the actions and ideas discussed.

What the Coachee Does
The coachee identifies what he or she wants to try or accomplish between coaching conversations and suggests when the next conversation should be scheduled.

Appendix A

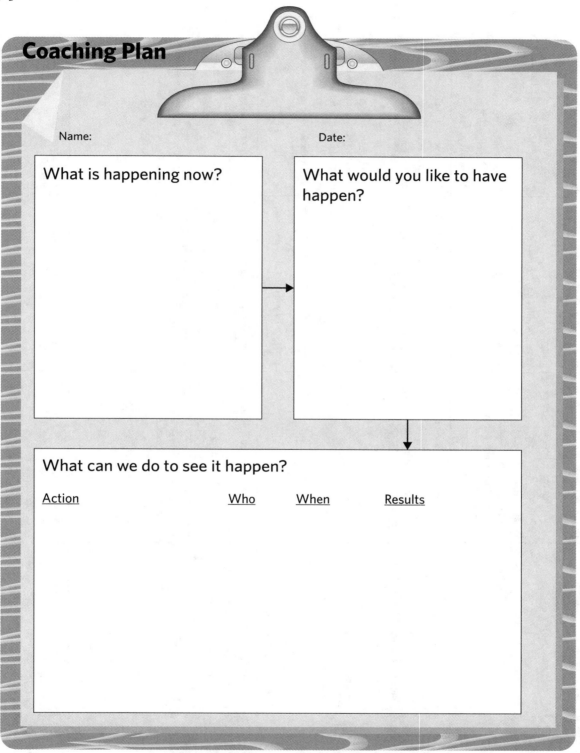

Coaching Plan

Name: Date:

What is happening now?

What would you like to have happen?

What can we do to see it happen?

Action   Who   When   Results

Appendix B

Framework for Reflective Questioning

Question content	Question type			
	Awareness	Analysis	Alternatives	Action
Knowledge/ Understanding (What you know)	What do you know about . . .? What is your current understanding of (topic, situation)? *Probes (examples):* How did you come to believe this?	How does that compare to what you want to know about . . .? How is that consistent with (standards, evidence) . . .? What do you know now after trying . . .? How does that compare with what you originally thought?	How could you find out about . . .? What different things could you do to learn more about . . .? What are other ways to view this for next time?	How do you plan to learn more about . . .? What option do you choose? Why? How are you going to put that into place? *Probes (examples):* What resources do you have? What supports will you need? Where will you get them?
Practice (What you did)	How are you currently doing . . .? Why? What kinds of things did you do (have you done so far)? Why? What kinds of things did you try? Why? What kinds of things are you learning to do? What did you do that worked well? *Probes (examples):* What is the present situation in more detail? Where does that occur most often? When did you first notice this?	How is that consistent with what you intended to do (wanted to do)? Why? How is that consistent with standards? Why?	What else could you have done to make practice consistent with standards? Why? What would you do differently next time? How might you go about doing that? What different ways could you approach this? *Probes (examples):* What would it take for you to be able to do . . .? What would you need to do personally in order to do . . .?	What do you plan to do? When will you do this? What option did you choose? *Probes (examples):* What types of supports will you need? What resources do you have? What would it take for you to be able to do . . .? What would you need to do personally in order to do . . .?
Outcomes (What the result was)	How did that work for you? What happened when you did . . .? Why? How effective was it to do that? What did you achieve when you did that? What went well? *Probes (examples):* How do you feel about that? What do you think about . . .? How much control do you have over the outcome?	How did you know you needed to do something else? How did that match (or was different from) what you expected (or wanted) to happen? Why? How do these outcomes compare to expected outcomes based on standards of practice? What *should* happen if you're really doing (practice)? What brought about that result?	What else might happen when you do . . .? Why? What different things could you have done to get expected outcomes? What might make it work even better next time?	Which option could get the best result? What do you plan to do differently next time? *Probes (examples):* What types of supports will you need? What resources do you have/need? Where will you get them?
Evaluation (What about the process)	What opportunities were useful to you in achieving . . . (or in learning . . .)? In what way? How was it useful? Why? What supports were most helpful? What about the supports were most helpful?	*Probes (examples):* How do you feel about that? What do you think about . . .? How was that consistent with what you expected?	What other opportunities would be useful?	What opportunities do you want to access? How will you access those opportunities? *Probes (examples):* What resources do you need? Where will you get them?

Chapter 6

Strategies for Learning the Coaching Process

Implementation fidelity is defined as "a specified set of activities designed to put into practice an activity or program of known dimensions" (Fixen, Naoom, Blasé, Friedman, & Wallace, 2005, p. 5). This chapter includes two activities or strategies that may be used to assess the extent to which a new coach adheres to the characteristics or dimensions of the practice while he or she is learning how to use coaching. These strategies may also be used as an ongoing evaluation of coaching practices after they have been mastered. The first activity uses the *Coaching Practices Rating Scale*, which is completed by the coach or by a supervisor, mentor, or colleague following direct observation or video-recorded analysis of a coaching interaction or series of interactions. The second activity uses the *Coaching Log* to document and analyze a coaching interaction.

COACHING PRACTICES RATING SCALE

Effective coaching requires the use of all five research-based characteristics of coaching practices (i.e., observation, action/practice, reflection, feedback, and joint planning) that were described in Chapter 5. Coaches should continually evaluate the extent to which they operationalize the characteristics of coaching. The authors have developed a tool to examine the frequency with which a coach demonstrates indicators of coaching practices, based on the coaching characteristics, called the *Coaching Practices Rating Scale*.

The purpose of the Coaching Practices Rating Scale is to determine how consistently a practitioner is adhering to and using coaching practices when he or she is working with either families or colleagues, in order to strengthen his or her competence and confidence using evidence-based early childhood intervention practices. The items on the Coaching Practices Rating Scale were developed from the findings of a research synthesis on how people learn (Bransford, Brown, & Cocking, 2000; Donovan, Bransford, & Pellegrino, 1999). A pool of items was developed by a work group of practitioners at the Family, Infant and Preschool Program in Morganton, North Carolina, who were examining how coaching could be used to support parents' and practitioners' use of natural learning environment practices (Dunst, Hamby, Trivette, Raab, & Bruder, 2000; Dunst, Trivette, Humphries, Raab, & Roper, 2001). The group examined each item to determine that it was consistent with the evidence, to eliminate redundancy, and to ensure that items covered the characteristics of both coaching practices and how people learn (Bransford et al., 2000; Donovan et al., 1999). The first version of the Coaching Practices Rating Scale was reviewed by two individuals who were familiar with the coaching literature and who provided feedback regarding item content. The work group used this information to make changes to the scale items. The scale was then piloted with six early intervention teams in two states. Feedback from the team members guided modification of individual items.

A person may complete the Coaching Practices Rating Scale on the basis of participation in or observation of a single coaching session or a series of coaching interactions between a coach and care provider, two colleagues, a supervisor and supervisee, or a mentor and mentee. To use the scale after a single coaching session, the person who is scoring indicates whether the characteristic was present or absent. To use the scale after a series of coaching observations, the person who is scoring indicates how often the coach implemented the practice using the following scoring system: 0 = *No opportunity to measure or use the practice*, 1 = *Use of the practice none of the time*, 2 = *Use of the practice some of the time*, 3 = *Use of the practice about half of the time*, 4 = *Use of the practice most of the time*, 5 = *Use of the practice all of the time*. A rating of 0 indicates that the rater was unable to observe the behavior described or that no opportunity occurred in the coaching session(s) to rate the item, whereas a rating of 1 indicates that an opportunity for use of the behavior occurred but the coach did not use it. The second page of the scale provides space for the observer to describe how the practice was used in order to justify the rating and provide more detailed feedback to the coach.

The Coaching Practices Rating Scale (see Appendix A at the end of this chapter) provides a quick opportunity for a person to examine the use of the coaching characteristics. After the scale has been completed, the coach can identify the indicators that need to be used more frequently in his or her coaching practices. Ratings that are below "most of the time" and "all of the time" signal areas of practice that should be strengthened.

Example of a Completed Coaching Practices Rating Scale

The following transcript provides an example of a coaching conversation between a coach, Devonna, and a mother. A video recording of the conversation was observed by Devonna's mentor, Janee, who then completed the Coaching Practices Rating Scale in preparation for a coaching conversation to assist Devonna in improving her coaching practices.

Devonna: At our meeting where we developed Amee's plan, we talked about how we could expand the activities you are doing with Amee and figure out ways for her to be more a part of those activities. One idea that we discussed was to encourage her to use her words.

Mother: Right.

Devonna: One thing that you said you were going to do was to encourage Amee to say some of the words she hears when she is watching TV. What have you tried regarding that during the past week?

Mother: Oh yes, I was able to do that and she was saying words. I like them to watch appropriate TV. We watch *Dora, Sesame Street,* and always *Full House.* I really like how that guy is so nice to those kids and the kids just listen.

Devonna: How much TV does your family watch?

Mother: Oh, wow, *Dora* has two shows—half an hour each. We watch *Sesame Street* which is an hour and *Full House.* Well, that is at least four hours. And of course we are watching the holiday specials. *Nick at Nite* is having 25 days of Christmas.

Devonna: How did encouraging Amee to talk during the TV shows go?

Mother: It went well. She was saying words like "no," "stop it," "I want that."

Devonna: When did she say "I want that?"

Mother: When she was watching the commercials. Ricky was saying, "I want that," and then she started saying it, too.

Devonna: It sounds like this is working well.

Mother: Yes, she really likes to say what Ricky says. She likes to talk, not like Ricky.

Devonna: That's good. You said that she likes to imitate what her brothers say?

Mother: She likes to follow her brothers.

Devonna: What do you want to keep on doing or do differently in the future?

Mother: I think I want to keep on having Amee talk during the TV shows. Also, after Ricky leaves for school, we have playtime and I encourage Amee to talk during that time.

Devonna: What do you do during playtime?

Mother: We play with blocks and draw.

Devonna: How do you encourage her to use her words during those activities?

Mother: I ask her a question about what she is doing and then wait a few seconds for her to answer. If she doesn't, then I tell her the word. Like I will say "What do you want to drink?" I wait and if she doesn't say anything, I'll say "milk" or "juice." Then I encourage her to try to say the words.

Devonna: Wow, you really learned a lot when you were helping Ricky learn to use his words.

Mother: Yes, I remembered what we were doing with Ricky. Amee likes to stack the blocks and say "tada." She is saying "no, no, no."

Devonna: Another possibility you brought up was—

Mother: [interrupts] Having the boys stop baby talking to her. She is just so small. She is our little princess. The boys don't care if she talks or not. They just give her everything.

Devonna: How do you think you will ask the boys to stop baby talking to Amee?

Mother: Well, I'm not going to ask them, I'm just going to tell them to stop talking baby talk to her. Raymond thinks it is funny but he needs to know that this is not helping Amee learn to talk.

Devonna: What do you think you can do to have the boys encourage Amee to talk?

Mother: I can't think of anything. I think I can say, "Let her do it." She helps me with the chores. She unloads the dishwasher, but she is not much help. I worry because she always wants to unload the silverware and I'm afraid she will cut herself with the knife. I will tell them to stop talking baby talk. I think they should ask her questions and then let her answer. She follows the boys' lead, mainly Ricky. She can say what they say.

Devonna: That will give Amee more opportunities to practice using her words.

Mother: Yes, even Jay [Amee's father] will get involved. He didn't really think Ricky has a speech problem. I thought girls didn't have speech problems. My niece Allie talks really well. Her mother is a teacher and has been teaching her since she was 2. She could have probably skipped kindergarten and gone on to first or second grade. She is always asking, "Why can't Ricky talk?" I just explain that it is hard for Ricky to talk and that is okay. Allie is very talkative and bossy. She tells her kindergarten teacher what the class should be doing. She says "I think we should do this and then that." Whenever Ricky would talk to Jay and he couldn't understand, he would just say "never mind." Ricky would just be quiet. But that is not Amee—she wants to talk. Last night the wind blew over the snowman and Santa, and Amee was trying to tell Jay. Jay was just saying it was okay. Amee got really mad and said "come here" as clear as a bell. Then Jay looked out the window and saw that the wind had blown over Santa and the snowman. He told Amee he was sorry and went out to fix them. When she gets angry, she really surprises you with what she will say. [Amee comes up to her mother, pulls her hand, and says "Mommy." The mother then says "up" and then waits. Amee says "Mom" and then the mother waits about 10 seconds and says "Up Mommy." Amee repeats, "Up Mommy." The mother gets up.]

Devonna: That was good the way you encouraged Amee to put the two words together.

Mother: I told you I remembered what I needed to do to get them to talk. [Amee takes her mother by the hand into the kitchen, points at her juice cup, and says, "I want that."]

Devonna: Amee is now using the phrase "I want that" at other times instead of just TV time.

Mother: When she wants something, she wants something. Like I said before, Amee wants to talk.

Devonna: I can see that. Let's review what the plan is for next week. You said that you and your family are going to encourage Amee to say words during TV time and playtime. You said you were going to do that by encouraging her to imitate the words you say and by asking her questions and if she doesn't say anything, you'll give her the answer and encourage her to say it back to you. You also said you are going to talk to the boys about not talking baby talk to Amee and to let her answer.

Mother: That's right.

Because Janee and Devonna had difficulty scheduling a time when Janee could accompany Devonna on a visit, Janee watched a video of Devonna's visit with the family and then completed the Coaching Practices Rating Scale. The completed scale in Figure 6.1 is the product of Janee's observation. Since this was an observation of a single coaching interaction between Devonna and the mother rather than a series of observations with this parent or multiple parents and care providers, Janee rated each indicator using the single observation column. Janee drew a box around the + for each indicator that she saw in the video and drew a box around the − for each indicator that she did not see in the video. Janee provided additional information and justification of her rating of each item on the second page of the scale. Shortly after Janee viewed the video and completed the Coaching Practices Rating Scale, she and Devonna sat down together to discuss her ratings of the visit.

Janee observed that 7 of the 14 indicators on the scale were present. The first 2 indicators on the Coaching Practices Rating Scale relate to adult learning and use of family-centered practices. Although watching television is not the ideal activity to promote child learning and in this case, language development, Devonna still recognized that this was an activity that could have development-enhancing qualities and one that the family did frequently; therefore, it could be a starting point. Janee credited Devonna with acknowledging the mother's current knowledge and abilities and being constructive rather than judgmental about this activity setting. In Indicator 11, Janee noted that Devonna did not use this situation as an opportunity for having the mother reflect on the amount of time that Amee watches television followed by informative feedback about what research tells us about television watching and language development. Such feedback could have helped the mother to make an informed decision about the amount of time she allows Amee to watch television. Janee used this as an opportunity to explore with Devonna why she perhaps did not use informative feedback and to determine whether Devonna just did not think about it, whether she did not know how to share this information with the family, or whether it was a matter of timing so that Devonna would be perceived by the mother as helpful rather than judgmental.

Coaching Practices Rating Scale

Name: _Devonna (Coach)_   Date: _12/08/09_

Rater: _Janee (Devonna's mentor)_   Period covered: _12/08/09_

> **Coaching** is an adult learning strategy in which the coach promotes the learner's ability to reflect on his or her actions as a means to determine the effectiveness of an action or practice and develop a plan for refinement and use of the action in immediate and future situations. The scale is used to determine the extent to which the practitioner uses the practices with families or colleagues in ways that promote self-assessment, self-reflection, and self-generation of new and existing knowledge and skills.

Think about the coaching conversation(s) for the period covered. For each practice indicator, indicate how often the practice was used:	Single observation — Present (+) Absent (−)	No opportunity to measure	None of the time	Some of the time	About ½ the time	Most of the time	All of the time
		Multiple observations over time					
1. Acknowledged the learner's existing knowledge and abilities as the foundation for improvement.	⊕ −	0	1	2	3	4	5
2. Interacted with the learner in a nonjudgmental and constructive manner during coaching conversations.	⊕ −	0	1	2	3	4	5
3. Identified with the learner the targeted skills that he or she wanted to learn and a timeline for the coaching process.	⊕ −	0	1	2	3	4	5
4. Developed with the learner a plan for action/practice necessary to achieve targeted skill(s) following each coaching conversation.	⊕ −	0	1	2	3	4	5
5. Observed the learner demonstrate _knowledge and understanding_ of the targeted skill(s) or practice(s).	⊕ −	0	1	2	3	4	5
6. Observed the learner's _use_ of the targeted skill(s) or practice(s).	⊕ −	0	1	2	3	4	5
7. Created opportunities for the learner to observe the coach and/or others model the target skill(s) or practice(s).	+ ⊖	0	1	2	3	4	5
8. Promoted use of multiple opportunities for the learner to practice implementation of the targeted skill(s) or practice(s) (e.g., role plays, in context).	+ ⊖	0	1	2	3	4	5
9. Used both planned and spontaneous opportunities to strengthen the learner's knowledge and skills.	+ ⊖	0	1	2	3	4	5
10. Asked probing questions to examine the learner's knowledge and abilities.	⊕ −	0	1	2	3	4	5
11. Prompted learner to reflect on his or her knowledge and use of the targeted skill(s) and practice(s) compared with research-based practice standards.	+ ⊖	0	1	2	3	4	5

Figure 6.1.   Sample completed Coaching Practices Rating Scale.

(continued)

Figure 6.1.   *(continued)*

Think about the coaching conversation(s) for the period covered. For each practice indicator, indicate how often the practice was used:	Single observation Present (+) Absent (−)	Multiple observations over time						
		No opportunity to measure	None of the time	Some of the time	About ½ the time	Most of the time	All of the time
12. Provided feedback about the learner's knowledge and skills following the learner's reflection on his or her performance.	+ ⊖	0	1	2	3	4	5
13. Provided and/or promoted access to new information and resources after the learner reflects on his or her performance.	+ ⊖	0	1	2	3	4	5
14. Engaged the learner in reflection on the usefulness, effectiveness, and need for continuation of coaching.	+ ⊖	0	1	2	3	4	5

Think about the coaching conversations for the time period covered. For each practice indicator, note how the practice was used.

Coaching practice indicators	Description of practice
1. Acknowledged the learner's existing knowledge and abilities as the foundation for improving knowledge and skills.	*Devonna used television watching, playing with blocks, and drawing as activity settings that the mother used with Amee for learning opportunities. Devonna built on what the mother already is doing to promote language development.*
2. Interacted with the learner in a nonjudgmental and constructive manner during coaching conversations.	*Devonna focused on the mother's interests and followed her lead during the conversation. She did not pass judgment about the amount of television watching but used it as a potential interest-based learning opportunity.*
3. Identified with the learner the targeted skills and a timeline for the coaching process.	*This was discussed as part of the development of the individualized family service plan.*
4. Developed with the learner a plan for action/practice necessary to achieve targeted skill(s) following each coaching conversation.	*Devonna started the conversation with the plan from the previous visit, but she focused on the skill of using words in the context of watching television (activity setting). She could have started with the activity that they had previously discussed. At the end of the session, Devonna reviewed the plan that they had discussed during the visit for the mother to do.*
5. Observed the learner demonstrate knowledge and understanding of the targeted skill(s) or practice(s).	*Mother explained how she wanted to have brothers interact with Amee in a different way.*
6. Observed the learner's use of the targeted skill(s) or practice(s).	*Mother modeled "up Mommy" in order for Amee to get what she wanted.*
7. Created opportunities for the learner to observe the coach and/or others model the target skill(s) or practice(s).	*None*
8. Promoted use of multiple opportunities for the learner to practice implementation of the targeted skill(s) and practice(s) (e.g., role plays, in context).	*No practice opportunities. The mother spontaneously used some of the strategies that had been discussed previously within the context of what was happening at the moment.*

Coaching practice indicators	Description of practice
9. Used both planned and spontaneous opportunities to strengthen the learner's knowledge and skills.	*Devonna helped the mother to recognize spontaneous opportunities for promoting child learning as they occurred during the visit. Devonna did not use any activities that she and the mother previously planned or that intentionally happened during this visit.*
10. Asked probing questions to examine the learner's knowledge and abilities.	*Devonna asked awareness, analysis, and alternatives questions. She did not ask any action questions; rather, she shared the plan at the end of the visit that had been emerging about what the mother planned to do.*
11. Prompted learner reflection on his/her knowledge and use of the targeted skill(s) and practice(s) compared against research-based practice standards.	*Devonna provided opportunities for reflection, but she did not have the mother reflect on any research-based information or standards. She did not provide an opportunity to have the mother reflect on the amount of television watching considering the amount the parent reported. Perhaps the mother is unfamiliar with the impact of watching television versus interaction with a parent or caregiver on child language.*
12. Provided feedback about the learner's knowledge and skills following the learner's reflection on his/her performance.	*Devonna did not provide feedback on the types of utterances that the mother reported child used (i.e., "no," "stop it"). She affirmed that having her help with toys, having the brothers to stop baby talk, and giving her choices to answer questions gives her opportunities to use words. She used evaluative feedback (i.e., "that's good"). She didn't ask mother to reflect before providing feedback.*
13. Provided and/or promoting access to new information and resources after the learner reflects on his/her performance.	*Devonna did not share any new information with the mother during this conversation.*
14. Engaged the learner in reflection on the usefulness, effectiveness, and need for continuation of the coaching process.	*Devonna did not evaluate their use of the coaching interaction style during this conversation.*

Devonna did not directly discuss the targeted skills (Indicator 3) that she is working on with the mother and that the mother is using to promote her child's participation in interest-based activity settings, nor the timeline for their work together. Janee knew they had discussed these details at a recent individualized family service plan meeting; therefore, she noted that this indicator was present. Janee also noted use of Indicators 5 and 6, which were related to observation by Devonna and showed the mother's knowledge and use of strategies to promote Amee's learning and use of words. Devonna did not model any new ways that Amee's mother could be responsive to her while watching television, playing with blocks, drawing, or playing with her brothers in ways that would promote her language development. Devonna and Amee's mother also did not intentionally practice any of the ideas or strategies that they discussed during this visit. Rather, the mother's use of the strategies occurred serendipitously during the visit when Amee wanted her mother to go into the kitchen and get her juice.

Because this was a single observation, not all of the indicators related to observation and action/practice may be present. If, however, over the course of multiple sessions Devonna never modeled or demonstrated for the parent and only relied on serendipitous events in order to observe the parent's use of targeted skills and practices, then she would not be fully adhering to the characteristics of a coaching interaction style. Modeling is an important way for the coach to further promote the parent's or care provider's ability to mediate child learning within the context of identified activities that occur frequently. It is also an opportunity to address the parent's priorities for child learning and development and to encourage the parent or care provider to practice during a typical routine or activity, as well as taking advantage of spontaneous moments. During their conversation about use of the indicators, Janee explored with Devonna how it might look with this parent if these indicators were present.

Janee's viewing of Devonna's video demonstrated that she used a variety of reflective questions (Indicator 10). Devonna also used affirmative and evaluative feedback (Indicator 12), but she tended to provide feedback prior to asking the parent to reflect on her understanding or the action that had just taken place first. Janee also noted that Devonna missed some opportunities to provide informative feedback (Indicator 13) about the types of utterances the mother reported that Amee was using and possibly about the amount of television watching that was taking place. Such feedback could help the mother work toward her desired outcome for Amee to use her words to ask for food, drinks, and toys. Devonna also did not reflect with the mother near the end of their visit about how coaching was working to build her knowledge and skills to continue to support Amee's learning. Because Janee was completing the Coaching Practices Rating Scale on the basis of only one observation, Janee discussed with Devonna the indicators that she did not directly observe during this visit to ensure that across visits they would be present. In this way, Devonna could reflect on her use of all of the coaching practice indicators and develop a plan to ensure that she was fully adhering to the characteristics of coaching with this parent.

COACHING LOG

The Coaching Log (Appendix B at the end of this chapter) is a tool that may be used to analyze a single coaching conversation by a person who is learning the coaching process and someone who has more experience coaching (i.e., a supervisor, mentor, or colleague). To use the log, the coach writes a transcript of the coaching conversation as soon as possible after the conversation occurred. The transcript portion of the log looks like a script indicating what the coach said and observed and what the coachee said. The log is not intended to be a word-for-word documentation of the conversation, but rather the coach's best recollection of the conversation for analysis purposes only.

After the coach has written the dialogue, he or she then codes the log according to the coaching characteristics. Each time the coach identifies the use of joint planning, observation, or action in the log, he or she places a checkmark in the column on the log that corresponds to the characteristic. The coach codes only his or her observations and dialogue, not those of the coachee. For each reflective question that the coach uses, he or she records the number corresponding to the type of question: 1 = *awareness*, 2 = *analysis*, 3 = *alternatives*, and 4 = *action*. The coach also codes the specific type of feedback that he or she provided: I = *informative*, A = *affirmative*, E = *evaluative*, and D = *directive*. The final column on the Coaching Log is a place for the coach to record his or her own reflections on how well the dialogue matched the coaching characteristics and what he or she might do differently next time.

For example, a coach may note that she used closed questions that resulted in a yes or no response from the coachee. She then rewrites the closed questions to make them open-ended and makes a plan to stop herself the next time she starts to ask a closed-ended question. The rewritten questions can serve as examples of how she might rephrase yes/no questions in the future.

The new coach generally writes coaching logs until a supervisor or mentor determines that the person's coaching practices are consistent with the characteristics of coaching. In many programs, experienced coaches continue to complete and share logs with a supervisor or mentor periodically as a way to keep their coaching skills sharp and to ensure ongoing adherence to the coaching practices.

Example of a Completed Coaching Log

The completed log between Lucia (the coach) and Eleana's mother in Figure 6.2 provides an example of how to document a coaching conversation on the Coaching Log. The sample log includes the transcript of the conversation in the first column, coding of the characteristics of the coaching practices in the middle columns, and Lucia's reflections on her use of the coaching practices in the column to the far right. As soon as possible after the actual coaching conversation, Lucia wrote the transcript of the conversation to the best of her recollection and then coded her questions, comments, and actions to determine the extent to which they were consistent with the characteristics of coaching. During the coding process, she jotted down her own reflections about what she did, including ideas about what she could do differently in the future. At a later date, she will discuss this Coaching Log with her supervisor, who is helping her to refine her coaching practices. After she and her supervisor determine that she is competent and confident in the coaching practices, she will discontinue writing the logs. Until that time, she will try to write one log per week for analysis and later discussion.

The text boxes on the sample log between Lucia and Eleana's mother in Figure 6.2 are provided to demonstrate how to complete the log. They provide an explanation of the coding of the transcript of the conversation and indicate how Lucia developed the comments that she made in the "coach's reflection/review" column.

Analysis of Coaching Logs

The purpose of analyzing coaching logs is to assist a coach with improving coaching skills by reviewing his or her coaching practices with someone else. This type of analysis may also be completed by using video or audio review; however, completion of the Coaching Log following the visit is less intrusive for the person who is being coached and provides a written transcript that allows word-by-word analysis of the coaching conversation. Even if the transcript is only the coach's best recollection of what happened during the conversation, it still can provide useful content for analysis. The Coaching Log may be completed either by a person who is learning to use a coaching interaction style or by a coach who wants to assess the extent to which he or she is continuing to adhere to coaching practices. The person who writes the log can ask a supervisor, mentor, or colleague to assist in analyzing the Coaching Log as long as the person who assists in the analysis is knowledgeable about the characteristics of coaching.

The following section provides examples of actual Coaching Logs that were completed by individuals who were learning the coaching process. These individuals have become highly competent coaches. Names have been changed to protect the confidentiality of the coaches and of the individuals they were coaching. The term "master coach" is used in the examples to denote the person who is assisting the coach who wrote the log with the analysis of the coaching practices. A reader who is interested in assisting others with the analysis of their coaching logs should pay particular attention to the questions or question stems that a master coach could use to support the coach's development of his or her coaching skills (in bold) and to the content of the informative feedback that the master coach provides related to the coaching practices.

COACHING LOG

Coach: _Lucia_   Learner: _Mother_

Date of interaction: _5/16/07_   Beginning time: _3:00 p.m._   Ending time: _4:15 p.m._

Location of interaction: _Home_

Who was present? _Lucia, Mother, Eleana_

Topic(s): _Eleana playing in the Jumperoo_

Was the coaching session planned?   <u>Yes</u>   No

	Characteristics					
Transcript of coaching conversation/observations	**P** ✓	**O** ✓	**A** ✓	**R** ★	**F** •	**Coach's reflections/review** (analysis of coaching process and promotion of parent's understanding and ability to promote child participation)
**Lucia:** Last visit we talked about finding options for Eleana (and you) for where she can be placed safely to play during the day, other than on her back, because when she is on her back, she cannot really participate in your family activities or even play. We talked about several different ideas and you were going to try borrowing a jumparoo from a friend. Tell me how that worked. _**Mother:** Oh yes, we got the Jumperoo from our friends and I want to look at that with you. Eleana loves it, but I want to make sure it is OK for her._ _**Lucia:** What do you think about it?_ _**Mother:** Well, I am happy that she has another place to be. Since she can't sit by herself, I don't have anywhere to put her other than the highchair, and I want to keep that for while I am in the kitchen, so that she learns to associate it with meals._	✓			1 2		Lucia started the coaching conversation by revisiting the previous joint plan, so she placed a ✓ in the column for "joint plan." She also asked the mother an awareness question (1) ("Tell me about . . .") that was related to the previous joint plan. Lucia asked the mother an analysis question (2) to have her compare having Eleana in the Jumperoo with her positioning in other activities and situations.

P = Joint Planning, O = Observation, A = Action, R = Reflection, F = Feedback
*Codes for Reflective Questions: 1 – Awareness, 2 – Analysis, 3 – Alternatives, 4 – Action; •Codes for Feedback: A – Affirmative, D – Directive, E – Evaluative, I – Informative

Figure 6.2.   Example of a completed Coaching Log.

	Characteristics					Coach's reflections/review (analysis of coaching process and promotion of parent's understanding and ability to promote child participation)
Transcript of coaching conversation/observations	P ✓	O ✓	A ✓	R ★	F •	
Lucia: So we can talk about both things—we can look at Eleana in the jumperoo and also talk more about what options you have for positioning during the day.					A	Lucia provided affirmative feedback (A) to the mother indicating that she heard and understood what the mother was saying.
Mother: Let's put her in the Jumperoo now and then she'll probably be happy to play there so we can talk more.						
Lucia: I see what you are saying. She seems to really like this. What are you seeing that you like or that you are concerned about?		✓		2	A	Lucia again affirmed (A) the mother by indicating that she understood what she was saying, observed Eleana in the Jumperoo (✓), and then asked her an analysis question (2) to contrast what the mother liked or did not like.
Mother: I love that she is happy here. I think it is good for her legs to be standing up, and sometimes she bounces herself a little bit. I wanted you to tell me if it is at the right height for her. Is it good for her to stand? She can't really sit yet and isn't even close to crawling, so is this OK? Is it OK for her developmentally? I hadn't really noticed until just now, but it looks like she leans to the side a lot.						
Lucia: My favorite part of what you just said is that Eleana is happy in the jumperoo. I think that makes this a win-win for Eleana and for you because as a mother with daily demands other than holding Eleana, you do need other options for her.					A	Lucia provided affirmative feedback (A) regarding the mother's analysis of the situation.
I'd like to talk about your specific positioning questions, but would it be OK if I share my opinion about whether the Jumperoo is developmentally OK?				1	Yes/no question	Lucia asked a closed-ended yes/no question, but it is appropriate because she is asking permission to share information.

P = Joint Planning, O = Observation, A = Action, R = Reflection, F = Feedback
*Codes for Reflective Questions: 1 – Awareness, 2 – Analysis, 3 – Alternatives, 4 – Action; •Codes for Feedback: A – Affirmative, D – Directive, E – Evaluative, I – Informative

(continued)

Figure 6.2.   *(continued)*

Transcript of coaching conversation/observations	P ✓	O ✓	A ✓	R ★	F •	Coach's reflections/review (analysis of coaching process and promotion of parent's understanding and ability to promote child participation)
						Characteristics (spanning P O A R F)
Mother: Sure. I want to know what you think.						
Lucia: I relate this to the same issue we talked about when we adapted the highchair so that Eleana could sit in it successfully to participate in meals and snack time. She wasn't quite able to sit up all by herself yet, but you gave her the opportunity to be in an age-appropriate (upright) position and learn things in a different way than if she were lying on the floor.					*I*	Lucia provided informative feedback (I) to the mother by linking the current situation to what they had done in the past and then adding new information. She concluded with a closed-ended awareness question (I) and caught herself doing this when she added her reflections on the log.
This affects not only her fine motor skills in manipulating toys differently but also her thinking and problem solving skills in approaching a different type of toy. So the more variety of positions you can set up for Eleana as part of your regular activities, the more enriched her learning opportunities will be. And the Jumperoo gives Eleana one more platform for learning. Does this make sense?				*1*		*Another yes/no question. I am finding that I tend to ask "Does that make sense?" a lot. Probably too much!*
Mother: Yes—absolutely. And it helps me feel good about using the Jumperoo as more than just a babysitter. I am noticing while we are talking through, that she leans to her right side all the time.						
Lucia: Why do you think she is leaning to her right?		✓		*2*		Lucia and the mother made an observation of Eleana (✓), and then Lucia asked the mother to analyze (2) the reason that Eleana might be leaning.
Mother: She really likes the spinner toy on that side.						
Lucia: So that is her favorite toy and what she is motivated to reach for. What could you do differently to change Eleana's orientation to the toy?				*3*		Lucia related the mother's assessment back to child interests and then asked an alternatives question (3) for the mother's ideas about what to do.

P = Joint Planning, O = Observation, A = Action, R = Reflection, F = Feedback
*Codes for Reflective Questions: 1 – Awareness, 2 – Analysis, 3 – Alternatives, 4 – Action; •Codes for Feedback: A – Affirmative, D – Directive, E – Evaluative, I – Informative

	Characteristics					Coach's reflections/review (analysis of coaching process and promotion of parent's understanding and ability to promote child participation)
Transcript of coaching conversation/observations	P ✓	O ✓	A ✓	R ★	F •	
Mother: *Oh, yeah—the seat rotates. I can't believe I didn't even think of that. That is simple. She hasn't figured out that she can turn herself yet, but I can move her around so she has to reach more to her left side [tries it]. . . . there, that helps.* **Lucia:** *And if you notice that Eleana persists in leaning to one side, which she may at times, what other things could you try to help her stand more upright?* **Mother:** *I could put a small blanket on the side she leans to, like we did in the highchair when she first used that.* *And what do you think about the seat height? We tried it a little lower but then decided to raise it.* **Lucia:** *What do you see in the taller position that you like?* **Mother:** *In the lower position she was more just sitting, whereas in this position she stands and bounces sometimes. I think it is good for strengthening her legs too. I just want to make sure this is OK for her.* *I mean are we skipping developmental steps by putting her up in a standing position before she is crawling?* **Lucia:** *I can see why you would ask that. But as for the developmental steps, normal development isn't divided into individual skills. There is always crossover between different skill types, like thinking and play and language, as well as movement and learning.* *Along the same lines, children don't completely learn one skill before they start to "work on" or learn another skill. So while Eleana is still*				3 2 I I		Lucia asked another alternatives question (3) to help the mother consider a back-up plan. Lucia invited the mother to analyze (2) the position first in order to build her confidence in making some of these types of observations and decisions. Lucia provided informative feedback (I) about development. Lucia provided additional informative feedback (I) about development followed by affirmative feedback (A) to let the mother know that what she is doing is consistent with what we know from research about child development.

P = Joint Planning, O = Observation, A = Action, R = Reflection, F = Feedback
*Codes for Reflective Questions: 1 – Awareness, 2 – Analysis, 3 – Alternatives, 4 – Action; •Codes for Feedback: A – Affirmative, D – Directive, E – Evaluative, I – Informative

(continued)

Figure 6.2. *(continued)*

Transcript of coaching conversation/observations	Characteristics					Coach's reflections/review (analysis of coaching process and promotion of parent's understanding and ability to promote child participation)
	P ✓	O ✓	A ✓	R ⋆	F •	
working to perfect sitting by herself, we should be helping prepare her for the next skill set. You are doing that by giving her tummy time which gives her learning and play opportunities. It also "prepares" her for the skill set of crawling. *Having the chance to spend time in a standing position gives Eleana the opportunity to "prepare" for play and learning in the upright standing posture and to "prepare" for the motor skill of standing and walking.*					*A*	
Mother: *Great—I understand. I also wanted to talk with you about how Eleana can be with me when I work out in the yard. Right now, the only time I feel like I can do that is when Eleana is napping because she cannot sit by herself.*						
Lucia: *What options have you considered?*				*3*		Lucia first asked the mother an alternatives question (3) to see what she knows or has tried, after which Lucia planned to add information and ideas as necessary.
Mother: *The stroller is the only thing that will work, but I want her to be able to sit near me and play. And to be down on the ground with me—not up in a stroller.*						Lucia asked an analysis question (2) with a suggestion embedded in it, which she recognizes when she reflects on her log.
Lucia: *How would it work if you put a blanket on the grass for Eleana, just like you put a blanket on the living room floor for her to play?*				*2*		*Oops! I was running well over my hour so it got harder not to just dole out answers at this point!*
Mother: *Sure, that would work, but I really want her to be able to sit up like other kids her age.*						Lucia provided informative feedback (I) in the form of a suggestion. Lucia's reflection provides another option.
Lucia: *I have known other parents that have used a laundry basket for their child when the child isn't quite safe sitting alone.*					*I*	*There I go again making suggestions. I should have really explored whether she had other ideas first or maybe have gone through the criteria for how she wants Eleana to be a part of this activity, and then I could share my ideas, too.*

P = Joint Planning, O = Observation, A = Action, R = Reflection, F = Feedback
*Codes for Reflective Questions: 1 – Awareness, 2 – Analysis, 3 – Alternatives, 4 – Action; •Codes for Feedback: A – Affirmative, D – Directive, E – Evaluative, I – Informative

	Characteristics					
Transcript of coaching conversation/observations	**P** ✓	**O** ✓	**A** ✓	**R** ★	**F** •	**Coach's reflections/review (analysis of coaching process and promotion of parent's understanding and ability to promote child participation)**
Mother: Are you serious? *Lucia: Yes—do you want to try it? Do you have a laundry basket? We could look at it together.*			✓	1 1		*Asked a yes/no question* *Asked another yes/no question*
[Mother brings out her wicker basket and puts Eleana in it. With almost no prompting the mother gets excited about the possibilities that she sees. She notices that she needs a blanket to cover the open wicker ends that might poke Eleana. She then puts another folded blanket behind Eleana so she is sitting more upright, and puts a couple toys inside for her to play with.]		✓				Lucia asked two yes/no awareness questions (1), but they are used to ask permission, which is appropriate.
Mother: I am so glad that I mentioned this today. This is great. *Lucia: I'm glad you brought it up, too. I hope you will continue to bring up anything like this. We can work together to figure most anything out. But what is great is that you are the one that problem solved this—not me.*					I	Lucia provided informative (I) feedback related to how they can work together.
Mother: Thank you. I am thrilled to try this out. I can use this in the house too, when we are in different rooms. It gives us another option. *I know you need to go, but next week could you help me figure out how to start bathing Eleana in the tub? She is getting a little too big for the bath seat in the sink, but I know she can't sit in the tub yet. I'm not sure what to do now.* *Lucia: Of course. That would be a great place for us to start when I come next time. Now before I go, tell me your plan for having Eleana be able to participate in some of your activities this week while she is sitting up.*	✓			4		Lucia moved to establishing the joint plan (✓) by asking an action question (4) related to the plan for what is going to happen between visits. The mother responded by outlining her view of the plan.

P = Joint Planning, O = Observation, A = Action, R = Reflection, F = Feedback
*Codes for Reflective Questions: 1 – Awareness, 2 – Analysis, 3 – Alternatives, 4 – Action; •Codes for Feedback: A – Affirmative, D – Directive, E – Evaluative, I – Informative

(continued)

Figure 6.2.   (continued)

Transcript of coaching conversation/observations	Characteristics					Coach's reflections/review (analysis of coaching process and promotion of parent's understanding and ability to promote child participation)
	P ✓	**O** ✓	**A** ✓	**R** ★	**F** •	
Mother: *I am going to have Eleana playing in her Jumperoo when I need to do some work around the house that she cannot really be part of. At meals and when I give her a snack, I am going to have her up in her highchair so that she links that to meals. Now when I am outside doing the yard work, Eleana can sit right beside me in the basket and we can talk about all the pretty flowers and the weeds that I have to pull out of the flowerbeds. I am going to have her in the basket in the house sometimes, too. Then she can be near me and we can talk about what we are doing.*	✓					
Lucia: *Well, I think you have quite a plan there. Next time, we will also plan to talk about ways she can participate more during bath time in the tub. I left my appointment book at the office. Is it okay if I call you to set up our next visit?*	✓					
Mother: *Sure, that will be fine. I will see you later!*						

P = Joint Planning, O = Observation, A = Action, R = Reflection, F = Feedback
*Codes for Reflective Questions: 1 – Awareness, 2 – Analysis, 3 – Alternatives, 4 – Action; •Codes for Feedback: A – Affirmative, D – Directive, E – Evaluative, I – Informative

COACHING LOG

Coach: _Janice_ _____ Learner: _Mother_ _____

Date of interaction: _5/19/09_ _____ Beginning time: _10:15 a.m._ Ending time: _10:55 a.m._

Location of interaction: _Park_ _____

Who was present? _Janice, Mother, Kayla_ _____

Topic(s): _Walking at the park to play on the equipment_ _____

Was the coaching session planned?   _Yes_   No

	Characteristics					
Transcript of coaching conversation/observations	**P** ✓	**O** ✓	**A** ✓	**R** ★	**F** •	**Coach's reflections/review (analysis of coaching process and promotion of parent's understanding and ability to promote child participation)**
[I meet Mother at the park, as planned, to come up with ways to help Kayla and Mother work on walking at the park.]						
Janice: How are you doing?				1		
Mother: Good. Kayla was excited when we pulled up to the park. [Kayla is smiling and pointing.]						
Janice: It sounds like she really likes the park. What do you do when you get to the park?				1		
Mother: Well, normally I let Kayla's older sisters play for a few minutes on what they want to—then have them come and stay close to me so Kayla can play on the smaller equipment. Then we go back and forth from the big to the little playground.						
Janice: How is that working for you?				2		
Mother: Pretty well. When my husband can come with us, we take turns playing with Kayla, so that is nice too.						
Janice: That sounds great. Do you ever try Kayla on the bigger equipment?				1	E	Y/N (yes/no question)

P = Joint Planning, O = Observation, A = Action, R = Reflection, F = Feedback
*Codes for Reflective Questions: 1 – Awareness, 2 – Analysis, 3 – Alternatives, 4 – Action; •Codes for Feedback: A – Affirmative, D – Directive, E – Evaluative, I – Informative

Figure 6.3. Coaching at the park. _(continued)_

Figure 6.3.   (*continued*)

Transcript of coaching conversation/observations	Characteristics					Coach's reflections/review (analysis of coaching process and promotion of parent's understanding and ability to promote child participation)
	P ✓	O ✓	A ✓	R ⋆	F •	
Mother: No, I am not ready to do that yet. Maybe later when she is more stable and walking.						
Janice: What would you like to accomplish today at the park?			✓		2	
Mother: I would like to try to help her walk more on her feet instead of on her knees. Like maybe when she gets off the slide she could walk, with my help, to get back on the slide.						*Wow. Mother knew exactly what she wanted to do.*
Janice: Let's give it a try.	✓	✓				
[Mother carries Kayla to the slide, lets her go down, then grabs her hand to have her walk. Kayla takes a step and then picks up her feet and grunts to get down. Mother sets her on the ground. She walks on her knees to the stairs.]						
Mother: She got very good at swinging when we were trying to help her walk.						
Janice: Have you tried only holding one hand instead of two?				1		*I missed a step of asking "what else have you tried to get her to stop swinging" before I jumped to my question.*
Mother: No, how would you do it?						
Janice: Here, I will show you.			✓			
[I catch Kayla at the bottom of the slide and put one hand out to help her get off the slide. She grabs it and stands up and takes a couple of steps, then goes to her knees.]						
Janice: Would you like to try?				1		*Y/N*
Mother: Sure. [Kayla does the same thing. Mother tries a couple more times and Kayla gets less and less willing to hold a hand and goes more quickly to her knees.]*						
Mother: I thought this was a good idea to do to get Kayla to walk.						

P = Joint Planning, O = Observation, A = Action, R = Reflection, F = Feedback
*Codes for Reflective Questions: 1 – Awareness, 2 – Analysis, 3 – Alternatives, 4 – Action;   •Codes for Feedback: A – Affirmative, D – Directive, E – Evaluative, I – Informative

Transcript of coaching conversation/observations	Characteristics					Coach's reflections/review (analysis of coaching process and promotion of parent's understanding and ability to promote child participation)
	P ✓	O ✓	A ✓	R ★	F •	
Janice: I think it is a good idea to keep giving Kayla opportunities to practice walking, like this one, just remember young children need a lot of repetition to master something. [Kayla keeps crawling on her knees to the stairs, then stands up and puts a foot on step and climbs up. She climbs to the top, then comes back down and goes up again.]					A I	*Wanted to support Mother in her ideas and let her know just because it did not work today that it could work another day.*
Mother: Wow. She likes these stairs. [Then Mother encourages her to go down the slide. Kayla just keeps going up and down stairs. Mother picks her up and tries placing her on the slide. Kayla protests and moves back toward the stairs.]						
Janice: Looks like Kayla wants to play on the stairs! Are you okay with letting Kayla keep playing on the stairs?		✓		1		*Y/N*
Mother: Yes, it is what she wants to do. She is getting very independent and wants to do things her way. [Kayla goes up and down the stairs several times. Mother and I stay close by watching and help to guide her feet a little bit when needed.]		✓				*Although Mother had a plan, Kayla's plan was different and provided opportunities for new skills that were different from Mother's plan but worked well.*
Mother: She has really stayed with this. I am surprised she likes this so much. Is this helping her?						
Janice: Yes, she is using it to practice and build up her muscles. Did you see any changes as she got more comfortable with it?				1	I	*Y/N*
Mother: Yes, she started using the railing to hold on to instead of the stairs. She tried a couple of times holding one hand on each side instead of putting both hands on one. She did not look like she is totally comfortable with it.						*It was great to see what Mother learned from the experience.*

P = Joint Planning, O = Observation, A = Action, R = Reflection, F = Feedback
*Codes for Reflective Questions: 1 – Awareness, 2 – Analysis, 3 – Alternatives, 4 – Action; •Codes for Feedback: A – Affirmative, D – Directive, E – Evaluative, I – Informative

(continued)

Figure 6.3.   *(continued)*

Transcript of coaching conversation/observations	P ✓	O ✓	A ✓	R ★	F ●	Coach's reflections/review (analysis of coaching process and promotion of parent's understanding and ability to promote child participation)
			Characteristics			
Janice: As she gets more comfortable with it, she will do it more.		✓			I	
Janice: What did you find helpful today that will help you next time you come to the park?	✓			2		*Not sure when I asked what Mother would say to the question.*
Mother: I think I will let Kayla show me what she wants to do and support her in doing it.						*Almost sounds like Mother is coaching Kayla.*
Janice: Sounds great. Remember young children need lots of exposure and practice to learn new skills.					I E	*I felt a need to share once again that opportunities for practice is what will help Kayla to continue to develop.*

P = Joint Planning, O = Observation, A = Action, R = Reflection, F = Feedback
*Codes for Reflective Questions: 1 – Awareness, 2 – Analysis, 3 – Alternatives, 4 – Action; •Codes for Feedback: A – Affirmative, D – Directive, E – Evaluative, I – Informative

Follow-Up Meeting on Coaching at the Park (Figure 6.3)

Master Coach: Janice, **what are your thoughts about how you used your coaching practices** with Kayla's mother during this visit?

Janice: Well . . . [thinking] . . . for one thing, I am still asking too many yes/no questions. I catch myself doing it, but I am having a hard time getting out of that habit. Another thing is that I think I am too quick to show the parent how to do something rather than asking her ideas first. I just want to jump in and do it rather than help them think it through first and build on their ideas. Old habits are sure hard to break!

Master Coach: I would agree with you about the yes/no questions, but when you asked Kayla's mom, "Would you like to try it?" that was necessary because you didn't want to make an assumption that she would or should try it. Rather, you were inviting her to try what you had just shown her. When we start looking at the log more closely, we can talk about that more specifically. **Tell me more about** your previous joint plan.

Janice: Our plan was that we were going to meet at the park because it is something they like to do together and they go there several times a week.

Master Coach: Sounds like that is a natural learning environment for them and it is something that happens frequently, so it would provide lots of opportunities for Kayla to practice her developing skills and learn some new ones. **What was Kayla's mother going to do in between your visits as part of your joint plan**?

Janice: Oh, we didn't really talk about that.

Master Coach: We want to make sure child learning and development are happening not only when we are there, but also when we are not there. **So how could you and Kayla's mother identify the activity settings in which she is going to promote Kayla's participation** during the week and specifically identify the ways in which her mom is going to be responsive to her learning and development?

Janice: I need to do a better job of coming to the joint plan. As you probably saw in this log, I still need to work on this. Maybe we can come up with some ideas to help me when we get to that part of this log.

Master Coach: OK, let's remember to talk about that more here in a few minutes. On the first page of your log after your initial awareness question, you asked another awareness question followed by an analysis question when you asked about what they typically do and how that is working. **What was your motivation behind those questions**?

Janice: I needed to find out how their trips to the park go and if that's how the mom wants it to go or if we could work on some ways to make it better. I guess I'm kinda doing some assessment here.

Master Coach: "How is that working for you" can be an effective analysis question. In fact, a famous talk show host often asks his guests that question. [Both the coach and Janice laugh] **What would you have said or done if** Kayla's mom had said, "Oh, it's going fine"?

Janice: I'm not sure. I guess I would have gone back to her priority for wanting Kayla to walk on her feet instead of her knees when she gets off the equipment, but I didn't ask about that until later at this visit.

Master Coach: Our goal really is to ask the fewest number of questions possible while obtaining the maximum amount of information from the person we are coaching and helping that person to reflect on what they want to have happen and how they might get there. **What are some other questions you could have asked** to meet this coaching goal?

Janice: I could've asked, "What does your trip to the park typically look like?" and "How does that compare to how you want it to look?" I could also have actually asked these questions on my previous visit when we were planning the trip to the park. That way, we would have been better prepared to just start right into supporting Kayla's play on the different equipment at the park and I also could have been thinking about how I could be helpful to Kayla and her mom on this visit. I wouldn't have needed to ask her what she wanted to accomplish that day either, because we would have already discussed it on the prior visit, or it would have come out when she told me how her ideal trip to the park compared with what's happening now.

Master Coach: So what I am hearing you say is that you are getting a lot more ideas about joint planning and ideas for asking fewer questions. Those questions you just came up with could definitely have provided you with the answers to some of the additional questions you asked. **What was your motivation for asking about** Kayla going on the bigger equipment?

Janice: I wouldn't have needed to ask that if I asked her about her typical visit and how that compares with what she wants. I was trying to see whether the bigger equipment would be a consideration, but I didn't really need to ask it and it was another yes/no question.

Master Coach: Let's move on with your log. I noticed that you invited participation of the parent when you said, "Let's give it a try." You do this several times throughout the log.

Janice: Yes, I wanted to see what it typically looked like.

Master Coach: Then you asked, "Have you tried only holding one hand instead of two?" I see in the coach's reflection column that you thought you missed a step. **What could you have asked there**?

Janice: I should have asked, "What else have you tried to get her to stop swinging?" That would have been an alternatives question and a strategy that we could have tried or built on the next time Kayla went down the slide. Then the mom could have experienced more success with this activity.

Master Coach: I agree with you. Asking, "Have you tried only holding one hand instead of two?" is embedding a suggestion in the form of a question, even if it is something the parent has already tried that you think they should try again.

Janice: I know. That's part of my problem with just wanting to jump in and start giving a lot of suggestions.

Master Coach: That would be faster, but based on what we know from the research about adult learning, it doesn't necessarily result in the parent doing what you suggest, especially if it doesn't fit with the parent's current thinking. That's why we always try to find out what they know and have tried before we give any suggestion. Then when we do provide suggestions, we follow up by asking how that would fit into what they might typically do. Then, Kayla's mother asked you how you would do it.

Janice: Right. If I'd asked her what else she'd tried, we could have gone on from there or brainstormed some other ideas together, but I asked a yes/no question and got a "no" response. So she wanted to see me try what I had suggested, which I did and it worked maybe a little better. Kayla didn't do her swinging thing and did take a few steps before hitting her knees.

Master Coach: When the person you are coaching asks you to do something, you have two options. One, you can model it for them, or two, you can ask them if they would be willing to try it with your support. Modeling is absolutely a part of the coaching process. You just want to make sure that you reiterate what you are going to do, why you are going to do it, and what you want the person you are coaching to observe. If you go with the second option and invite the person you are coaching to try it with your support, then you've jumped ahead a step, which is fine if they are willing to try it. As part of that option, you could talk through what they are going to try, and then as they try it, you can provide them with verbal feedback in the form of step-by-step instruction or affirmations. **Using this information, what would you have done differently**?

Janice: In that situation, I would still have modeled for her, but I should have first told her what I was going to try and why, as well as having her watch how it kept Kayla from swinging and helped her place her feet on the ground.

Master Coach: Okay. Then you asked Kayla's mom if she wanted to try it, which is an invitation to practice. As we mentioned earlier, it's an appropriate use of a yes/no question because you wanted to avoid making an assumption that she would want to practice. The mom tried it a few times, but then seemed to think that it wasn't working. You affirmed the mother's efforts and provided some informative feedback, which was absolutely consistent with use of the coaching practices. In retrospect, **what other options did you have here**?

Janice: We could have brainstormed some other ideas for helping to keep Kayla on her feet and tried them, but ultimately, Kayla had a different idea, so we followed her lead. She liked just playing on the stairs, so we were following her interest in this activity. I asked another yes/no question here, but I think it was okay because I wanted to make sure it was okay with the mom if Kayla played on the stairs.

Master Coach: What would have happened if she had said "no?"

Janice: Unless it had been a safety concern, which it wasn't, I would have provided some informative feedback to her mom about responsive teaching and learning, like recognizing the child's interests, following the child's lead, and using that as a way of developing existing skills and learning new ones.

Master Coach: That is absolutely consistent with the practices we have been talking about. You also use informative feedback very effectively, such as when you talked about the repetition of playing on the stairs and shared information with the mother about how that was helping Kayla's muscle development.

Janice: I just shouldn't have asked that yes/no question. I am just the queen of the yes/no question.

Master Coach: How could you have reframed that question to make it open-ended?

Janice: Let's see . . . I could have asked, "What changes did you see as she got more comfortable with it?" The mom helped me out though; she didn't just stop when she answered my question with a "yes."

Master Coach: You then moved toward the end of your coaching conversation by asking, "What was helpful today that will help you next time you come to the park?" That is an analysis question which is used to evaluate the coaching process. Sometimes many coaches forget to ask those types of reflective questions. **How did this help you get to your joint plan**?

Janice: I thought it was good that she was going to let Kayla show me what she wants to do and support her in doing it. She really seemed to understand what happened during the visit.

Master Coach: She sure did! **How could you have gotten to an even more specific joint plan**?

Janice: I'm not sure. This is where I need some help.

Master Coach: We want the plan to be as specific and concrete as possible, so both we and the parent will know exactly what she is going to be trying and doing between the visits. Some possible action questions might be "Exactly what will it look like when you let Kayla show you what she wants to do and support her in doing it?" "What will it look like at the park this week?" "What do you think she might do?" "What will you do to support her?" "What will it look like at home?" "When do you think this might happen?" "What will you do to support her then?"

Janice: OK, I see what you mean. I need to have the parent talk really specifically about what they are going to try during some of the activities that we have discussed or even done, as well as other possible activities. Like we said earlier, I could also do some planning with the parent for the next session, especially if we are going out into the community.

Master Coach: Yes. **How else can I support you** today in your work with this family or in other coaching opportunities?

Janice: This has been really helpful.

Master Coach: So **what's your plan for continuing to move your coaching practices forward**?

Janice: Somehow I knew you were going to ask that question and I have been thinking about it as we have been talking. First, I am going to keep working on reducing the number of yes/no questions I ask except when I don't want to make an assumption. Second, I am going to ask parents for their ideas first before I jump into giving or trying my own. That doesn't mean that I can't or won't give ideas, but I need to build on their ideas whenever possible because they will be more likely to use them. Third, I am going to keep asking parents to try things that we are doing and talking about. That seems to work for me and the parents. Fourth, when I model something for a parent, I am going to be more deliberate about it and be sure that I explain what I am going to do and then debrief it with them and explain how it might work for them. Finally, I am going to make sure that I do a better job of joint planning with the parents to ensure that they have something which they will be doing between our visits and to make it is as specific as possible.

Master Coach: Wow! That's quite a plan. When should we check back in with each other?

Janice: I see this family on Thursday. Would you have some time to talk after the team meeting on Friday?

Master Coach: Sure. Let's get together then.

Summary of Follow-Up on Coaching at the Park Scenario

The role of the master coach in this scenario was to help the coach-in-training reflect on her use of the coaching characteristics by reflecting on an actual coaching visit that she had documented using the Coaching Log. Instead of telling the coach-in-training what was good and what needed improvement on the basis of a review of the Coaching Log, the master coach mirrored and modeled the coaching practices used with the coach-in-training in the same way that the coach-in-training would use the practices with a coachee, which in this scenario was a parent. The goal

COACHING LOG

Coach: _Katrina_   Learner: _Mother_

Date of interaction: _5/22/09_   Beginning time: _8:45 a.m._   Ending time: _9:45 a.m._

Location of interaction: _Home/Park_

Who was present? _Katrina, Mother, Vernon_

Topic(s): _Bath time and swinging_

Was the coaching session planned?   Yes   No

Transcript of coaching conversation/observations	P ✓	O ✓	A ✓	R *	F •	Coach's reflections/review (analysis of coaching process and promotion of parent's understanding and ability to promote child participation)
		Characteristics				
Katrina: _How have things been going?_				1		_It felt awkward to jump in with "Last time we talked about bath time...." That would have been my next question but Mother jumped right into it._
Mother: _Good. We've been trying the bath time things that we talked about last time. So we've been saying a lot of "bath" and "bubbles" and "pop." He is imitating "ba" and trying to say "bubbles." "Pop" seems to be harder for him. I don't know if that's because the /p/ sound is at the beginning and end._						
Katrina: _I completely agree. "Pop" definitely could be harder because the /p/ sound occurs at the beginning and end._					A	
So what do you feel has helped Vernon imitate those words during bath time?				2		
Mother: _I don't know if it is anything I did. Oh, he also started saying "hello!" I don't know why he did but he says it all the time now._						

P = Joint Planning, O = Observation, A = Action, R = Reflection, F = Feedback
*Codes for Reflective Questions: 1 – Awareness, 2 – Analysis, 3 – Alternatives, 4 – Action; •Codes for Feedback: A – Affirmative, D – Directive, E – Evaluative, I – Informative

Figure 6.4.   Coaching about bath time/swinging.

Transcript of coaching conversation/observations	Characteristics					Coach's reflections/review (analysis of coaching process and promotion of parent's understanding and ability to promote child participation)
	P ✓	O ✓	A ✓	R *	F •	
Katrina: That's great! "Hello" is one of those routine words that Vernon is hearing often. It sounds like that really supports Vernon when he hears the same words often. We know that it helps children when they hear the words over and over and over again. It sounds like a lot of repetition to us, but it is helpful to the child. That's how he learns the words. During bath time, did you feel that you were able to use the same words often?				1	E A I	*Trying to help increase Mother's awareness of the strategies she's using.* *Yes/no question*
Mother: Yeah, I found that there are a lot of great words we use often during bath time!						
Katrina: Were you able to use any of the visual or tactile strategies we had discussed with those "lip" sounds?				1		*Yes/no question*
Mother: You know, we tried and Vernon started to look away from us. So we stopped.						
Katrina: Okay, so the increased awareness was hard for him.				A		
Mother: Yeah, he seems to know what we are trying to do.						
Katrina: So really using the word often seems to support him the best. That's the key!					A I	
Mother: I think so.						
Vernon: Outside. Swing.						
Mother: Oh, you want to go outside? Let's go get some socks.						
[We move outside to this great neighborhood playground that is conveniently located right behind their house. While we are outside, Mother and I model some words around the activity (e.g., "push," "up," "pump"). Once inside the house again . . .]						*It is still hard for me to do a lot of real direct coaching when we move outside to an active activity, especially when we are working on articulation.*

P = Joint Planning, O = Observation, A = Action, R = Reflection, F = Feedback

*Codes for Reflective Questions: 1 – Awareness, 2 – Analysis, 3 – Alternatives, 4 – Action; •Codes for Feedback: A – Affirmative, D – Directive, E – Evaluative, I – Informative

(continued)

Figure 6.4.   *(continued)*

Transcript of coaching conversation/observations	P ✓	O ✓	A ✓	R ★	F •	Coach's reflections/review (analysis of coaching process and promotion of parent's understanding and ability to promote child participation)
			Characteristics			
Katrina: What did you notice about Vernon's speech while he was swinging?				2		
Mother: He tried to say "pump." He does seem to know though when we are trying to get him to say a word! He is really good at avoiding it!						
Katrina: Yeah, he did seem to have some great strategies to communicate without using the modeled words. I did notice that he tried to say "push" when we just modeled the words instead of giving him a choice or asking him.					A	
Mother: Oh yeah, I guess he did.						
Katrina: I also noticed that when he was imitating "pump," he was able to produce the word better during the first attempt to imitate it. After that he would use the /t/ sound during other productions of "pump."					1	*I could have asked an awareness question such as "what other words did you observe Vernon trying to say?"*
Mother: Yeah, I guess I've seen that too. He does say words better right after I say them.						
Katrina: Now that the weather is getting better, do you think that this is an activity that you and Vernon will be doing more often?				4		*Yes/no question*
Mother: Yeah, I think so. He also swings with his grandpa and dad a lot.						
Katrina: Great! That could provide a lot of opportunities for him to practice saying words during that activity. How will you share with them some of the words we tried?				1	E I	*How do you help incorporate the people that can't be at the session?*
Mother: Yeah, I think that it would be great for them to model some of the words as we did today. I will show them how to do this.						

P = Joint Planning, O = Observation, A = Action, R = Reflection, F = Feedback
*Codes for Reflective Questions: 1 – Awareness, 2 – Analysis, 3 – Alternatives, 4 – Action;   •Codes for Feedback: A – Affirmative, D – Directive, E – Evaluative, I – Informative

Transcript of coaching conversation/observations	Characteristics					Coach's reflections/review (analysis of coaching process and promotion of parent's understanding and ability to promote child participation)
	P ✓	O ✓	A ✓	R ★	F •	
Katrina: So, this week, try modeling those words associated with swinging like "push" and "pump." You could also keep modeling those bath time words, too! *Mother: Yeah, I think he is doing well with that!*	1				D	*I felt like Mother wanted something more to do because Vernon doesn't always swing with her and I also wanted to let her know that she can still use strategies from previous sessions.* *I do struggle with coaching when articulation is the primary goal. I feel like I tend to be broader because there are so many things that can be targeted. The family goal tends to be "we will understand him more" which is extremely broad. I guess I need to work on having parents learn the steps to being more understandable.*

P = Joint Planning, O = Observation, A = Action, R = Reflection, F = Feedback
*Codes for Reflective Questions: 1 – Awareness, 2 – Analysis, 3 – Alternatives, 4 – Action; •Codes for Feedback: A – Affirmative,
D – Directive, E – Evaluative, I – Informative

of the master coach was to have the coach-in-training analyze her practices by comparing them with the coaching characteristics. The master coach always started by asking a question to promote the coach-in-training's reflection on an aspect of her log. First the master coach asked her to reflect, and then the master coach provided feedback. In this scenario, the feedback was related to use of yes/no questions, joint planning, the types of questions used, modeling, and providing informative feedback to the parent. The master coach tried to use affirmative and informative feedback rather than evaluative feedback (e.g., good, right, I like how you did that, I agree). Instead, the master coach affirmed that what the coach-in-training did matched the characteristics of coaching and mentioned specifically how it matched. In the same way that the coach-in-training should use the coaching characteristics with a coachee, the master coach asked the coach-in-training what specific plan she had developed as a result of the coaching conversation, how else the master coach could be helpful to her, and when they would meet again to follow up on her plan.

Follow-Up Meeting on Coaching About Bath Time/Swinging (Figure 6.4)

● Master Coach: What would be the most helpful way I can support you in our analysis of this log?

● Katrina: I would like to just jump right in. I know there are some places in the log where I could improve my practices, but let's just start at the beginning. Is that okay with you?

● Master Coach: Sure. Your first reflection is that it felt awkward to jump in with "last time we talked about bath time . . ." **Tell me more about your thinking right there and how it relates to starting with the previous joint plan.**

Katrina: I asked a really general question, but I was just trying to get the conversation started, and then I was going to get more specific about the previous plan, but she answered that question by talking about the previous plan.

Master Coach: She did. Her response could be feedback to us that she understands the coaching process and has become accustomed to sharing what has happened related to the joint plan. Both of you recognize the need to start with your previous joint plan. She also started with the context, which was bath time, rather than just focusing on the skill of correct articulation.

Katrina: Right. We have been talking about how speech happens within the context of real-life activities and one of the activities that they do where she feels like he has a lot of opportunities for talking and using his words is bath time. The mother says this is a real quality time between the two of them and he really likes playing in the bathtub, which also makes it a nice time to support his speech development. This mother is also really thinking about why some words might be harder for him to say than others, so with my next statement, I just had to affirm the conclusion that she had already drawn.

Master Coach: The next question you asked was, "So what do you feel has helped Vernon imitate those words during bath time?" **What was your purpose in asking this analysis question?**

Katrina: That is a parent self-attribution question, so I wanted her to realize that what *she* is doing by imitating his words is helping him learn how to say them. She did not seem to pick up on this, and in fact, she just went on by telling me how he is saying "Hello."

Master Coach: You took that as an opportunity to affirm her and then provide her with some informative feedback about communication development. **How does the next question that you asked** . . . let me see . . . I think it was, "During bath time, did you feel that you were able to use the same words often?" **match the coaching practices?**

Katrina: I guess I was still trying to get her to acknowledge that she was repeating the words a lot and that was directly helping him. I was trying to do that during my informative feedback, too. I should have just been very explicit here and told her. I didn't need to ask that question and besides, it was a yes/no question anyway.

Master Coach: **How could you have made it an open-ended question?**

Katrina: I'm not sure.

Master Coach: One option could be, "During bath time, how many times did you use the same words over and over? What words were they?"

Katrina: Okay. She never did really elaborate on the words that she used.

Master Coach: **Tell me the purpose for asking the next yes/no question,** "Were you able to use any of the visual or tactile strategies we had discussed with those lip sounds?"

Katrina: [laughs] I know . . . another yes or no question. I could have said, "Tell me how you used some of the visual and tactile strategies that we talked about last time." When Vernon and his mom were reading a book together during my last visit, we talked about some cues that she could give him when she repeated some of the high-frequency target words that we had discussed, so I wanted to see how that worked during bath time.

Master Coach: So you provided some affirmative feedback to the mother about her observations related to these strategies and provided a bit more information or reinforcement of the notion that repetition seemed to work best. So . . . then both you and the mother followed his lead by attending to his interest to go outside, which changed the activity setting to swinging on the swing in the backyard. I saw in your reflection column that you find it difficult to provide coaching during an active outside activity. **What about that is difficult for you?**

Katrina: Well, the first thing is that it is active, so a lot is happening at once and the mom is running over to the swing with him and then they start the swinging activity and they are talking and stuff, so it just seems unnatural to coach.

Master Coach: They are *talking*! Imagine that! So am I hearing you say it really is a good time for speech development and practice to occur? [Both Katrina and the master coach laugh.]

Katrina: No, I didn't say that, but I get your point. [They laugh again.]

Master Coach: Would it be helpful if I share information and observations with you about this?

Katrina: Please do. I can use all the help I can get. This is when coaching is hard for me.

Master Coach: You indicated that you used some modeling for the mother and that both you and the mother were using some modeling with Vernon. I didn't see in your log how you set up the model with the mother. One strategy for doing this would be as the mom was getting Vernon ready to go outside, you could brainstorm with the mom about your plan for using what you have been talking about related to bath time while he is playing on the swing. You could see whether she wants to take the lead or wants you to take the lead. During the very active activity, both of you can implement this plan. If it doesn't go as the two of you had planned, then you can ask her if she has another idea, you could ask her to try a new idea, or you could have her watch you try a new idea. Then, as the activity winds down, you can debrief just as you did. The key is for you to help the mother think about how she can be responsive to Vernon during the activity. In this case, her responsiveness would be related to his speech and communication. The two of you can figure out how this activity could provide lots of opportunities for the parent's priorities to be addressed. Now, if there isn't time for all of this to take place, a back-up plan is always to debrief your observations by having the parent reflect on what occurred, similar to what you did.

Katrina: Thanks. That is helpful to hear. I frequently forget to set up my modeling like you described. I am going to work on that.

Master Coach: How did what you asked when you said, "What did you notice about Vernon's speech while he was swinging?" **fit with what I just shared**?

Katrina: It was an analysis question that I used to debrief the activity and tie back to her priority for him related to his speech. She was able to identify words with the target sound that he was practicing during the swinging activity.

Master Coach: And you provided affirmative feedback that was based on her shared observation.

Katrina: I may have shared too much of my observation there. I wrote in the reflection column of the log that I could have asked her some awareness questions about other words that he was trying to say and how it happened that he said them, like by repeating us right after we say the word or when we ask him to say the word. I could then ask her on the basis of this experience what strategy she might use during these activities, which could lead to part of the joint plan.

Master Coach: Well, I couldn't have said that better myself. [They laugh.] **Tell me how you would rephrase the yes/no question** of, "Do you think that this is an activity that you and Vernon will be doing more often?" You coded it as an action question, but when it is closed-ended like this, it is really just an awareness question.

Katrina: I could have asked, "What ideas have you gotten from this activity?" or "How will you use what we have done today?" That brings up my question about how the person you are coaching can share what they are doing that is making the difference with other people.

Master Coach: What do you think about how you asked that question?

Katrina: Now that I think about it, I believe the question was good, but she thought I was asking a yes/no question, so I could have asked it again or rephrased it, and then that could be part of her plan.

Master Coach: Okay. Now let's talk about the joint plan at the end. **How was the plan consistent with the coaching practices**?

Katrina: We had a plan at the end?

Master Coach: Whose plan was it?

Katrina: [Reads the plan she had written on the log] Oh my goodness! I am just telling her what to do, but I did feel like she wanted something more to do.

Master Coach: One way to come to the joint plan is for you to review what you have talked about and done during the visit, then ask the parent how she might use this during the week and/or how it could extend into other activities. Another way is to have the parent share her plan. That could be as basic as asking the parent to tell you on the basis of all the things you have talked about and done what she plans to do between now and the next time you are together. You can follow up by asking how she will know it works and what the back-up plan is if it doesn't.

Katrina: Right. I came across kind of directive rather than reflective.

Master Coach: That's a nice way to put it. That is where the log came to an end. **What have we not touched on today that you would like to discuss**?

Katrina: This helped me think about how speech really comes about through practices within the context of everyday activities. We can identify the sounds to support, teach the child and parent how to produce the sound, and then figure out with the parent all the different ways she can promote high-frequency use of the words and sounds in the activities that happen frequently and that the child enjoys doing.

Master Coach: Well, you know we just cannot end our conversation without talking about our joint plan. **What is the plan**?

Katrina: Of course not, so one thing I am determined to work on is being better at setting up opportunities for my modeling like when we were outside swinging. I also am going to try the idea of developing a plan with the parent while we are getting ready to transition to a more active situation. I could stand to work on reducing the number of yes/no questions, too. Thanks for the information you shared about promoting speech development through my coaching and support of the parent and child. I knew that, but sometimes I just need to be reminded or affirmed that what I am doing is consistent with the research-based practices. I also appreciated the reminder about ways to get to a joint plan. I tend to get in a hurry at that point because it is the end of my visit, so I just jump in and share the plan. I am going to encourage the parent to tell me what her plan is and then I can ask her about adding to it if necessary. I could also ask about our next visit—something like "What would you like to focus on during our next visit?"

Master Coach: It sounds like you are thinking of a two-part plan. One part of the plan is what the parent or care provider will focus on between visits, and the second part of the plan is when you need to return and what you will do together during the next visit. **What support would you like from me**?

Katrina: I have another family who I am going to see tomorrow whose priority is for the grandfather to be able to understand the child when he visits during the holidays. We have been focusing on their book reading time, mealtime routines, and when he and his brother are playing with their puppy. I would like to write a log about that visit and maybe talk with you about it sometime next week. Can I e-mail you some possible times to meet after I get it written?

Master Coach: Sure. That sounds good.

COACHING LOG

Coach: _Sheila_   Learner: _Teacher A and Teacher B_

Date of interaction: _2/12/09_   Beginning time: _2:05 p.m._   Ending time: _3:10 p.m._

Location of interaction: _Happy Days Child Development Center_

Who was present? _Sheila, Teacher A, Teacher B, Jane_

Topic(s): _story reading and children's seating logistics_

Was the coaching session planned?   Yes   No

	Characteristics					
Transcript of coaching conversation/observations	**P** ✓	**O** ✓	**A** ✓	**R** ★	**F** •	**Coach's reflections/review (analysis of coaching process and promotion of parent's understanding and ability to promote child participation)**
Sheila: _At our last session the plan was to try the seating arrangement that we had discussed for story reading, including how you were going to introduce this to the children. I video recorded Teacher A's Reading Two (R2) of Whistle for Willie for us to review together as a team today. We also have Jane here today at your request because of a situation that happened during your story reading and you want her to look at the tape and provide feedback._	✓					
So, tell me about your new seating arrangement.				1		_This seating arrangement was a huge shift in their thinking; it is nice to hear their excitement. Jane gives them some affirmative feedback regarding this particular child (Kevin) so they are really feeling positive about their classroom and teaching._
Teacher A: _It is going great, it is working. Kevin is even talking! He never says anything in any group situation._						

P = Joint Planning, O = Observation, A = Action, R = Reflection, F = Feedback
*Codes for Reflective Questions: 1 – Awareness, 2 – Analysis, 3 – Alternatives, 4 – Action; •Codes for Feedback: A – Affirmative, D – Directive, E – Evaluative, I – Informative

Figure 6.5.   Coaching and early literacy.   (continued)

Figure 6.5. *(continued)*

Transcript of coaching conversation/observations	P ✓	O ✓	A ✓	R ★	F •	Coach's reflections/review (analysis of coaching process and promotion of parent's understanding and ability to promote child participation)
				Characteristics		
Teacher B: Yeah, he commented on the button when I read Corduroy today. Anson said that he couldn't see the button on the page and Kevin spoke up and said "it's right there," just like the button on Corduroy. This was my first reading of Corduroy and I didn't even practice it.						
Sheila: Hmmmmmm, I'm going to make a note that this was your first reading of Corduroy and we can talk about that after we review the video.						I don't want to let this go, but it wasn't in our plan. I think I did the right thing by adding it on to the end.
To what do you attribute Kevin's contribution to the conversation?				2		
Teacher A: His best buddy is talking a lot too, that's Anson.						
Sheila: Where does Kevin sit in relation to Anson?				1		
Teacher B: He is a row behind and kind of off to the side						
Teacher A: I think he feels more comfortable and Anson isn't touching him or getting in his space. None of the kids are really putting their hands on each other.						
Sheila: It sounds like Kevin is feeling safer in this environment you have created and he doesn't have to worry about his personal space being invaded.					A	
Sheila: You also chose to use name tags to help children find their seat for story time, tell me about that.				1	A	
Teacher A: I put the chairs out and their name tags on the chairs and collect the tags before I start reading. It is going good.						
Sheila: What other benefits from using the name tags do you see?				2		

P = Joint Planning, O = Observation, A = Action, R = Reflection, F = Feedback
*Codes for Reflective Questions: 1 – Awareness, 2 – Analysis, 3 – Alternatives, 4 – Action; •Codes for Feedback: A – Affirmative, D – Directive, E – Evaluative, I – Informative

Transcript of coaching conversation/observations	Characteristics					Coach's reflections/review (analysis of coaching process and promotion of parent's understanding and ability to promote child participation)
	P ✓	O ✓	A ✓	R ★	F ●	
Teacher B: Well, I'm surprised that Anson can recognize his name and I think they are all more interested in the story.						
Sheila: What is your plan for story time seating arrangements?	✓			4		*I'm not really sure how to end this and move on. This seems like a really stupid question; of course they are going to continue.*
Teacher A: Oh, we are going to keep it this way, I think it is working.						
Sheila: I will write that into the joint plan that you will continue with this arrangement and continue to monitor how it is working for all the children.	✓					
Sheila: Let's look at the video. Here is the Story Reading Two Consistent/Inconsistent form. You have seen this form from the last tier two training and we have been using it in the classroom to observe readings. Please use this when you are looking at the video to see where the reading is consistent or inconsistent with the guidance that you have been given for Reading Two.		✓	✓		I	*I wasn't sure how this would go; they were both concerned about being video recorded I have not had a coaching session where we have talked about Reading Two with them so I was not sure what they would focus on when we looked at the observation tool I used. I tried to keep it simple, I only want them to focus on and work on one or two strategies.*
Teacher A: I already know of some of the things that I will want to work on.						
Sheila: So you have been spending some time thinking about your reading. Let's look at the video and see how it compares with the thoughts that you are having about your reading. [We look at the video.]					A	
Sheila: Teacher A, how does this reading compare with what you know to be strategies for Reading Two?				2		
Teacher A: I was right, I didn't really respond to Savannah when she mentioned that part about David. I shouldn't have said no to her when she talked about the reflection.						
Sheila: What could you have said differently?				3		

P = Joint Planning, O = Observation, A = Action, R = Reflection, F = Feedback
*Codes for Reflective Questions: 1 – Awareness, 2 – Analysis, 3 – Alternatives, 4 – Action; ●Codes for Feedback: A – Affirmative, D – Directive, E – Evaluative, I – Informative

(continued)

Figure 6.5.   (continued)

Transcript of coaching conversation/observations	Characteristics					Coach's reflections/review (analysis of coaching process and promotion of parent's understanding and ability to promote child participation)
	P ✓	O ✓	A ✓	R ⋆	F •	
Teacher A: Well, if I just didn't put the "no" in front of that sentence. I noticed I did that in a few other places too.						
Sheila: Remember that the guidance for responding to children's comments for Story Reading Two is to help build their understanding of the plot and big ideas of the story. So when we are responding to children we need to keep that in mind too. What else could you have said in your response to Savannah so that you are building her understanding?				3	I	*I think next time I should go over the consistent part of the form. It seemed to be hard for them to focus on the whole form. Maybe only use the consistent side.*
Teacher A: I guess I could have said something about why David was looking in the mirror at his reflection, so that he would be more grown up. I did say that after, but I guess I could have said it when Savannah made her comment.						
Sheila: What else did you notice about your reading?				2		
Teacher A: I don't know, I tried not to say "Do you remember . . ." I need to work on that one too.						
Sheila: What about the first consistent strategy? [This refers to retelling in a nonlinear manner.] How does the reading compare to this strategy?				2		
Teacher B: Well, it was linear but it isn't supposed to be.						
Teacher A: Yeah, I forgot about that.						
Sheila: Where in the story do you see opportunities for nonlinear retelling? [long silence]				2		
Sheila: Would it be helpful to look through the book together? [They nod in agreement.]			✓	1		

P = Joint Planning, O = Observation, A = Action, R = Reflection, F = Feedback
*Codes for Reflective Questions: 1 – Awareness, 2 – Analysis, 3 – Alternatives, 4 – Action; •Codes for Feedback: A – Affirmative, D – Directive, E – Evaluative, I – Informative

Transcript of coaching conversation/observations	P ✓	O ✓	A ✓	R ★	F •	Coach's reflections/review (analysis of coaching process and promotion of parent's understanding and ability to promote child participation)
			Characteristics			
It sounds like we have two strategies for Reading Two to add to our joint plan: thinking about responding to children in a way that supports further understanding of the plot and looking for places in the story where you can retell in a nonlinear fashion.	✓					I'm in a panic at this point because we are running out of time and it will be a whole week before I see these two in a coaching session again.
We have one more topic for today. Teacher B, you mentioned that your Reading One of Corduroy went well but you didn't practice, tell me what went well.				1		These transitions from one topic to the next feel awkward to me. I don't remember having this issue before.
Teacher B: I said I didn't practice but I was prepared. I used sticky notes but I found I didn't need to use them. I remembered a lot of the vocabulary and comprehension asides. I read over the manual once and wrote what I needed to say on the sticky notes.						
Sheila: That seems to be a good strategy for you to use for Reading One. Reading Two does not have a manual, so what is your plan to prepare for Reading Two?	✓			4		
Teacher B: I think I'm going to do like Teacher A and think about where I can retell by flipping back and forth in the book and make sure that I am helping to understand the story when I am retelling.						
Sheila: It sounds like the joint plan applies to both of you as you prepare for story reading. I will be in your classroom next Tuesday. What reading will you be doing?				1		I'm curious to see how they give feedback to each other; I will note that for next time.
Teacher B: Reading Two of Corduroy.						
Teacher A: I think you should video her, it was really helpful for me to see how I read. I do a better job than I thought.						
Teacher B: Thanks a lot!						

P = Joint Planning, O = Observation, A = Action, R = Reflection, F = Feedback
*Codes for Reflective Questions: 1 – Awareness, 2 – Analysis, 3 – Alternatives, 4 – Action; •Codes for Feedback: A – Affirmative, D – Directive, E – Evaluative, I – Informative

(continued)

Figure 6.5.   (*continued*)

Transcript of coaching conversation/observations	P ✓	O ✓	A ✓	R ★	F ●	Coach's reflections/review (analysis of coaching process and promotion of parent's understanding and ability to promote child participation)
Sheila: *Tell me about your concerns related to being recorded on video.* **Teacher B:** *No it is fine, after seeing hers, I think I can handle it.* **Sheila:** *Okay, I will add that I will video record your Reading Two of Corduroy on Tuesday.*	✓			1		*I think this is a big step for her to agree to the video recording. She has been very nervous about being observed but she uses the strategies she has learned and talks constantly to the children in her class. We will view her video in the next session.*

P = Joint Planning, O = Observation, A = Action, R = Reflection, F = Feedback
*Codes for Reflective Questions: 1 – Awareness, 2 – Analysis, 3 – Alternatives, 4 – Action; •Codes for Feedback: A – Affirmative, D – Directive, E – Evaluative, I – Informative

Summary of Follow-Up on Coaching About Bath Time/Swinging

In this scenario, the master coach assisted the coach-in-training to reflect on how her interactions with the parent were consistent with the coaching practices. The coach-in-training had noted some specific concerns about her coaching in the coach's reflections/review column on the log. In particular, she was concerned about starting the coaching conversation by referring back to the joint plan, how to help the parent understand that what she is doing helps the child's communication development, how to use coaching in a more active outdoor or community-based setting, how to include other people who are not present in the plan, and how to use coaching when supporting the child and parent around articulation. The master coach asked the coach-in-training to reflect on her practices by reviewing what she had written on the log that was directly related to her areas of concern and question. The master coach provided informative feedback as needed, especially around how the use of a coaching interaction style and the natural learning environment practices can promote improved articulation.

Follow-Up Meeting on Coaching and Early Literacy (Figure 6.5)

Sheila: This is only my second coaching session with this team because snow days and illness have prevented the team from getting together, but I have coached both of the teachers as individuals on several occasions. Jane was also present for this coaching conversation. She is the in-house Special Education Consultant and the team has asked that she be present for the feedback. One purpose of this conversation was to discuss their new seating arrangement, which was why Jane attended. We also wanted to review the video of Reading Two and have them reflect on how the reading compares with the early literacy curriculum that is the foundation for our work together. I started the conversation with that previous joint plan.

Master Coach: Yes, you did! You coded your "tell me about . . . " statement as an awareness question. **How does that type of coding fit with your intention and the way the teacher responded?**

Sheila: It was really more of an analysis question, wasn't it? I was asking her to compare the new seating arrangement with their previous one.

Master Coach: That's the way I think I would have coded it. On the second page of your log, you had a reflection regarding Teacher B's statement about not practicing her reading. **Why did you choose not to address that statement at that point, as it is inconsistent with the curriculum?**

Sheila: As you could see from the log, I had to take a cognitive pause. I made a note and told her that we would revisit it. I chose not to address it right then because we were achieving such great momentum at that point and I didn't want them to probe that and perhaps provide feedback that could be perceived as negative at that point. I also wanted to follow the line of the conversation related to Kevin's participation, so I asked them the analysis question about that.

Master Coach: Okay, I am following your thinking. **What is another option for** your response when she attributed Kevin's talking to the presence of his friend?

Sheila: I definitely could have acknowledged this observation on her part by giving her some affirmative feedback or I could have shared information about how his buddy is serving as a language model for Kevin, but after my next question, they came up with some other ideas as to why he might be communicating more.

Master Coach: I noticed that, too. **Tell me about your motivation for mentioning** that they were now using name tags to help the children find their seat during story time.

Sheila: I had observed that they were now using the nametags. I thought that was a great strategy to use that fits with our early literacy practices. I was so happy to see it that I really just wanted to tell them how great that was, but I remained calm and wanted to have them reflect on that.

Master Coach: After the first response of one of the teachers, you followed up with an analysis question about what other benefits they see from using the name tags. **Give me some insight into your thinking.**

Sheila: I asked that because I wanted them to compare what they did with the early literacy practices.

Master Coach: And how did that work for you?

Sheila: It didn't really work, so I just moved on.

Master Coach: What could you have done differently there?

Sheila: Hmmmm. I could have given them affirmative feedback about using the nametags and then since they didn't pick right up on it, I could have provided informative feedback and tied their actions back to what we know about early literacy strategies such as this one.

Master Coach: Okay. I saw your reflection about trying to wrap up one portion of the conversation in order to move to another and you felt like you didn't do a very good job of it. **Now that you've had time to think about it, what other question could you have asked or how could you have rephrased the question that you asked there?**

Sheila: They thought I was asking if they were going to continue with the seating arrangement, but actually I was trying to get to a joint plan about the seating arrangement, so her response was feedback to me that my action question was not very clear. So . . . [thinking] . . . I could have asked them what we should put on our joint plan about their continued use of the seating arrangement. I need to help them be more specific and I need to be more explicit with that type of questioning.

Master Coach: From reading the log, it looks to me like you are using a "plan as you go" approach to developing the joint plan. **How is that working for you and these teachers?**

Sheila: Although I have not had very many coaching conversations with these two teachers, I have been using this approach. It seems like this strategy helps us bring closure to one part of our conversation before we move on to the next.

Master Coach: Well, that is certainly one of several ways to get to the joint plan. The next portion of your log relates to reviewing the video of Story Reading Two. **What was your rationale in giving them the form to use to review the video?**

Sheila: One of the points we talked about during our coaching training was that whenever you model or whenever you ask someone you are coaching to make observations, you should give them a job to do. That really stuck with me. For this video review, I wanted to make sure we analyzed what was consistent and inconsistent about Reading Two, so that is the form that I used. This form would also remind them about the characteristics of Reading Two. After the video review, we would then have a place to start our discussion.

Master Coach: Sounds like you could teach that portion of the coaching training!

Sheila: I was so excited that the teacher had already thought of some areas of practice that she wanted to improve! I think I messed up there though.

Master Coach: Tell me more about that.

Sheila: I gave her some affirmative feedback regarding her reflection, but then I moved right on to watching the video, even though I asked her to compare her thoughts to what we see in the video. Then I asked that analysis question right after we watched the video.

Master Coach: What are you thinking you would have done differently?

Sheila: I could have asked her to go ahead and share what she would do differently and then draw our attention to the parts in the video where she would have done things differently.

Master Coach: All right.

Sheila: Right before I shared the informative feedback about responding to the comments of the children for Story Reading Two, I should have given her some affirmative feedback about her reflection in response to my alternatives question about what she would have done differently, but I was focused on what I was going to say next and just missed it.

Master Coach: Your log continues with some alternatives questions and analysis questions that are tied back to the early literacy practices.

Sheila: I stumped them with my analysis question about where in the story they saw opportunities for nonlinear retelling. I should have talked about the purpose of retelling in a nonlinear way. I'm not sure they understand why it can be useful. In fact, I could have just asked what they remembered about nonlinear retelling first, and then I could have shared the information. That's when we went right back to the book to find it together.

Master Coach: Whenever a coach is using a curriculum like this, having them refer back to it is a very important learning tool. It helps the teachers become more comfortable finding the answers to their own questions over time. That is what capacity building is all about. As we move to the next to the last page of your log, that is where you went back to the teacher not practicing before Reading One. You noted in your reflections on the log that the transition felt awkward to you. **What specifically made the transition feel awkward to you?**

Sheila: I think I felt like I was being directive. We were getting close to the end of our allotted time together and I wanted to make sure I went back to the comment about not practicing.

Master Coach: If it is okay with you, I would like to give you some feedback about that. [Sheila nods in agreement] Your purpose for being in the classroom and working with these teachers is very specific. You are there to support them with implementing the early literacy curriculum that this program has chosen to use. Your role is to help them take what they are learning from the trainings and implement it in the classroom. The curriculum serves as your guide and framework, so you will always refer them back to that foundation for the practices. Certainly, you want to be responsive to them and answer their questions about implementation of the curriculum and set-up of the classroom environment, but your role is also to make sure they can implement the curriculum. It is consistent with the coaching practices in this venue to bring up additional topics that relate to the curriculum. As their coach, you really have to provide opportunities for reflection and feedback on your observations as well as theirs.

Sheila: That makes sense to me. I just don't want to feel like I am controlling the conversation or being too directive with them.

Master Coach: I think that is a filter that you can use to continually assess your coaching practices. Your reason for being there is to assist them in meeting their objectives related to implementation of the early literacy curriculum in their classroom as a follow up to their training on the curriculum.

Sheila: Okay, thanks for that feedback. I think the rest of my log went fairly well as we moved to the final part of our joint plan around making a video of the other teacher.

Master Coach: Your practices there appeared to be consistent with the coaching practices and protocol for assisting the teachers to implement the curriculum. Speaking of joint plans, we better think about ours before our time runs out for today.

Sheila: I want to pay particular attention to my use of affirmative and informative feedback. I think I missed some opportunities to tie their actions and reflections back to the curriculum. I also need to check with the teachers to make sure that they have some baseline knowledge about content areas, such as the nonlinear retelling, before asking analysis questions related to the topic.

Master Coach: What about your concern that you might be too directive at times?

Sheila: I am going to think more about that and assess whether I think I may be too directive when I am trying to make sure that we are addressing all areas of the curriculum as well as my observations and their actions related to their implementation. Can we talk about my progress during our next meeting?

Master Coach: Any other topics you would like to cover today? If not, shall we plan to meet at this time next week for our regular coaching meeting?

Sheila: Nothing else I can think of for today. Thanks.

Summary of Follow-Up on Coaching and Early Literacy

The focus of this Coaching Log analysis conversation was to help the coach-in-training apply the characteristics of coaching practices with classroom teachers using an early literacy curriculum as the content for the coaching. The master coach assisted the coach-in-training with thinking about missed opportunities for providing affirmative feedback (e.g., teacher practices matched early literacy curriculum) and informative feedback (e.g., more information about a particular early literacy practice or strategy). The master coach also provides informative feedback to the coach-in-training about how a coaching interaction style works when it is used with a specific curriculum or set of practices.

CONCLUSION

This chapter provided descriptions and examples of how to use the Coaching Practices Rating Scale and the Coaching Log to help practitioners learn how to implement coaching practices and adhere to the characteristics of coaching by seasoned coaches. Whereas the Coaching Practices Rating Scale is typically used for self-assessment or review by a supervisor or mentor to record a coach's performance over a series of coaching interactions, the Coaching Log can be used for in-depth analysis of a single coaching interaction. When these tools are used for a short period of time initially and then are used intermittently as individuals work to refine their coaching practices, both of them can be effective for practice adherence and learning.

RESOURCES

Rush, D.D., & Shelden, M.L. (2006a). Coaching practices rating scale for assessing adherence to evidence-based early childhood intervention practices. *CASEtools 2*(2), 1–7. Retrieved from http://www.fippcase.org/casetools/casetools_vol2_no2.pdf

This article provides background on the development and use of the Coaching Practices Rating Scale to measure adherence to coaching practices.

Rush, D.D., & Shelden, M.L. (2006b). Validity of the coaching practices rating scale. *CASEinPoint 2*(3), 1–6. Retrieved from http://www.fippcase.org/caseinpoint/caseinpoint_vol2_no3.pdf

This article describes a pilot study that was used to determine the content validity of the Coaching Practices Rating Scale for assessing practitioner adherence to coaching practices.

Appendix A

Coaching Practices Rating Scale

Name: _____   Date: _____

Rater: _____   Period covered: _____

Coaching is an adult learning strategy in which the coach promotes the learner's ability to reflect on his or her actions as a means to determine the effectiveness of an action or practice and develop a plan for refinement and use of the action in immediate and future situations. The scale is used to determine the extent to which the practitioner uses the practices with families or colleagues in ways that promote self-assessment, self-reflection, and self-generation of new and existing knowledge and skills.

Think about the coaching conversation(s) for the period covered. For each practice indicator, indicate how often the practice was used:	Single observation	Multiple observations over time					
	Present (+) Absent (−)	No opportunity to measure	None of the time	Some of the time	About ½ the time	Most of the time	All of the time
1. Acknowledged the learner's existing knowledge and abilities as the foundation for improvement	+ −	0	1	2	3	4	5
2. Interacted with the learner in a nonjudgmental and constructive manner during coaching conversations	+ −	0	1	2	3	4	5
3. Identified with the learner the targeted skills that he or she wanted to learn and a timeline for the coaching process	+ −	0	1	2	3	4	5
4. Developed with the learner a plan for action/practice necessary to achieve targeted skill(s) following each coaching conversation	+ −	0	1	2	3	4	5
5. Observed the learner demonstrate *knowledge and understanding* of the targeted skill(s) or practice(s)	+ −	0	1	2	3	4	5
6. Observed the learner's *use* of the targeted skill(s) or practice(s)	+ −	0	1	2	3	4	5
7. Created opportunities for the learner to observe the coach and/or others model the target skill(s) or practice(s)	+ −	0	1	2	3	4	5
8. Promoted use of multiple opportunities for the learner to practice implementation of the targeted skill(s) or practice(s) (e.g., role plays, in context)	+ −	0	1	2	3	4	5
9. Used both planned and spontaneous opportunities to strengthen the learner's knowledge and skills	+ −	0	1	2	3	4	5
10. Asked probing questions to examine the learner's knowledge and abilities	+ −	0	1	2	3	4	5
11. Prompted learner to reflect on his or her knowledge and use of the targeted skill(s) and practice(s) compared with research-based practice standards	+ −	0	1	2	3	4	5

(continued)

(continued)

Think about the coaching conversation(s) for the period covered. For each practice indicator, indicate how often the practice was used:	Single observation	Multiple observations over time						
	Present (+) Absent (−)	No opportunity to measure	None of the time	Some of the time	About ½ the time	Most of the time	All of the time
12. Provided feedback about the learner's knowledge and skills following the learner's reflection on his or her performance	+ −	0	1	2	3	4	5
13. Provided and/or promoted access to new information and resources after the learner reflects on his or her performance	+ −	0	1	2	3	4	5
14. Engaged the learner in reflection on the usefulness, effectiveness, and need for continuation of coaching	+ −	0	1	2	3	4	5

Think about the coaching conversations for the time period covered. For each practice indicator, note how the practice was used.

Coaching practice indicators	Description of practice
1. Acknowledged the learner's existing knowledge and abilities as the foundation for improving knowledge and skills.	
2. Interacted with the learner in a nonjudgmental and constructive manner during coaching conversations.	
3. Identified with the learner the targeted skills and a timeline for the coaching process.	
4. Developed with the learner a plan for action/ practice necessary to achieve targeted skill(s) following each coaching conversation.	
5. Observed the learner demonstrate knowledge and understanding of the targeted skill(s) or practice(s).	
6. Observed the learner's use of the targeted skill(s) or practice(s).	
7. Created opportunities for the learner to observe the coach and/or others model the target skill(s) or practice(s).	
8. Promoted use of multiple opportunities for the learner to practice implementation of the targeted skill(s) and practice(s) (e.g., role plays, in context).	
9. Used both planned and spontaneous opportunities to strengthen the learner's knowledge and skills.	
10. Asked probing questions to examine the learner's knowledge and abilities.	

(continued)

Coaching practice indicators	Description of practice
11. Prompted learner reflection on his/her knowledge and use of the targeted skill(s) and practice(s) compared against research-based practice standards.	
12. Provided feedback about the learner's knowledge and skills following the learner's reflection on his/her performance.	
13. Provided and/or promoting access to new information and resources after the learner reflects on his/her performance.	
14. Engaged the learner in reflection on the usefulness, effectiveness, and need for continuation of the coaching process.	

Appendix B

COACHING LOG

Coach: _____ Learner: _____

Date of interaction: _____ Beginning time: _____ Ending time: _____

Location of interaction: _____

Who was present? _____

Topic(s): _____

Was the coaching session planned?   Yes   No

Transcript of coaching conversation/observations	Characteristics					Coach's reflections/review (analysis of coaching process and promotion of parent's understanding and ability to promote child participation)
	P ✓	O ✓	A ✓	R ★	F •	

P = Joint Planning, O = Observation, A = Action, R = Reflection, F = Feedback
*Codes for Reflective Questions: 1 – Awareness, 2 – Analysis, 3 – Alternatives, 4 – Action; •Codes for Feedback: A – Affirmative, D – Directive, E – Evaluative, I – Informative

The Early Childhood Coaching Handbook by Dathan D. Rush, Ed.D., CCC-SLP, and M'Lisa L. Shelden, PT, Ph.D.
Copyright © 2011 by Paul H. Brookes Publishing Co., Inc. All rights reserved.

Chapter 7

Coaching Families

A key component of practice for an early childhood practitioner involves understanding how to work effectively with the adults—particularly the parents—who are involved in the lives of children who are eligible for supports and services. Early childhood legislation requiring the involvement of the parents of eligible young children at many levels spans a period of almost 45 years. Specifically, early childhood programs such as Head Start (Economic Opportunity Act of 1964 [PL 88-452]), Part H (now known as Part C Early Intervention) of the Education of the Handicapped Act (Education of the Handicapped Act Amendments of 1986 [PL 99-457]), Even Start (Elementary and Secondary Education Act of 1988 [PL 100-297]), and Early Head Start (EHS) (Head Start Transition Project Act of 1990 [PL 101-501]) all originally required the involvement of parents and considered parent participation to be critical to successful intervention and effective program outcomes. Subsequent reauthorizations of each of these programs continue to support and enhance the role of parents in promoting child learning, providing parent-to-parent support, and participating in program leadership, evaluation, and policy development. In addition, over the last 2 decades the fields of early childhood education and special education, early literacy, occupational therapy, physical therapy, and speech-language pathology have encouraged early childhood practitioners to reinvent their roles with family members. These directives advocate for nonhierarchical collaborative partnerships that focus on caregiver priorities.

Several articles specifically state that the role of a practitioner should change from being the primary person responsible for promoting child learning to serving as a coach supporting parents and other caregivers. In this new role, the practitioner works alongside the parent(s) to jointly identify strategies to support child participation and learning as well as to support the adults' identification of, access to, and evaluation of needed resources (Campbell, 1997; Chai, Zhang, & Bisberg, 2006; Dinnebeil, McInerney, Roth, & Ramasway, 2001; Hanft & Pilkington, 2000; Rush, Shelden, & Hanft, 2003). Over time, researchers also have shown that active engagement of parents contributes to enhanced outcomes for children who are enrolled in early childhood programs (Mahoney, 2009). Studies have demonstrated specifically that parent-mediated strategies, particularly parent responsiveness, are more effective in promoting enhanced child development than those same strategies implemented by early childhood practitioners (Mahoney, Boyce, Fewell, Spiker, & Wheeden, 1998). Research has also shown that parent participation in intervention is key and that supporting parents in competently and confidently interacting responsively with young children during their daily routines may be more critical to intervention effectiveness than the time children spend with professionals (Mahoney, 2009; Mahoney & Perales, 2005).

Despite this emphasis on parental involvement, directives to redefine practice, and evolving research related to the participation of parents in educational and therapeutic programs, many practitioners have continued to focus on intervention strategies that are therapist–child focused (Campbell & Sawyer, 2007; Peterson, Luze, Eshbaugh, Jeon, & Kantz, 2007). In therapist–child-focused interventions, the parent is often relegated to being an observer and carrying out follow-up activities involving implementation of home programs, worksheets, or decontextualized activities focusing on skill development. The purpose of this chapter is to describe how to use coaching to support family members, particularly parents of young children, to promote child learning as a natural part of everyday activities. We will also address parenting support topics and issues that focus on the mobilization and provision of resources that the family prioritizes. More specifically, this chapter is designed to illustrate how coaching can be used to assist the parents and other family members of children who need supports and services from a variety of early childhood venues, regardless of the specific content of the program (e.g., EHS, Part C Early Intervention, early childhood special education, Early Reading First Initiatives, Even Start, Parents as Teachers).

FAMILY CONTEXTS: OPERATIONALIZING NATURAL LEARNING OPPORTUNITIES IN THE HOME AND COMMUNITY

If not entirely based on providing support in the natural setting of the eligible child, many early childhood programs (e.g., Head Start, EHS, Part C Infant–Toddler Program, Even Start) require a home visitation component (Economic Opportunity Act of 1964 [PL 88-452]; Elementary and Secondary Education Act of 1988 [PL 100-297]; Head Start Transition Project Act of 1990 [PL 101-501]; Education of the Handicapped Act of 1986 [PL 99-457]). One of the most renowned programs is the Part C program (previously Part H) of the Individuals with Disabilities Education Act (IDEA) of 1997 (PL 105-17) of particular importance in this legislation, originally passed in 1986, was the requirement that all supports and services for infants and toddlers with disabilities must be implemented in natural learning environments in order to enhance the capacity of parents and other care providers to promote the growth and development of the children in their care. Although numerous early intervention programs existed prior to implementation of federal legislation for a national system of statewide programs, many of these programs were center-based and directed by professionals. Furthermore, at that time the majority of early intervention professionals had no training to prepare them for working with families in home and community settings (Bailey, Hebbeler, Scarborough, Spiker, & Malik, 2004; Bailey, Palsha, & Huntington, 1990; Bailey, Simeonsson, Yoder, & Huntingon, 1990; Hebbeler et al., 2007). The natural learning environments provision of Part C of IDEA (U.S. Department of Education) continues to be a sticking point for many early interventionists at the present time. Natural environments are defined in Part C of IDEA as "settings that are natural or normal for the child's same age peers who have no disabilities" This provision was required in order to assist parents and other caregivers in supporting the child's increased or enhanced participation in everyday activities.

Natural learning environment practices include instructional approaches to early intervention that are implemented by practitioners to support parents and other caregivers in using everyday activities as the sources of infants' and toddlers' learning opportunities (Campbell, 2004; Campbell & Sawyer, 2007; Dunst, Hamby, Trivette, Raab, & Bruder, 2000; Dunst, Trivette, Humphries, Raab, & Roper, 2001; Humphrey & Wakeford, 2008; Keilty & Galvin, 2006; Kellegrew, 2000; McWilliam, 2000; Spagnola & Fiese, 2007). Examples of typical activity settings for children include but are not limited to playing in the sprinkler in the backyard, eating a family meal, riding in the car alongside an older sibling who is going to school, playing with a new pet, going on a hike with family and friends, getting ready for bed, watching television or a movie, and playing on a screened-in porch at Grandma's house. Natural learning environment practices also support parents and other care providers in recognizing and using child interests as a means for capitalizing on the abundant learning opportunities that exist in the lives of all children (Dunst, Herter, & Shields, 2000; Raab, 2005). Research indicates that parent support of child participation in typical, everyday, interest-based natural learning opportunities has positive consequences for child development and learning (Dunst, Bruder, Trivette, & Hamby, 2006; Trivette, Dunst, & Hamby, 2004).

Reflect

Think about a family you know. Choose a specific child from that family and consider all of that particular child's interests. Now imagine a typical day for that child and think about all of the opportunities afforded the child to experience his or her interests. As you are thinking about interest engagement, make a mental list of all of the learning opportunities that happen naturally as a part of everyday activities that are based on a child's interest.

Parent responsiveness is a key component of maximizing child engagement as a means for promoting learning opportunities throughout a child's daily activities. Use of responsive parenting strategies has shown to enhance development of pivotal behaviors across domains (Beckwith, Rodning, & Cohen, 1992; Bornstein, Tamis-LeMonda, & Haynes, 1999; Vereijken, Ricksen-Walraven, & Kondo-Ikemura, 1997). Mahoney and colleagues (1998) found that intervention to promote child development is only successful if it is focused on the parents and increases child opportunities for responsive interactions with their parents. They also demonstrated that intensity of intervention is an important factor, but does not refer only to the amount of contact with professionals. The success of the intervention depends on the frequency with which parents and other care providers use responsive strategies to interact with and promote their children's participation in real-life activities. In a review of studies involving approximately 700 children and their parents, Mahoney cites two key findings:

> "(1) parents are the major influence on their children's development even when their children participate in intervention; and that (2) the effectiveness of intervention is highly associated with parents becoming more responsive with their children during the course of intervention." (2009, p. 90)

Examples of responsive strategies used by parents include playing frequently with the child, imitating the child's actions and communications, waiting expectantly, following the child's lead, giving the child frequent opportunities to make choices, building on the child's interests, turning routines into games, and assigning intent to the child's facial expressions and vocalizations. When parents use responsive interactions with their children during daily activities and routines, learning opportunities are maximized during all waking hours, as opposed to limiting child learning to instruction of specific behaviors or increasing the amount of "stimulation" a child receives (Bruder & Dunst, 1999; Kim & Mahoney, 2005; Mahoney, 2009; Mahoney, Boyce, Fewell, Spiker, & Wheeden, 1998; Mahoney & Perales, 2003, 2005; McWilliam, 1996).

Many early childhood practitioners are taught intervention strategies that focus directly on practicing and improving the child's delayed or absent developmental skills

Observe

Take time to observe a family you are currently supporting and consider specific opportunities for increasing parent responsiveness. Using interest-based activity settings as the venue will increase your odds of success.

instead of using parent-mediated interventions that emphasize parent responsiveness by building on child interests as the primary means for supporting child learning throughout naturally occurring activities within a child and family's life. Consider a young child with significant language delays who is enrolled in a home-based EHS program and receives home visits on a weekly basis. Because his mother works fulltime, he spends most days with his grandfather. Using a more

Remember

The characteristics of natural learning environment practices are:

- Child interests
- Everyday opportunity
- Parent responsiveness

traditional approach to promote communication skills, the EHS home visitor has been working with the grandfather on using sign language with his grandson to support the child's attempts at communication. The EHS home visitor identified three signs on which to focus (e.g., COOKIE, DRINK, MORE). The practitioner then instructed the grandfather to practice these three signs throughout the day as much as possible.

In contrast, an early childhood practitioner who understands the use of interests, everyday activity settings, and parent responsiveness as the means for promoting child learning would approach the situation differently. This EHS home visitor understands that the family members are concerned about the child's delays in language development. The home visitor takes the time to identify activity settings and interests that already exist as part of the child's days, particularly the ones that he spends with his grandfather because he is with his grandfather almost every day of the week. The grandfather has discovered that his young grandson enjoys looking at photographs, which he keeps in an old trunk in the attic. Each time the youngster visits, he immediately tugs on his grandfather's arm, pulling him toward the stairs to the attic. The grandfather enjoys spending time with his grandson and eagerly follows his lead, carrying him up the stairs to open the trunk. The EHS home visitor would encourage the grandfather to continue this activity and explains the importance of following the child's lead. She also would discuss all of the valuable learning opportunities afforded to the child because of the grandfather's responsiveness. If the grandfather is interested, they could explore together additional strategies that the grandfather might use to support the child's communication during the photo-viewing activity setting. For example, the practitioner and grandfather might note that the signs for UP and PICTURE would fit naturally into their discussions about the photographs in the attic. The grandfather might decide he would like to ask the child questions about the old photos or simply comment on the pictures. The grandfather already tells funny stories that the child obviously loves to hear about the pictures. The home visitor could explore with the grandfather the idea of using shorter utterances or phrases with the child and waiting expectantly for the child to attempt a word or use a sound that approximates a word. The home visitor could demonstrate for the grandfather how to use facial expressions that promote elaboration and attention of the child or how to repeat the word the child is trying to say. Each of these strategies encourages the development of communication skills and promotes social–emotional growth and development, fine and gross motor development, and cognitive development. The home visitor would work with the grandfather to support his confidence and competence related to using the new strategies and continue to

Reflect

How do the natural learning environment practices described in the scenario with the grandfather and the young child compare with the way that you currently work with families?

promote his enjoyment of the activity with his grandson. Over time, the early childhood practitioner would explore other activity settings that the child and grandfather enjoy in order to expand on the breadth of learning opportunities throughout the child's day.

Coaching to Support Parent-Mediated Child Learning

To support families in promoting child growth and development, the coach initiates conversations that explore parent priorities for the child and family. These coach–parent or coach–care provider conversations identify existing activity settings, routines, rituals, and special circumstances that are a part of the child's life. The coach also explores other possible activity settings in which the family members would like to participate but are not doing so. Coaches talk with families about family and child interests and how they currently support interest expression within daily routines and activities.

Regardless of whether the content of the supporting program is Part C Early Intervention, EHS, Early Reading First, Even Start, or Parents as Teachers, identifying parent priorities, child interests, and everyday routines and activity settings is a critical component of supporting the child and family. For instance, in Early Intervention, identifying interests and everyday activity settings is a required component of writing the individualized family service plan (IFSP). In EHS, these routines, activity settings and priorities serve as the content for the Family Partnership Plan. In Early Reading First or Parents as Teachers, identifying child interests is a primary area of focus for promoting early literacy activities within a child's home or early childhood program. The following tools are particularly effective in gathering information about family and care provider priorities as they relate to child participation in everyday activity settings and needed or desired resources and supports:

- The *Asset-Based Context (ABC) Matrix* (Wilson & Mott, 2006). The *ABC Matrix* is a contextually based assessment tool for implementing an approach to early childhood intervention practices that emphasizes the importance of children's learning in natural environments. It is designed for use by practitioners and parents to identify children's interests and assets and promote children's learning opportunities and participation in everyday life experiences and activities. Information is gathered through conversations with parents or primary care providers and through interactions with and observations of the child in natural settings. The Asset-Based Context Matrix is available at http://www.fippcase.org/casetools/casetools_vol2_no4.pdf.

- The *Interest-Based Everyday Activity Checklists* (Swanson, Raab, Roper, & Dunst, 2006) consist of three different checklists: one for children birth to 15 months of age, one for children 15–36 months of age, and one for children 36–60 months of age. These assessment/ intervention tools are designed as checklists and are used to identify interest-based child learning opportunities that occur as part of everyday family and community life and to increase child participation in the activities. This resource is available at http://www. fippcase.org/casetools/casetools_vol2_no5.pdf.

- *The Routines-Based Interview* (McWilliam & Clingenpeel, 2003). This tool is a conversational process that replaces a discussion of passes and failures on test protocols as the basis for choosing intervention priorities. The discussion is intended to result in a plan for helping the parents and care providers focus on their priorities for the children in their care. The interview involves six steps that begin with talking about the day-to-day life of the child and family. As they talk about everyday situations, the family members and care providers are asked to choose the things that are most meaningful to them. This tool is available from research@sisken.org.

Activity Settings
• What does your child and family do every day or almost every day? • What are those things that have to be done, such as meals, dressing, bathing? • What does your child and family do certain days, on weekends or times of the week/year? • What are the special events in which your child and family participate? • What are the special activities or events as part of your child and family's life?
Child/Family Interests
• How does your child/family choose to spend time? • What are your child's favorite toys, people, and events? • What things are interesting or enjoyable to your child and family?
Child/Family Assets
• What does your child and family work especially hard at doing? • What are your child and family especially good at doing? • What are your child and family's strengths, skills, and accomplishments?
Functional/Meaningful Interactions
• What does your child do to get started in play? • What does your child do to keep play or an interaction with you or other going? • How does your child get what he or she wants? • How does your child get to where he or she wants to go?
Opportunities
• What activities does your child get to do every day? • How often does your child get to do his or her favorite things? • Where are the places your child gets to do the things he or she likes and can do? • Who does your child get to play or interact with on a regular basis?
Participation
• What does your child actually do during an activity that he or she likes to do and is good at doing? • What are the specific ways in which your child participates in interactions with objects and people?
Possibilities
• What are the ways that your child's current opportunities and participation can be expanded? • What interactions and skills would you like your child to develop?

Figure 7.1.   Asset-Based Context Matrix assessment questions. (From Wilson, L.L., & Mott, D.W. [2006]. Asset-based context matrix: An assessment tool for developing contextually based child outcomes. *CASEtools, 2*[4], 1–12. Copyright © 2006 by Family, Infant and Preschool Program.)

Figure 7.1 is an excerpt from the Asset-Based Context Matrix (Wilson & Mott, 2006) containing examples of assessment questions to identify interest-based child and family activity settings, current and desired participation in and across family and community routines, and opportunities for learning that occur with high frequency.

The answers to the questions on the Asset-Based Context Matrix (Wilson & Mott, 2006) contain critical information that will help practitioners support family members of young children to promote the growth and development of the children in their care. Discussion of the topics addressed by these questions occurs at the point of initial contact and at any time that the child's or family's circumstances change. The coach must remain up to date and knowledgeable about the family priorities, routines, and interests in order to provide ongoing support of the parents and other caregivers to promote child participation in and across all the contexts that are important to the child and family. Parents, other care providers, and early childhood practitioners can ensure that the child frequently practices newly developing skills by optimizing child participation in regularly occurring interest-based activities (Campbell, 2004; Campbell & Sawyer, 2007; Chai et al,, 2006; Dunst et al., 2000; Dunst et al., 2001; Humphrey & Wakeford, 2008; Keilty & Galvin, 2006; Kellegrew, 2000; McWilliam, 2000; Raab, 2005; Spagnola & Fiese, 2007). Interest, opportunity, and parent responsiveness are key factors for success

Practice

Use one of the tools described in this chapter with a family you are currently supporting to identify interests and activity settings for the child enrolled in your program:

- The *Asset-Based Context Matrix* (Wilson & Mott, 2006)
- The *Interest-Based Activity Checklists* (Swanson, Raab, Roper, & Dunst, 2006), or
- The *Routines-Based Interview* (McWilliam & Clingenpeel, 2003).

in promoting child growth and development. Additional information and clarification on use of natural learning environment practices in early childhood intervention appears in *Agreed upon Mission and Key Principles for Providing Early Intervention Services in Natural Environments* (Workgroup on Principles and Practices in Natural Environments, 2007). See http://www.nectac.org/~pdfs/topics/families/Finalmissionandprinciples3_11_08.pdf, http://www.nectac.org/~pdfs/topics/families/AgreedUponPractices_FinalDraft2_01_08.pdf, and http://www.nectac.org/~pdfs/topics/families/Principles_LooksLike_DoesntLookLike3_11_08.pdf.

The following scenario illustrates the use of natural learning environment practices and a coaching interaction style with a young family that is living in a trailer park in a suburb outside a large metropolitan area in the Midwest. The family members include Cindy, the mother; Ellie, age 4; Maggie, age 2, and Wendy, age 2 months and eligible for early intervention. Wendy's physician referred her to early intervention because she has a diagnosis of lissencephaly. The team goes through the process with the family and identifies the following IFSP outcomes:

1. Cindy will feel comfortable taking all three girls to the playground at the trailer park.
2. Cindy will know how to care for Wendy to keep her from becoming sick.
3. Cindy will pursue her GED.

The team identifies Paula, a physical therapist (PT), as the provider for the family. The visits will begin with Paula obtaining an understanding of Cindy's current capabilities and understanding regarding Wendy's care. Paula and other team members will support Cindy in learning how to position Wendy, feed her, bathe her, watch for ear infections, and so on. This process will require assessing Wendy's needs and assisting in obtaining special equipment for her. Assume that Paula is well into her visits with Cindy (i.e., it is month two) and Cindy is ready to take a family trip to the playground in the trailer park. The joint plan was for Cindy to gather the items she would need to take to the playground and "talk up" the event with all three girls between visits. Cindy was also agree to write down any questions she had about the event and brainstorm "what ifs." Weather permitting, they planned to head to the playground during Paula's next visit.

When Paula arrived, Cindy was packed and ready to go. Wendy was in her stroller with her jacket, hat, and mittens on. Maggie and Ellie were in the process of zipping up their coats as well. Cindy had packed a backpack with a small blanket and snacks for the girls. Cindy was obviously excited about the event and commented that the weather was perfect. Cindy had written down only one question about the trip. She was worried about what to do if Wendy wet her diaper. She knew that it was not good for Wendy to be wearing a wet diaper, but felt that it might be even worse to change her while they were outside. Paula asked Cindy several questions to help Cindy decide what to do. She asked, "What do you think might work?" (reflection/analysis question), "What are your options?" (reflection/alternatives question), and "What would you like to try today?" (reflection/action question). After this interaction, Cindy decided that she would check on Wendy frequently during their trip to the playground and that if she did wet her diaper, the family would just head back home.

Cindy reminded Maggie and Ellie about the rules for walking outside and the girls immediately clasped hands and headed out the front door. Paula and Cindy thought through several options for Cindy to get the stroller out the door and decided that having Ellie hold the front door was the best option. Once they were out the door, Cindy could carry the stroller down the four steps from the trailer. As they walked to the playground, Cindy was able to maneuver the stroller and keep track of the girls. Paula commented on Cindy's ability to keep the girls engaged and focused on being safe by asking them questions (affirmative/informative feedback).

When they reached the playground, Ellie ran toward the swings. Maggie also wanted to swing, so Paula and Cindy followed her to that area. Ellie climbed into the swing and Cindy gave her a push to get her going. Maggie cried out to get in a swing. The playground swingset did not have an infant/toddler swing. Cindy asked Paula what she should do. Cindy could figure out how to swing Ellie and Maggie safely, but then Wendy would just be sitting in the stroller. Paula asked Cindy, "What is your vision of a successful fun time for all of the girls?" (reflection/analysis question). Cindy shared multiple possibilities. After Maggie and Ellie were tired of swinging, they moved toward the small slide. Maggie and Ellie were able to go up and down the slide on their own, so Cindy used this opportunity to get Wendy out of her stroller. Cindy asked several questions about how to hold Wendy on the slide and wanted to try out a couple of ideas (observation by the coach), but she was not pleased with the results. Paula asked Cindy, "Why do you think this isn't working?" (reflection/analysis question) and "What could you do differently?" (reflection/alternatives question).

Following this discussion, Paula offered some suggestions (informative feedback) and demonstrated some alternatives while Cindy watched for what was different (observation/modeling by the coach). After the demonstration, Cindy tried out the idea and was able to successfully hold Wendy while being able to see her face and talk to her as she helped her slide down the bottom few feet of the slide. Maggie and Ellie thought it was great fun to see baby Wendy on the slide and wanted to help mom with sliding. After a few more successful slides, Cindy checked and Wendy did have a wet diaper, so the group headed back home.

After they returned from the trip to the playground, Paula and Cindy discussed what Cindy felt went well (reflection/analysis question) and what additional supports or ideas she would like to pursue (reflection/action question). The joint plan that follows is a result of that conversation:

1. Cindy will talk with the trailer park manager about installing infant/toddler swings for the playground.

2. Cindy will place a flyer in the trailer park office to see whether other mothers of young children are interested in meeting at the playground.

3. Paula will bring some catalogs of playground equipment (infant/toddler swings) to the next visit.

4. Although Cindy is not ready to go to the playground alone with the girls, she would like to go again on Paula's next visit.

The scenario with Cindy illustrated the use of coaching to support a young mother's ability to promote child participation in an activity setting that the family enjoyed. Paula planned to begin her next visit with the family by focusing on specific aspects of their joint plan. Sometimes it is challenging for a coach to know how to initiate that next conversation with the parent or care provider. Staying focused on the intent and purpose of the real-life activity setting is essential for success.

Remember

When you are initiating coaching with a family, whether the family is new to the program or already enrolled, it is critical to follow these steps:

1. Explain the use of coaching practices. Be sure to include an explanation of why you are using coaching and how it will look. Refer to Chapter 5 for a detailed description of how to explain coaching.

2. Using conversational interview techniques, identify the parents' priorities for the child and family.

3. Systematically converse with parents and other care providers and observe the child and family in order to identify child interests and activity settings.

4. Support the parents in their ability to mediate participation of the child in interest-based settings in order to support the intended outcomes of your program (e.g., early intervention, early literacy).

SPECIFIC COACHING PRACTICES TO USE WHEN WORKING WITH FAMILIES

Sometimes new coaches have particular difficulty in two areas: 1) knowing how to revisit the joint plan at the beginning of the coaching conversation and 2) understanding the level of involvement of the coach to support action by the coachee.

Starting the Coaching Conversation and Revisiting the Joint Plan

Individuals who are serving in a coaching role typically use one of five types of questions to initiate the coaching conversation and refer back to the previous joint plan. These questions are the generic grand-tour question, skill-focused question, strategy-focused question, strategy-focused question tied to an activity setting, and activity-focused question.

The most commonly used question, which is used especially often by new coaches, is the generic grand-tour question. Examples include "How are things going?" "How have you been doing?" or "How's Betsy doing?" Generic grand-tour questions typically do not refer directly to the previous joint plan; instead, the reference to the plan is implied. The problem with this type of question is that the coachee could essentially take the conversation anywhere. Although it may be appropriate for the coach to follow the coachee's lead or need relative to the conversation, generic grand-tour questions are not conducive to revisiting the joint plan to determine the level of the coachee's active participation toward the goal and reflection on the success of the plan.

The second type of question often used to start a coaching conversation is a skill-focused question that relates directly to the child's deficits and the skills that are being addressed. Common skill-focused questions include "How many words does he have now?" "How is she doing with pulling to stand?" or "How is she holding the spoon now?" Use of skill-focused questions by a coach places emphasis on isolated skills acquisition or milestones rather than on functional use and the context in which the skill is used. These questions initiate skill-based conversations rather than conversations that would promote, through modeling by the coach and/or practice by the coachee, the child's participation within the context of everyday activities in which the skill would be used. Asking a skill-focused question naturally leads the parent to report about skills use and places emphasis on the skill rather than on the child's participation in real-life activities that would support acquisition and use of the desired skill and also many other skills.

The third type of question that is commonly used to start coaching conversations is strategy focused. Examples include "How has it been going with using choices this week?" "Tell me how it worked to put his toys up on the couch so he would have to pull up on the side of the couch to get them" and "How did it go using the highchair this week?" When the focus is placed on the strategy, as with skill-focused questions, the emphasis becomes use of that strategy rather than the child's participation in activities that incorporate that strategy. Strategies for promoting a child's participation that also improve a desired skill or address a parent's priority for the child are often part of coaching conversations, but they should occur only within the context of functional and meaningful activity settings that are unique to the child and family.

Closer to the goal of emphasizing child participation within everyday contexts is the use of strategy-focused questions that are tied to an activity setting. An example of this type of start to a coaching conversation might be "How have you been doing with giving your child choices for drinks during mealtime?" In this type of question, the strategy (i.e., use of choices) is attached to the activity setting (i.e., mealtime) in which it could regularly occur for this child and parent. The emphasis is still on a particular strategy that the coachee had planned to use between coaching conversations, but the question is contextualized. This type of question still places importance on a strategy, which could limit the ways in which the coachee could be responsive to the child.

The recommended method for opening a coaching conversation and referring back to the previous joint plan is to ask about the context(s) or activity setting(s) that was or were to be the coachee's focus between the coaching conversations. The activity setting(s) could yield multiple possibilities for skill development and use of any strategy or strategies discussed in previous conversations. The emphasis, however, is on the child's participation in an activity setting and all that both the child and parent could be doing to promote learning and development. Examples of activity-focused initiations to the coaching conversations include "Tell me about how your mealtime routine went this week" and "Last time I was here you were going to focus on how you could support Elizabeth's involvement in your family mealtime. Tell me how that went." This opening could be followed by more specific probes, such as "What did you try that went well?" "What could you have done differently?" "How did what you did match to what we had talked about and tried last time I was here?" "What was Elizabeth learning during mealtime this week?" and "What did you do that made the difference in mealtime with Elizabeth?" When a coach begins a coaching conversation by revisiting the previous joint plan that highlights a particular activity setting or everyday context that had been discussed, the emphasis is on the parents' and child's involvement in the activity, during which certain strategies may have been attempted and a variety of skills ultimately were addressed.

Continuum of Involvement by the Coach Regarding Action by the Coachee

In order to support a parent's ability to maximize child participation in natural learning opportunities, the coach must pay particular attention to how his or her presence influences the real-life situation in which the coachee typically engages without the coach's contributions. A coach must also be mindful of effective adult learning

> **Remember**
>
> The recommended method of opening a coaching conversation with a family is to refer to the previous joint plan and ask about the context or activity setting that was to be the coachee's focus between the coaching conversations.

strategies that affect a parent's ability to experience success within a context that may be very challenging. The involvement of the coach within or regarding a particular action by the coachee rests on a continuum from direct to indirect involvement, hands on or hands off, and most intrusive to least intrusive interaction. All points on the continuum are possible ways in which the coach may be involved with the coachee and the child. No one method should be used to the exclusion of the others; rather, all options should be included in the coach's repertoire, available for use by the coach depending on the situation and level of support required by the coachee.

The most direct, hands-on, and invasive strategy that a coach may employ is to use the child to model a particular strategy or action while the parent observes. Modeling by the coach can never occur if the parent is not an engaged participant who is able to make specific observations. Modeling is often used by a coach to try to figure out the strategies or level of support that might work best. When a coach makes the decision to use modeling, the coach must ensure that this technique does not in some way give the message that the parent is unable to do the task, but rather helps the parent see alternate methods for doing the action or strategy. When it is possible, the coach should take time before modeling to discuss what he or she is going to try and to obtain input and ideas from the parent that may be incorporated into the model. Modeling should be followed immediately by reflection on what the coach did and how it might look if the parent tried it, with an invitation for the parent to attempt the strategy or action.

For example, a mother named Donita needed support in giving her infant, Tina, oral feedings without having Tina immediately regurgitate the formula. A swallow study had been conducted on Tina and had ruled out swallowing problems. Mary, the speech-language pathologist (SLP), modeled for Donita how to hold Tina, give her the bottle, withdraw the bottle to allow Tina time to swallow the formula, and then present the bottle again. The strategy was quite successful and Tina was able to retain all of the formula without any signs of distress, discomfort, or regurgitation. Unfortunately, when Mary looked up she saw that Donita had a tear running down her face. Donita asked, "Why didn't I know how to do that? I'm her mother." Before modeling, Mary could have talked with Donita a bit more about what she was going to try, or, in this particularly sensitive situation, she could have chosen to intensively support Donita through the process of doing the feeding herself, which is the next level on the continuum.

In a situation that is still directive but somewhat less hands-on and less intrusive by the coach, the parent is directly involved with the child while the coach provides verbal support via prompts during the activity. Sometimes these prompts may be in the form of a question that directly relates to strategies or actions that the coach and/or parent have recently discussed or tried in the past. Other times the prompts may be suggestions made by the coach as the parent is directly engaged with the child. To use this approach with Donita, Mary asked Donita whether she wanted to try feeding Tina with Mary's direct support. If Donita felt uncomfortable doing so, Mary could ask Donita's permission to show her an option for feeding Tina. But Donita did agree to try to feed Tina, so Mary said to her, "We have been talking about ways to hold Tina that will allow her to drink from the bottle more easily. Which one would you like to try now?" After Donita positioned Tina, Mary said, "Now, gently stroke her lip with the nipple of the bottle and watch how she'll open her mouth to take the nipple." When Donita tried this and achieved some success, Mary said, "Okay, let's gently remove the nipple from her mouth and be sure that she is able to swallow the formula and rest for a minute. How will we know when she's ready for more?" When Donita responded, Mary said, "We are learning to read her cues. Let's see if she wants a little more." Donita fed Tina for a few more moments, and then Mary asked her to remove the nipple again. As Donita became more competent and confident in reading Tina's cues, Mary had Donita try it more on her own while Mary observed. Mary made some additional suggestions and asked Donita a few questions about how the activity was proceeding. When the feeding was completed, Mary and Donita debriefed. When using this coaching strategy, the coach is in the moment with the coachee and makes suggestions as appropriate or asks the coachee to reflect on what they have tried that has worked in the past. The key to using this strategy is to provide suggestions only long enough for the coachee to become comfortable with the strategy or actions to try. The trial is always followed by reflection on how the suggestions or prompts worked and how the parent would continue to use this strategy within this activity or similar activities, as well as how the parent would build on what was working.

The third strategy on the continuum of involvement by the coach regarding action by the coachee is a type of reflection in action (Schon, 1987). This strategy consists of indirect involvement of the coach and hands-on interaction by the parent during the activity. In this strategy, the parent is directly involved with the child while the coach is observing but withholding questions or feedback until there is an appropriate opportunity to promote the parent's reflection on what is taking place. For example, consider a situation in which a father, a child, and a coach are at the park and the parent is helping the child go down the slide. The father lifts the child up to the top of the slide and then carefully holds the child as he goes down the slide. After the child has gone down the slide the first time, the coach might ask the father how he could help Joshua climb up the steps with his father's support, as his goal is for Joshua to be more independent. The coach and father brainstorm some options and the father implements the best option while the coach watches. Then the coach and father debrief and reflect on what parts went well and what the father will do differently on the next attempt up the steps. The coach also might ask the father how Joshua is letting him know that he wants to go down the slide again and how he might help Joshua use words like "more slide" to let his dad know what he wants. The father then repeats the activity of helping Joshua climb the steps of the slide and encouraging him to ask for "more slide." The coach and father continually reflect on how they can modify this activity to promote Joshua's continued learning and skill acquisition across developmental areas. Rather than directly modeling how to help Joshua go up the steps and promote Joshua's word use during this sliding activity, or guiding Joshua's father through the individual steps of the activity, with this approach the coach observed the father's actions and prompted him to think about ways to use the activity to address his priorities for his son.

A fourth coaching strategy on the continuum of coach involvement involves a type of reflection on action (Schon, 1987) in which the coach directly observes the parent and child during an activity or situation and then engages the parent in reflection/debriefing about what happened following the activity. For example, the coach is with a parent and child in their home when the child takes a toy away from her baby brother. When the mother tries to intervene, the child throws the toy across the room, narrowly missing the coach's head. The parent apologizes to the coach and expresses her frustration regarding the girl's behavior, especially her interactions with her younger brother and other situations in which she seemingly does not get her way and proceeds to tantrum. Within this coaching opportunity, the coach and parent reflect on the actions of the child and parent that the coach just observed. They reflect on how the ideal situation would look, ways to promote positive sibling interactions, and approaches for addressing the tantrums whenever and wherever they occur.

The strategy that is the least directive, least hands-on, and least intrusive on the coaching continuum is a debriefing and reflection session between the parent and coach focusing on an action or practice opportunity that happened between coaching visits. The coach did not have the opportunity to observe the parent's actions or practice, but he or she listens to the parent report what happened. Depending on the parent's understanding of the coaching process, the need for or intensity of the reflective questioning of the parent by the coach may vary. A parent who is becoming more competent and confident in supporting his or her child's participation in interest-based activity settings within the family and community settings may relay what happened to the coach and mention other modified actions that he or she took which led to the intended outcome. A parent who is less confident or knowledgeable may need to be prompted with more reflective questions and informative feedback by the coach in order to analyze what worked or did not work and consider other options that he or she could have tried.

The coach chooses where to start on the continuum depending on 1) the context (i.e., whether the action is occurring or could occur while the coach is present), 2) the situation (i.e., whether it is a situation in which the coach can or should be more directive and hands-on or less directive and hands-on), and 3) the level of confidence, knowledge, and skill of the coachee (i.e., does the parent require some prompting or immediate reflection within the context of the immediate situation or can reflection follow the current activity or situation?).

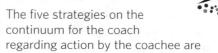

Remember

The five strategies on the continuum for the coach regarding action by the coachee are

1. Coach models while the parent observes, immediately followed by reflection by the parent.

2. Coach provides verbal support and prompts while the parent directly engages in the activity.

3. Coach observes parent, but withholds any questions or feedback until an appropriate opportunity for parent reflection occurs *during the activity* (reflection in action).

4. Coach directly observes parent and child and then immediately reflects and debriefs with the parent *following the activity* (reflection on action).

5. Coach and parent debrief and reflect on an action or practice opportunity that happened between visits.

SPECIAL SITUATIONS RELATED TO A COACHING STYLE OF INTERACTION

Many situations and circumstances arise for coaches working with families from diverse backgrounds and life experiences. Coaches are often challenged by complex situations that may be related to characteristics of the parent, child, or environment. Often referred to as barriers, or reasons practitioners believe that they cannot use a coaching style of interaction, these special circumstances are opportunities in which coaching is an effective strategy for building the confidence and competence of *all* parents and care providers.

Coaching Parents to Identify, Access, and Evaluate Needed Resources

Families of young children often have questions about how and where to locate needed resources. These needs and priorities often are related specifically to the child or children in the family, but they also may be based on broader family issues or the personal needs of other family members that directly or indirectly affect the child who is eligible for the program providing services. For example, a family might want to enroll their child in a community preschool program, but they might lack reliable transportation to ensure the child's regular attendance at the program. Another situation might include a mother whose children have been removed from her custody and placed in foster care. The mother might have questions about joint visits with the foster family or where to find local parenting classes.

Resource-based intervention practices are defined by a set of strategies that focus on mobilization and provision of supports and resources for individuals and families. These practices are designed to strengthen the capacity of the individual or family to 1) identify what is needed, 2) access the prioritized resources, and 3) evaluate the effectiveness of the support that is used. Resource-based intervention practices encompass a full range of community types of assistance consisting of both informal and formal sources of advice, guidance, material support, and other types of support or services needed to help individuals and families achieve desired outcomes (Dunst, Trivette, & Deal, 1994; Jung, 2010; McWilliam & Scott, 2001; Mott & Dunst, 2006). The use of coaching for implementation of resource-based intervention practices is ideal because parents are not just being told about a specific resource or service, but instead are taken through a series of questions to identify what they have already tried, what they might know about, or what has worked in the past when they may have faced similar circumstances, thus building their confidence in finding such resources in the future.

Consider a scenario involving a young family in a rural community in the southeast. After the birth of their new baby, the Whitaker family relocated to a small town in rural North Carolina to be closer to extended family members. The parents, Vito and Celine, both had experience in the furniture industry and were looking for cabinetry work. Their daughter Susannah was born 4 months ago with Down syndrome and was doing well after overcoming some early problems with feeding and gaining weight. The parents felt secure moving to a new location and the maternal grandmother was eager to care for Susannah as soon as the parents could find jobs and begin working. After they settled into their new home residing with Susannah's grandmother and enrolled the infant in the early intervention program, the Whitakers realized that jobs were scarce in their area. During the IFSP process with the early intervention program, the family asked their service coordinator, Ginny, for assistance in identifying employment opportunities. Instead of simply directing the family to the Employment Security Commission or providing them with a list of community resources, Ginny used coaching practices to assist the family.

Ginny first asked Vito and Celine what resources they had already accessed when they moved to the area (reflection/awareness question). The parents said that they had contacted existing factories that Celine's mother knew about and asked neighbors and her mother's friends for leads (informal supports). Finding nothing promising, Vito and Celine had contacted the Employment Security Commission and had begun a systematic search of the phone book to identify possible employers (formal supports). After Vito and Celine shared their current strategies, Ginny asked several questions to help them reflect on other possibilities that they might know about or consider: "How does your job search here compare to what you've done in the past?" (reflection/analysis question), "What other ideas do you have?" (reflection/alternatives question), and "What are your next steps?" (reflection/action question). Ginny also shared some additional information (informative feedback) about a resource in the community for temporary employment and a grant-funded retraining program at the local community college. Ginny helped Vito and Celine develop a plan for contacting the new resource and continuing their search in the community and nearby towns as well (joint planning). Ginny planned to follow up with Vito and Celine not only on how their plan was working, but also on how helpful the new resources were in assisting them in meeting their identified priorities.

In this scenario, Ginny's support of Vito and Celine built on their existing skills and strategies, assisted them in reflecting on what was working, and helped them generate alternative ideas for taking action. Coaching and resource-based intervention practices were used to support the couple's continued competence and confidence and to steer clear of dependency-creating strategies (e.g., Ginny calling known resources for the parents; Ginny driving the couple to a job counselor at the local community college). These practices promote the possibility that the next time the couple needs to solve a problem or work toward a goal, they will consider what they already know, what has worked in the past or might work in this situation, and how to evaluate their approach. In contrast, had Ginny done the work for them or told them what to do, their learning experience would have been limited to knowing that contacting Ginny is their strategy for answers.

> ### Remember
>
>
> Using resource-based practices involves
>
> 1. Identifying parent priorities and possible resources and supports to address these priorities;
> 2. Accessing the needed and desired resources; and
> 3. Evaluating the effectiveness of the resources and supports that were accessed.

Practitioners who use coaching as an interaction style with parents must ensure that the parents understand that the role of the coach is to support the parents' ability to promote child learning within the context of everyday life activities or assist them in identifying and accessing needed resources. Even if the practitioner has ideas that might be effective, the practitioner should start with what the parents know and already are doing that could be achieving the desired effect. Coaching is a way of finding out what the parents want, know, and are already doing, and of jointly generating ideas to foster child learning and development or accessing resources and supports. Just telling the parent what to do may not suit the parent's lifestyle, goals, or learning style. The parent might be willing to do what the practitioner says during the visit and perhaps for a short time later if it happens to be a match, but it is not a long-term strategy for personal success. Likewise, the practitioner implementing a strategy with the child or for the parent may address the issue at that moment, but it does not necessarily prepare the parent to handle the situation in different contexts or go beyond what was told or done. In contrast, coaching builds on what the parent is currently doing and teaches him or her to identify and implement other ideas and strategies without depending on the coach.

Coaching Families with Diverse Backgrounds

In early childhood intervention, practitioners often have opportunities to support families of young children from cultures and backgrounds and possessing life experiences that are very different than their own. Training related to cultural diversity for early childhood interventionists is limited (Hanson, 2004; Lynch & Hanson, 1993), and it must be based on the practitioner's understanding of his or her own cultural beliefs, experiences, and biases (Harry, 1992). Because early intervention, EHS, and many early literacy programs require home visiting as a major program component, practitioners obtain more information about a family's culture and lifestyle simply by being present in the actual environment than what they would learn if the family were bringing the child into a classroom or clinic-based setting. For example, just being present in a family's home provides the practitioner with wonderful opportunities for observing actual mealtime, bath time, and playtime activities and routines. These real-life, everyday activities are the venue for child learning. It is critical for practitioners to respect this private information.

Embedded within the notion of respecting diversity is an inherent requirement for the practitioner to be open to understanding and learning about family lifestyles, opinions, and choices. Practitioners can find themselves in situations with which they have no prior experience and they may have difficulty understanding or valuing a family's position or decision regarding a particular topic or parenting issue. A practitioner must be open and flexible enough to appreciate different ways, styles, and preferences for family routines, particularly with regard to the wide continuum of parenting styles and strategies that a home visitor might encounter in a typical day. For example, consider a situation where a mother has prioritized learning how to help her child, who is enrolled in EHS, try new and more nutritious foods. The home visitor and mother plan a mealtime observation for the next home visit. When the practitioner arrives at the family's apartment, the children are playing with toys on the family room floor and watching television while snacking from food trays that are placed on the ottoman. If this practitioner's experience with family mealtimes is limited to situations in which all family members are present and seated around the dining room table, a mealtime that is so different from his or her own might be somewhat confounding.

Consider another scenario in which an early literacy coach is supporting a parent on shared reading experiences before naptime. During the observation, the coach watches as the parent allows the child to make marks in the books and tear and chew on the book pages. This coach has never been in a circumstance where a parent does not seem to mind that the child is damaging the books. In both situations, how the coach reacts to the discomfort of a new and different experience is critically important. Recognizing the feelings of discomfort is an important first step on the part of the practitioner. Instead of concluding that the situation is wrong or judging that the circumstances need to be changed, the coach must first explore with the parent how the current situation compares with what the parent would like to see happening. What might be the same? What might be different? What ideas might the parent have for moving forward? The coach could also share evidence-based information about child learning and development as it relates to the situation or circumstance.

Circumstances can arise in which a cultural chasm can develop between an early childhood intervention practitioner and a family due to lack of information, knowledge, or understanding. For example, in many cultures, food plays an important role and food preparation, participation in mealtime activities, the role of women as providers of nutrition, and the actual partaking of the food can be associated with strong cultural and religious beliefs. Respecting and maintaining cultural complexities can be quite a challenge for practitioners working closely with family members. When children have special situations related to growth and development that hinder their ability to participate in typical activities with strong cultural roots, practitioners must work diligently to be open to understanding the feelings, emotions, and day-to-day practicalities faced by families when conflicts arise.

Consider the experience of Jamal, an infant living with his parents and paternal grandparents in an ethnic neighborhood in a major city in the Pacific Northwest. Jamal's parents, Hafazah (his mother) and Abidin (his father), moved to the United States about 10 years ago from Malaysia, shortly after their marriage. They had a great deal of difficulty in conceiving. Jamal was born prematurely and required neonatal intensive care support for several weeks before he came home from the hospital. About a month before Jamal's birth, Abidin's parents came to live with the family in the United States for an undetermined amount of time. Abidin's mother wanted to be close to Jamal and help with raising him. Abidin is employed in a neighborhood restaurant as a chef, working 6 days a week, and often returns home around midnight after closing the restaurant. Hafazah does not work outside the home and is with Jamal and his grandparents all the time. The grandparents rarely leave the home, except on Abidin's day off from work. Although Abidin and Hafazah speak fluent English, Jamal's grandparents do not.

Jill, SLP with the local early intervention program, has been assigned to support Jamal and his family members to help Jamal learn to eat better and gain weight. Jamal is the equivalent of 10 months old (corrected age for prematurity) and receives all his nourishment via breastfeeding from Hafazah. Hafazah is interested in learning how to introduce other foods to Jamal. She also is worried because Jamal is very quiet and does not make sounds. The family's IFSP outcome is that Hafazah will feel comfortable feeding Jamal foods other than breast milk. The following coaching conversation demonstrates Jill's willingness and openness to learn about Jamal's family in a way that is respectful to all involved.

Jill: Hi there. Thank you for agreeing to meet with me today, especially on Abidin's day off from work. I'm glad your parents are able to join us today as well.

Abidin: Thank you, Jill. I've explained to my parents what we are doing. They want to watch and hope to not be a bother to you.

Jill: Please tell them I am glad they are here. I appreciate their interest and patience with me as I learn more about Jamal and your family.

[Abidin shares what Jill has said with his parents.]

Hafazah: Jill, I bought some jars of baby food at the Walmart yesterday, but I've been too worried to try. Could we try today?

Jill: Definitely. Thank you for remembering to get some baby food. Tell me what you've been worried about.

[Abidin continues to interpret for his parents.]

Hafazah: I went to the store with my friend Heba. She has a baby girl and feeds her baby food all the time. She says I am behind by not feeding Jamal baby food. I do not want to be behind or be slow to Jamal, but I want him to grow and breast milk is good.

[Abidin interprets for his parents and his mother begins to talk to him in a somewhat loud tone. As this happens, Hafazah's facial expression changes and she looks down and becomes quiet. Abidin raises his voice with his mother. Abidin's father starts talking very loudly and Hafazah begins to cry. When Abidin's mother sees Hafazah's face, she walks hurriedly out of the room, talking in a loud voice. Abidin's father says something to Hafazah and Abidin and also leaves the room, talking loudly and waving his arms as if he is angry. Abidin offers Hafazah a handkerchief. She accepts and begins to cry more emphatically.]

Abidin: Jill . . . my parents . . . they do not understand about breastfeeding. My mother believes only newborn babies should drink from breast. My mother believes it is why Jamal is too small. She speaks down to Hafazah for wanting to breastfeed Jamal. She tries to make Jamal eat roti-jala. He chokes and Hafazah gets more upset. I tell her again and again, but she does not believe us.

Jill: Thank you for explaining all of this to me Abidin. Hafazah, are you OK? Do you want to continue with our discussion?

Hafazah: Yes. I'll be OK.

Jill: Please forgive my ignorance . . . what is roti-jala? I want to learn as much as I can about your family so I can be helpful.

Abidin: Jill, it is O.K. I am glad you are asking. Roti-jala is like a thin pancake . . . sort of like bread for us.

Jill: Tell me more about your mother's belief about breastfeeding.

Hafazah: I just get mad and so sad about this. The hospital taught me that feeding Jamal from the breast is the best thing to do for Jamal. Abidin learned that, too. She will not listen. She will not learn. She is old and she will not change. I know we do the best for our baby.

Abidin: My mother believes she is right. She wants the best for Jamal and she does not understand why we will not feed him more food.

Jill: I can see how upsetting this is for you. It can be very difficult when grandparents don't agree with parenting approaches. How have you tried to explain to her what you have learned about breastfeeding?

Hafazah: I told her what the nurses and doctor said. I asked her to come to the doctor with us. I asked her what she needed to believe me. She just says no, no, no . . . and walks away angry.

Jill: How can I help?

Abidin: I don't think you can help. This is too sad.

Jill: Let's explore your thoughts and ideas. Tell me . . . what other ideas do you have?

Hafazah: I have thought that if she could help with feeding Jamal that she might feel better. See for breastfeeding, it is mostly me. I can pump the milk, but I don't like to do it. My friend Heba, has baby food that she buys . . . that she helped me to buy. Could I make it instead of buying it? Could I make the baby food here at home?

Abidin: What? How can you make it?

Jill: Hafazah . . . tell me more about what you are thinking.

Hafazah: Could I blend foods in the food processor for Jamal?

Jill: Certainly! Where would you like to start?

Abidin: You could blend food up for Jamal and he could eat it? That is good.

Hafazah: I could start with fruits and vegetables like Heba said. I could see what Jamal likes. Could I blend up roti-jala? I could teach Mer Tuamu [her mother-in-law] how to blend the roti-jala . . . she would be happy. She would like to cook for Jamal. She needs to cook for Jamal to feel happy inside.

Jill: I can see that you've been thinking a lot about this. How do you think this will change things with your mother-in-law?

Hafazah: Using the blender or food processor will involve Mer Tuamu in feeding Jamal. Also, he will maybe not choke.

Abidin: I think this is great idea. If my mother is happy, my father will be happy.

Jill: [smiling] I've heard that comment many times. Hafazah, when would you like to start using the processor?

Hafazah: Could we do it right now? I have some fresh peaches from market.

Jill: Sure. How would you like to include your parents?

Abidin: Not now. It is too soon after bad talking. Hafazah, can you try it now without mother?

Hafazah: I agree. I am not happy with her right now. I want to try the peaches without her now.

Jill: Please let me know if I can help in any way. What about the roti-jala?

Hafazah: Oh! She would like to try roti-jala. I am OK with that.

Abidin: Are you sure? I will get them. .

[Abidin brings his parents into the kitchen. Hafazah shares with her inlaws her interest in using the food processor. Mer Tuamu quickly moves to the pantry and begins talking in an excited voice. Abidin and his father smile at one another. The women begin to prepare the food for the food processor while Jill observes.]

Jill: What do you know about blending foods?

Hafazah: [first to Mer Tuamu and then to Jill in English] We need water or liquid to help the peaches be smooth.

Jill: What types of liquid might you consider using?

Hafazah: Water or milk? Could I use breast milk?

[Abidin interprets for his parents. Mer Tuamu tosses her hands up and clearly is opposed to using breast milk to puree the peaches and roti-jala.]

Hafazah: Jill. Please tell her about breast milk. Maybe she will listen to you.

Jill: Hafazah, how about you start telling her and I will jump in if you need me to do so. Abidin, will you interpret for me?

[Abidin agrees.]

Hafazah: OK.

[As Hafazah explains why using breast milk is important to her and what nutritional benefits the milk has, she also shares her desire to have her mother-in-law more involved. She says that she too would like Jamal to learn to eat roti-jala, but that when he chokes it is bad and scary for her. She asks her mother-in-law to try it and Jamal's grandmother grudgingly agrees. They process the peaches and roti-jala using some breast milk that Hafazah has pumped and take the blended food to the kitchen table. Hafazah holds Jamal on her lap and supports him so he can try a bite of food.]

Jill: Before you start, could we talk about what you're planning to try?

Hafazah: Sure. I'm excited, but nervous.

Jill: Talk me through what you're planning to do.

Hafazah: I'm going to start with peaches on the tip of the small spoon. I'm ready if he starts to choke.

Jill: What might happen when you approach Jamal with the spoon?

[Abidin is interpreting for his parents and his mother responds to Jill's question.]

Abidin: My mother says he might hit the spoon or close his mouth.

Hafazah: Oh! If he closes his mouth, what should I do?

Jill: What ideas do you have?

[Mer Tuamu immediately responds.]

Abidin: My mother says to put a little taste on his lips . . . he will see if he likes it and will not choke.

Jill: That's a very safe way to approach this. Hafazah, are you comfortable with this?

Hafazah: Yes.

[She proceeds to try the peaches with Jamal. At first he turns his head away, but once the peaches are on his lips he begins to smack and use his tongue to get the food. His grandparents laugh out loud and talk excitedly. Abidin and Hafazah are very happy, too. Jamal continues to eat several small bites of peaches. Mer Tuamu points to the roti-jala and talks with Hafazah and Abidin.]

Abidin: She wants to dip the peaches into the roti-jala and try a bit. Can she give him the bite?

Jill: Hafazah, what would you like to do?

[Hafazah smiles and hands her mother the spoon. Mer Tuamu proceeds to feed him a few bites of peaches and roti-jala. Jamal is obviously excited and happy and is not choking on the pureed food.]

Jill: How do you think Jamal is doing with this?

Abidin: This is so nice. We are all happy and Jamal is eating. He does not choke.

[Jamal finishes the peaches and most of the roti-jala. His grandmother wipes his face and speaks to Hafazah. Hafazah smiles and prepares to breast feed Jamal.]

Hafazah: She said he is thirsty and needs to drink from me.

Jill: [to Mer Tuamu] Thank you for joining us. This was a very nice start for helping Jamal learn. It was kind of you to support Hafazah's desire to breastfeed Jamal.

[Abidin interprets for his mother.]

Mer Tuamu: He is good boy. I love him. I want him to eat. She is good mother. I want to help.

Jill: [to everyone] Well, we've had such a nice visit today and tried some new ideas. How will you use what we've tried today?

Hafazah: I want to feed Jamal food each time he is hungry. Mer Tuamu, will you help me?

Mer Tuamu: [with Abidin interpreting] I will fix lots of food. We will mash it. He will eat.

Jill: Based on what we've talked about today, it sounds like you're going to include feeding Jamal pureed food at each meal. When would you like me to visit again?

Hafazah: Could you come back in a few days? I am sure Mer Tuamu will want to try meats sooner than I will. I want help with that.

Jill: Sure. How about this Friday . . . in three days?

Hafazah: Yes . . . three days. We will be ready.

In this scenario, although Jill did not have prior experience working with families from Malaysia, her open and honest approach with the family was apparent to all involved. She listened, observed, asked questions, and was eager to learn about the priorities of all of the family members. Jill encouraged the family members to talk with one another and build on their interests, which was critically important for developing open communication around the IFSP outcomes and agreeable strategies and activities to achieve their goals. Jill made no assumptions during her visit and paid attention to what each family member communicated and to the nonverbal cues that were demonstrated during the conversations. Jill's attentiveness to the information that the family shared and her focus on reflective questions facilitated a positive interaction around highly sensitive subject matter. Jill's willingness to learn was demonstrated by her inclusion of all family members in the conversation as well as her patience during the interpretation of the Malaysian language and English. She also openly expressed her lack of knowledge related to the family's values and beliefs and asked for their patience with her as she joined with them to learn.

It is important for a practitioner to know as much as possible about a particular culture in order to be respectful and sensitive to a family's values and beliefs. It can, however, feel quite overwhelming to a practitioner to understand this information at the very same time that he or she is getting to know a family. Learning about cultures that differ from one's own is a requirement in order to implement family-centered practices. Some practitioners may also find it challenging not to stereotype families on the basis of what they have learned about a particular culture. In order to respect a family's culture in an individualized manner, the practitioner should strive to develop open and honest communication to form a successful partnership with the family.

A common notion about using a coaching approach pertains to diverse family situations. Practitioners from all types of programs often muse that coaching might work with some families but not with families who are challenged by addiction, poverty, mental health issues, intellectual disability, or other difficult circumstances. These beliefs are often held by practitioners who either have not fully embraced or do not clearly understand family-centered practices. The characteristics of family-centered practices and effective helpgiving include respect for the coachee, presumption that the coachee is competent, and promotion of the person's strengths and abilities rather than an attitude that limits them by their presumed deficits (Dunst & Trivette, 1996). If a practitioner or service coordinator is unable to set aside personal filters that place limited expectations on the family, then coaching cannot be successful. If the coach has a negative view of the family, even using a child-focused treatment model will not be effective because practitioners cannot provide enough therapy to make a difference; they will create dependence; and when practitioners are not present, the situation will most likely return to the way it was before they were involved. Family activity settings are as unique and different as families are. Of course, coaches in early childhood intervention must be able to recognize and evaluate extreme situations in which abuse or neglect may be a factor, as well as situations in which the coach's or a family member's personal safety are at risk. Embracing family differences as unique and different instead of right or wrong, however, is a positive way of maximizing learning opportunities for all involved.

> ## Reflect
>
> The next time you are out in the community (e.g., at a park, shopping), take note of different families. Think specifically about how the family members are both similar to and different from your family members and friends. Ask yourself the following questions:
>
> 1. How is that family similar to or different from mine?
>
> 2. How open am I to exploring my comfort level with these similarities and differences?
>
> 3. What have I learned about myself as I examine my comfort level with situations that differ from my own culture and life experience?

Coaching Families of Children with Severe Disabilities

Another belief among some early childhood practitioners is that coaching is limited to use with parents of children who have mild disabilities. Some practitioners believe that children with multiple or severe disabilities require more intensive and more specialized services than use of a coaching interaction style with parents and care providers might allow. Practitioners or service coordinators who hold this perception are operating in a deficits-based, service-based, professionally centered paradigm. They view their role as the intervener, focused on engaging the child in decontextualized, passive interventions that they believe the parents lack the time or ability to do. When focusing on child participation in meaningful activities as the outcome, however, parents are *very good* at knowing what their child likes, wants, and needs to do (Dunst et al., 2000). A coaching interaction style supports the parents in identifying what works, what might need to be done differently, and what level of support they need from the coach. Interventions are focused on parents' abilities to support the child's participation in real-life activities, not exercises or drilled practice of skills, or assumptions based on type of disability or degree of severity.

Consider the following example: Denise is a PT supporting a family in a large metropolitan area in the Northeast. Barbara, the mother, has recently moved to the area with her son James (age 9 years) and daughter Natalie (age 18 months). Natalie has infantile spinal muscular atrophy and is enrolled in the early intervention program. The family lives in a two-bedroom apartment downtown and uses the public transportation system to get around. Natalie is confined to the home due to her condition and is on a ventilator for breathing support. Barbara does not work outside the home. Natalie does have nursing supports provided in her home for 14 hours each day, 7 days a week. Barbara leaves the apartment during the day to take James to and from school and run errands to maintain the household. Because she is new to the area, she does not have any close friends, and the closest family member is a distant cousin who lives about 2 hours away. At the time of the IFSP meeting, Natalie was spending most of her time in her small bedroom in a rented hospital bed that the family had obtained through the in-home nursing supports. Natalie does have a wheelchair, but Barbara and the in-home nurses do not like to use it because they feel that Natalie is uncomfortable in the wheelchair. Throughout the assessment process, Denise and other early intervention team members identified Natalie's routines, everyday activities, and interests as well as identifying Barbara's priorities and any needs of the nurses working with Natalie. Although the process helped Barbara and the in-home nurses identify a few of Natalie's interests, Barbara commented on how little there was for Natalie to actually do during the day. The lead in-home nurse, Jennifer, explained that Natalie's day was quite busy with caregiving routines, medical procedures, and administration of Natalie's medications. Barbara felt very strongly that although the caregiving routines and medical issues were a big part of Natalie's day, she wanted Natalie to have more fun during the day and perhaps to go outside the apartment in her wheelchair. Barbara was clearly troubled by the passiveness of Natalie's day and commented several times on her new focus of helping Natalie to have fun. During the first home visit following the IFSP, Denise met with both Barbara and Jennifer.

Denise: Hello! It's good to see you both. Jennifer, thank you for agreeing to meet with us today.

Jennifer: You're welcome. I only have about 20 minutes until Lila [the other nurse caring for Natalie that day] has to leave. She's working with another client in this part of town and needs to leave for that shift.

Denise: Thank you Jennifer for letting me know about the time constraints. I'll be sure to finish our conversation by then.

Barbara: Couldn't we just move into Natalie's room when Lila needs to leave? It doesn't seem to me to be that big of a deal.

Jennifer: I need to be able to focus on Natalie's care and I'm afraid I'll be distracted with Denise here.

Denise: Oh . . . I'm glad you explained that, Jennifer. I appreciate your attentiveness to your duties with Natalie. I do hope that you'll feel comfortable spending more time with me with Natalie present because you spend so much time with her each day. Please let me know if you feel that I'm interfering with your ability to care for Natalie.

Jennifer: Thank you. I will. Let's go on into Natalie's room.

Barbara: Let's get started. I'm excited about figuring out how to get Natalie outside.

Jennifer: What??? No . . . no . . . no. Not on my watch. No way. I can't take responsibility for that.

Barbara: Jennifer . . . you're going to have to get over yourself. You do not make the rules. We've talked about this a million times. I don't want Natalie's entire life to be this room. If you can't be more flexible, I'll just have to hire someone who can be.

Jennifer: Well . . . maybe you should. I'm not going to compromise my professional opinion because you want to take the unnecessary risk of taking Natalie outside.

Denise: Excuse me, ladies. I don't mean to be rude, but I'd like to help out with this conversation. Jennifer, when we talked at the IFSP meeting, you agreed to the outcomes that we established and one of them clearly stated taking Natalie outside in her wheelchair. Is that your recollection of the meeting?

Jennifer: Yes . . . but I really didn't think you were serious. I mean, really. How in the world are we going to take Natalie outside?

Barbara: Jennifer! I'm so frustrated with you.

Denise: Please . . . let's stay calm. Barbara, may I try something?

Barbara: Yes . . . yes.

Denise: Jennifer, what would it take for you to be comfortable taking Natalie outside in her wheelchair?

Jennifer: Why do we even want to do this?

Barbara: Because . . . we talked about how much Natalie enjoys the sunshine and how she smiles when I talk about what is going on outside her window. You do it, too . . . sometimes. I've heard you telling her about the bus driving by or about a bird on her windowsill.

Denise: Yes. We were thinking about all of Natalie's interests. If we use Natalie's interests as a way to promote her participation then we know she will be more alert, pay attention longer, and be more motivated to engage and learn.

Barbara: I was shocked at how difficult it was for us to identify Natalie's interests. When I think of James at this age . . . well, I can easily tell you still to this day what he liked to do. I don't want to look back on this time for Natalie and only remember her medical care routines or how stressful giving her a sponge bath was. I want to remember things she liked to do and looked forward to doing.

Denise: Jennifer . . . how would you respond to Barbara's comments?

Jennifer: I understand the thinking behind it . . . I just don't know how we're going to safely do it.

Denise: What would it take for you to be comfortable with this, Jennifer?

Jennifer: Well, for starters . . . her wheelchair doesn't seem right. She seems unhappy and uncomfortable in it.

Barbara: I agree. I never have liked that wheelchair.

Jennifer: Also . . . we need a way to carry her oxygen tank on the wheelchair. We don't have a way to do that now.

Denise: OK. This is very helpful. I'm writing this down.

Jennifer: I don't want to do it by myself or have any of the nurses do this alone. It is too dangerous.

Denise: Barbara . . . what are your thoughts about that?

Barbara: I agree. I think it will take both of us to do this and maybe Denise, too. Maybe in the future, we can figure out how to do it safely with one person, but we're not ready for that now.

Denise: OK. I agree. It sounds like if we can figure out how to do this safely and make sure that Natalie is comfortable, then we're all in agreement about moving forward with taking Natalie outside in her wheelchair?

Barbara: Yes!

Jennifer: Yes . . . but I will tell you when I think I'm ready.

Denise: I can agree to that . . . Barbara, what about you?

Barbara: Yes . . . and thanks, Jennifer. I appreciate your willingness to talk about this.

Jennifer: I feel better.

Denise: Jennifer, I know you need to relieve Lila. Would it be OK for Barbara and me to join you in Natalie's room in a few minutes? We could get started looking at Natalie in her wheelchair.

Jennifer: Yes. Let me get settled with Lila and see how Natalie is doing.

Denise: Thanks, Jennifer. Barbara, let's talk a few minutes about Natalie's wheelchair. When we join Natalie and Jennifer, would you be willing to ask Natalie to show me how she sits in her wheelchair? As you know, we had planned on seeing her in her wheelchair before the IFSP, but when her gastrointestinal problems flared up, you thought it best to wait.

Barbara: Yes . . . I remember. Sure, I'm happy to ask her if she's OK with getting up in her chair.

Denise: How do you think she'll respond?

Barbara: She'll be OK. I'll make it fun . . . I'll explain that you really want to see her in the chair.

[After Lila leaves the apartment, Barbara and Denise join Jennifer in Natalie's room. Barbara and Denise greet Natalie and talk with her a bit about Lila's visit.]

Barbara: Hey Nat . . . would you be willing to show Denise how you sit in your wheelchair? She's never seen you up in the chair and she really wants to see you doing that.

[Natalie nods her head yes and grins.]

Denise: Wow! Thanks, Natalie . . . I'm so excited. OK. Barbara and Jennifer, how do you typically help Natalie get up into the chair?

Jennifer: It takes both of us. I lift Natalie and Barb manages the tubes and cords. The chair is heavy, so we get it in place first.

[Denise moves to the side and Barbara, Jennifer, and Natalie prepare to transfer Natalie to her wheelchair. After the transfer is complete and Natalie is safely settled the conversation resumes.]

Denise: How does that transfer compare to what you typically do?

Barbara: It's how we do it every time. What do you think?

Denise: It appeared to go pretty smoothly. Jennifer, your thoughts?

Jennifer: Well . . . it is how we do it. I think getting her in the chair is OK, but look at Natalie in her chair. She looks so uncomfortable. Natalie, where are you hurting?

[Natalie nods her head up and down to indicate yes and looks down at her hips.]

Barbara: Sometimes we put a pillow under her butt. It's OK for a while, but then she scoots a bit and she's uncomfortable again.

Denise: What do you think about her alignment?

Barbara: Her what?

Jennifer: How straight or crooked she is.

Barbara: Oh . . . she's always a bit crooked; if she's straight her head flops forward.

Denise: Would you mind showing me how you readjust her position?

Jennifer: Sure.

[Jennifer and Barbara move Natalie's shoulders and knees. She slides down in the chair a bit and her head flops back.]

Jennifer: Sorry, Nat. See, Denise . . . something isn't right.

Denise: What do you think is wrong?

Jennifer: It's like it doesn't fit her right. If she's straight in the chair, then her head flops forward or backward.

Denise: What ideas do you have about where the problem might be?

Barbara: The seat is too flat . . . I can move on my own and I don't like sitting in a flat seat with a flat back. Our bodies are curvy, not straight.

Jennifer: Yes . . . it's too flat and hard.

Denise: I was thinking the same thing. The seat and back surface are rather unforgiving. Barbara, when you ordered the wheelchair, what options for seating did you discuss?

Barbara: When we ordered the chair we were supposed to talk to someone about a seat cushion, but something happened with that. Jen, do you remember?

Jennifer: No. She already had her wheelchair when I started working with you guys.

Barbara: Hmmm. Maybe we missed something. I had totally forgotten about that. We hardly ever use it, so I guess it just slipped my mind. She needs a cushion, doesn't she?

Denise: I think you're right on target. A cushion would not only be more comfortable for Natalie, it would provide her with a more stable base for her hips. With a more stable base, I think we'll see some nice changes related to her head position. Natalie . . . how are you doing, sweetie?

[Natalie smiles meekly, but looks at her bed.]

Denise: Are you ready to move back to your bed?

[Natalie nods her head yes and smiles.]

Denise: You both told me that the transfer out of bed was pretty typical. What would you think about involving Natalie more in the process?

Jennifer: What do you mean involving Natalie more? She can't move.

Denise: Yes, Jennifer, you're correct. What ideas do you have for giving Natalie a role in the process?

Barbara: Can you show us what you mean?

Denise: Sure. Jennifer, would you mind if I stepped in this time to help transfer her back to her bed?

Jennifer: OK with me.

Denise: I'll try a few things. Would you guys watch what I'm doing to involve Natalie more in the transfer and see what you think?

Barbara and Jennifer: Sure!

Denise: [squatting down to be eye-level with Natalie] Natalie. Are you ready to move back to bed?

[Natalie nods yes.]

Denise: What do I need to do first?

[Natalie looks at her tubes and cords.]

Denise: So . . . mom or I should get the tube and cords ready to move . . . is that right?

[Natalie smiles and nods yes.]

Denise: OK. What's next?

[Natalie looks at her bed.]

Denise: We're ready to move to your bed?

[Natalie smiles and nods yes.]

Denise: How about you close your eyes really tight when you're ready to be picked up? Does that sound good?

[Natalie smiles and then very deliberately closes her eyes tightly. Denise and Barbara transfer Natalie back to her bed and settle her tubes and cords so she is comfortable.]

Denise: So Natalie . . . how was that? Are you comfortable?

[Natalie smiles and nods her head vigorously.]

Barbara: Hey Nat . . . I like you being in charge! What do you think, Jennifer?

Jennifer: [smiling] I agree. That was great.

Denise: So . . . your comments let me know that you agree having Natalie more in charge of her body is a good idea.

Barbara: Yes! I love it. I think we can use that idea for a lot of things, don't you, Jennifer?

Jennifer: Yes . . . about medicine she takes, when she wants ice chips . . . oh my . . . we can do a lot more—No, wait . . . we can do a lot LESS and have Natalie do MORE!

Denise: What specifically did you notice about the transfer?

Barbara: Well, you put Natalie in charge of the process. Even though you knew what to do, you asked Nat about the steps in the process.

Jennifer: I liked the way you squatted down where she could look right at you when you asked her to give you a sign when she was ready to go. I would think that would be less scary for her.

[Natalie nods her head vigorously, smiling.]

Denise: So, how do you think you'll use the ideas during the day?

Barbara: Well, when we need to move her, we'll do the same things you did . . . squat down where she can see us, ask her about the process, and then let her show us when she is ready.

Jennifer: I'm serious . . . I'm going to ask her those same questions about some of her medical procedures . . . like cleaning her trach, and caring for her stoma. She knows the routines, so I'll just focus on involving her more.

Barbara: Oh, me too! When she's getting dressed, or we're brushing her teeth, or even getting her bath, I can do the same. Thanks, Denise . . . these are great ideas.

Denise: You're very welcome, but most of the ideas belong to the two of you! Again . . . Jennifer, thanks so much for being open to the ideas.

Jennifer: I want what is best for Natalie. I hope you know that, Barbara.

Barbara: Of course I do, Jennifer. I just feel out of control sometimes. I know I can get bossy.

Jennifer: I understand. We just need to be honest with each other.

Denise: OK guys. We need to get a plan regarding the wheelchair cushion.

Barbara: Right. Hmmm . . . I don't know. I really don't want to go back through the hospital. The therapist there helped order the wheelchair. It's just never really been right and I don't want to go that route.

Denise: Jennifer, what resources do you know about?

Jennifer: Well, there's this medical equipment guy we use at our agency . . . he's OK.

Denise: Would you recommend him for this situation?

Jennifer: Actually, no . . . I don't think so.

Denise: OK. I've got a few vendors that I've worked with in the past. One company in particular has several cushion options that I think we could obtain pretty quickly.

Barbara: That sounds good to me. Denise . . . I'd like to take your lead on this. What do you think, Jennifer?

Jennifer: Yes . . . I agree. The quicker the better, right Natalie?

[Natalie smiles happily and nods her head in agreement.]

Denise: All right then, I'll contact the company and ask for an appointment as soon as possible. Is it OK for me to call you after I talk with them?

Barbara: Sure thing.

Denise: I also wanted to talk with you about something else. Do you have time?

Barbara: OK, what is it?

Denise: It is about Natalie's options for communicating with other people.

Jennifer: Oh, here we go . . . a talking machine right?

Denise: Jennifer . . . tell me more about your feelings.

Jennifer: I worked with a lady a long time ago that had an electronic communication device. It was a pain in the backside. It was huge, heavy, and sounded like a robot. We all hated it.

Barbara: When Natalie was in the hospital after things got so bad, a speech therapist mentioned something to me about her being able to use some things to get our attention. I think we tried a few things, but they didn't work so well, and then Natalie left the hospital. So I've just never followed up on it.

Denise: I've got a team member that I would like you to talk to more about this. She's got a lot of ideas, and Jennifer, I promise, it won't be huge or heavy . . . Plus, I think lots of options exist these days that don't sound quite as robotic. What do you guys think about this?

Barbara: I'm game! Are you, Natalie?

[Natalie nods yes and smiles.]

Jennifer: OK, but I'll believe it when I see it, Denise . . . no offense.

Denise: None taken. I understand. OK, let's make our plan from our visit today.

Jennifer: I'm going to involve Natalie more in all of her care routines.

Barbara: Me, too. We'll also use those ideas when we need to move her . . . asking her what's next, and asking her to tell us when she's ready.

Denise: I will call the vendor regarding the cushion and talk with my team member about coming to see Natalie and talk with both of you. I will call you after I talk with both of them. When should we plan the next visit?

Barbara: Since Natalie has a visit with the respiratory specialist on Monday . . . how about we wait until you call back. I can give you a better idea then. Is that OK?

Denise: Definitely. I will call as soon as I have information. Thanks for all of your hard work today. Natalie, I will see you soon! Bye!

In this scenario, the coach found herself in a complex situation involving a parent and a home health care nurse who had differing priorities and interaction styles. Denise used honesty and objectivity to support open communication between the adults who were involved most closely in Natalie's care. The coach was able to navigate the situation using active listening techniques, reflective questioning, observation, and joint planning to actively involve the parent, nurse, and child in the discussion. During the conversation, Denise was careful to clarify the opinions of all involved, promote an environment in which all parties were comfortable sharing information, and facilitate active agreement on a plan of action.

Coaching Families Using an Interpreter

Practitioners who use coaching in circumstances in which an interpreter is required to communicate effectively with the family members often have questions about how to partner with the interpreter while simultaneously developing their own relationship with the family. Prior to working with an interpreter in a coaching conversation, the coach must take time to explain the process of coaching to the interpreter. The coach must ensure that the interpreter understands that everything said by the coach to the parent and everything the parent says back to the coach must be interpreted. Because of the challenges related to communication, coaches in these situations often ask more yes/no closed-ended questions. Even though it is tempting to do this, coaches should strive to use a variety of open-ended questions to promote parental reflection.

Consider a situation in which a family is interested in including their youngest child when they go swimming at the YMCA. The older children in the family take swimming lessons there and the entire family attends free swim every Friday night. The youngest child, Sun, is enrolled in early intervention due to language delays. Her mom, Mi-sook, has been working with Martie, a SLP, for several months. Jin is the interpreter who is assigned to support Martie and Mi-sook.

Before they began home visits, Martie and Jin conversed several times about their roles. Martie explained the coaching process to Jin so that he would understand the nature and actual phrasing of the questions he would most likely be asking Mi-sook. Jin was very excited about the opportunity to learn more about coaching, but he expressed some concern that some of the specifics might be lost in translation. Jin wanted to make sure that it would be all right to clarify questions during their home visits to make sure he was communicating effectively. Martie assured him that having an open dialogue would be preferable. Over the course of their time working together, Jin, Martie, and Mi-sook have developed a conversational style that works well for all involved. Martie makes sure to speak directly to Mi-sook, not to Jin, when she wants to address her.

Martie: Hello, Mi-sook. It's good to see you. What were you able to find out at the YMCA about their policy allowing young children who wear diapers into the pool?

[Jin interprets question for Mi-sook, and continues to interpret each statement by Martie or Mi-sook.]

Mi-sook: It is OK for Sun to swim with us. She must wear special swim diapers. We bought some at the store.

Martie: Great! Since that is cleared up, what questions do you have about involving Sun in your visits to the pool?

Mi-sook: I want to know how to help her talk more while we swim.

Martie: OK. How will supporting Sun at Family Swim Night be different from how you support her during bath time?

Mi-sook: Oh . . . OK. We just blow bubbles, say her sounds and words back to her? Just like bath time?

Martie: Yes. What do you think about that?

Mi-sook: I thought I might need to be different or try new things. OK. I can do that.

Jin: [to Martie] I think she is worried about something. I'd like to ask her.

Martie: [to Jin] Sure. I feel the same way. Please ask her.

[Jin then holds a short conversation with Mi-sook while Martie waits for Jin to explain what is being shared.]

Jin: [to Martie] Martie, I asked Mi-sook if she was worried or nervous about something . . . She shared that she was worried about Sun going underwater and getting an ear infection. She remembers your discussion about Sun's ear infections and how it might have contributed to her language delays. She actually wants to know if she should let Sun swim in the pool.

Martie: Mi-sook . . . I'm glad you shared your concern. I hope you will always feel free to ask about anything that is on your mind. It will be great for Sun to join your family in such a fun time that you all enjoy and do together. Remember how we talked about how to keep water out of her ears during bath time?

Mi-sook: Yes . . . all right. I do not let her go under in the bathtub, but I am not sure I can keep it from happening at the pool.

Martie: What ideas do you have about keeping water out of her ears in case she goes under?

Mi-sook: My mother used to make us wear swim caps. Will that help?

Martie: That certainly would help protect her ears. I've also seen some parents use ear plugs. They now have moldable swim ear plugs that you can buy off the shelf. What do you think about using ear plugs?

Mi-sook: Will she be able to hear me?

Martie: Her hearing will be muffled. What are some things you can do to make sure she can hear during the time in the pool?

The conversation continues reviewing the strategies that Mi-sook can use to help Sun during Family Swim Night. At the end of the home visit, Mi-sook and Martie have a joint plan for what will happen until the next visit and specifically how Mi-sook and her family will support Sun's participation during the swim time. Following the visit, Martie and Jin discuss the visit and debrief the conversation regarding clarity and support for one another. Martie expresses her thanks to Jin for following up with Mi-sook when she hesitated about including Sun in Family Swim Night. They close their conversation by planning the logistics of their next visit.

Coaching Foster Parents and Biological Parents

Sometimes coaches have additional questions when a child in a foster care placement is found to be eligible for a specific program. In conjunction with supporting the foster parents, practitioners sometimes

Practice

The next time you work with an interpreter, share information about the coaching interaction style and explain how you will be asking questions to build on what the parent already knows and is doing.

struggle with how to support and include the biological parent(s). We know from research that supporting the adults in the life of a child is critical to maximizing the effectiveness of the intervention (Mahoney, 2009; Peterson et al., 2007). Using practices that support the adults within the context of everyday activities and routines is also essential to our success. Although it is somewhat cumbersome, practitioners must plan for and take time to identify interests, activity settings, and priorities of both family units in order to plan a program that is individualized to all involved. If an amicable relationship exists between the foster and biological parents and the social service program or judicial system allows, it is ideal to include parents in joint sessions in order to promote consistency for the child and success for the parents. These visits, however, must happen in a setting that is natural for the child and as comfortable as possible for both sets of parents. If the relationship between the foster parents is strained, separate visits with the biological parents and foster parents are necessary. The same person should coach both the biological parents and the foster parents. The coach should discuss interests, activity settings, and priorities with each set of parents and use coaching strategies to support both families in achieving their desired outcomes. If the biological parent is working on family reunification, the coach should use resource-based practice strategies to help the parent identify additional supports that he or she needs to access the needed and desired resources.

Coaching Parents Who Frequently Change the Topic

With any family, situations may occur that make a coach feel uncomfortable or confused about what to do. Coaching is a relationship-based practice that requires open and honest communication. Personality and interaction style come into play when a practitioner uses coaching strategies. A coach will be better able to handle uncomfortable situations if that coach knows his or her own strengths, tendencies, and vulnerabilities. For example, if the person being coached has a tendency to jump from topic to topic, the coach should feel comfortable asking the coachee whether 1) it is all right to develop a plan around one topic before moving to the next, 2) the coachee is ready to change topics or needs to finish the previous topic before moving on, 3) the coach should write the new topic down and then promise to come back to it after they have completed the current topic, or 4) the coachee prefers to reach a resolution and develop a plan for all topics at the conclusion of the conversation. Providing the coachee with options about how to focus on joint planning also helps the coach ensure that a plan is developed around the topics which are important to the coachee.

In other situations, the coachee may tend to drift off the topic of the coaching conversation. When this occurs, the coach may feel uncomfortable or even rude if he or she does not address the variety of topics or discussions that arise. Coaches should feel comfortable gently letting a topic drop or repeatedly guiding the coachee back to the topic of the conversation that necessitated the coaching visit.

In the following scenario, Christina, an occupational therapist working in an early intervention program, supports Pam, a young mother, to make grocery store trips go more smoothly. They meet at the grocery store parking lot. Christina sees Pam driving into the parking lot with Charlotte (age 2 years) climbing around in the backseat of the car. Christina hurries to greet the young family as they choose a parking spot close to the front door.

Christina: Hi, Pam! Hi, Charlotte! I'm glad we could make it work to meet at the grocery store today. I noticed our plan to have Charlotte ride in her car seat during car rides didn't seem to work out. I saw her climbing around in the car when you drove in.

Pam: Yes! She's driving me crazy. I tried what we talked about last Friday and gave her choices about what toys and what snack she wanted if she buckled into her car seat. It worked great until we were driving down the road and she unbuckled and started crawling around. I was almost here, so I didn't pull over.

Christina: OK. I'm glad that getting her into her car seat went more smoothly.

Pam: Yes . . . but she's demonic. She's hell bent on getting me arrested. Did I tell you that my little brother might get out of detox sooner than we thought? He's been following the rules and apparently they've run out of beds.

Christina: I'm glad to hear your brother has made progress. Let's talk about Charlotte climbing out of her car seat.

Pam: She hates her car seat. I'm just sick and tired of trying to make her ride in it. She pitches a fit every single time.

Christina: Yes. We've talked about this. Tell me again . . . why do you think this keeps happening?

Pam: I'm dying in this heat. Can we go ahead and go into the store? Come on, Charlotte. Let's go get a buggy.

[Charlotte giggles and climbs toward her mom to be carried into the grocery store.]

Christina: Sure. We can move inside, Pam, but let's get a plan for Charlotte and her car seat.

Pam: OK., but I've got to buy us a Mountain Dew on my way in. I'm thirsty and I know Charlotte is too!

[They head toward the door and make a stop at the soda machine.]

Christina: Pam, what are you planning on buying for Charlotte to drink?

Pam: A Mountain Dew. We'll share one.

Christina: What does Charlotte usually drink during the day?

Pam: Whatever I'm drinking. Our favorites are Sun Drop and Mountain Dew.

Christina: What has Charlotte's pediatrician told you about her drinking soda?

Pam: She told me it is bad for her . . . especially for her teeth. I also know it has a lot of caffeine . . . that's why I like it.

Christina: What do you think about the information that Dr. Perez shared with you?

Pam: I'm sure it probably is bad for her and me, too. I just hate having to worry about everything. Life used to be so easy.

Christina: What do you want to do about Charlotte drinking soda?

Pam: I shouldn't give her soda. I'll buy her something else. What should I get her?

Christina: How could we involve Charlotte in this decision?

Pam: Oh, yeah. I could ask her what she wants.

Christina: If you do that, what do you think she'll choose?

Pam: Mountain Dew or Sun Drop.

Christina: Remember . . . what did we do for snack time at home?

Pam: I just gave her a choice of milk or juice. . . . she always chooses juice.

Christina: How could you take what you learned about using choice-making at snack time and use it here at the soda machine?

Pam: I'll ask her if she wants juice or water. I think it's really dumb to pay for water, just so you know. I can also hold her up and let her push the button. I think she'll like that.

Christina: That's a nice way to include her in this activity. What do you think she'll do when she sees you've got a Mountain Dew?

Pam: She'll be mad. I'll have to give her some.

Christina: What are your options here?

Pam: Well. . . . I want a Mountain Dew. I'm not going to stop drinking it because of Charlotte.

Christina: What are your options?

Pam: I can just listen to her pitch a fit. I could not buy one, but then I'll be mad. Hey . . . I could get a Koozie for us both here at the store and maybe she won't know what I'm drinking. I'll do that.

Christina: That sounds like a way to give Charlotte healthy choices and still choose the beverage you want to drink. Let's give it a try.

[Pam purchases the drinks and Charlotte chooses water to drink.]

Christina: How do you think that went, Pam?

Pam: Fine. Fine. I want to get those drink holders, I'm really thirsty.

Christina: What did you notice regarding how Charlotte responded to you when she got to push the buttons?

Pam: She liked pushing the buttons. I let her do that sometimes on my cell phone. I forgot how much she likes that.

Christina: Remember how we've discussed that using what she likes and is interested in really helps her be involved in what you're doing in a positive way.

Pam: Charlotte's going to flip out if I don't give her a drink. Let's go get the Koozies.

[Pam places Charlotte in the shopping cart and heads off to find the Koozies. She places the purchased drinks in the Koozies and hands Charlotte her water.]

Christina: Pam, how can you prepare Charlotte for her drink?

Pam: What?

Christina: How can you help her be happy with her drink?

Pam: I don't know . . . I was just going to hand it to her and get on with shopping. This is taking forever.

Christina: How about I try something and you watch what I'm saying and how Charlotte responds? Is that OK?

Pam: OK by me.

Christina: Charlotte, look what mama got you . . . a big girl drink.

Charlotte: [with a big smile] Dink!

Christina: Yes! Charlotte's drink.

[Charlotte tries to open the bottle, but can't. Charlotte thrusts the bottle back at Christina.]

Christina: Charlotte, what do you need?

Charlotte: Open!

Christina: Open the drink?

[Charlotte nods her head yes. Christina waits expectantly.]

Pam: She wants you to open the bottle. Geez!

[Christina nods knowingly at Pam and continues to wait.]

Charlotte: Yes. Open dink!

[Christina loosens the bottle cap and hands the bottle back to Christina.]

Christina: Open the bottle. Charlotte wants a drink!

[Charlotte takes the drink and sips from the bottle and smiles.]

Charlotte: Char dink . . . mmmm!

Christina: Yes! Charlotte's drink is good.

[Charlotte appears to be quite happy having her own drink and does not appear interested in Pam's drink.]

Pam: Hmmm. . . . that went really well.

Christina: Why do you think it went so well?

Pam: Well, the koozie works! She can't see that I have a [whispers] Mountain Dew.

Christina: What else?

Pam: She likes having her own bottle . . . even if it's only water.

Christina: What did you notice about how I gave her the water bottle? What was different than what you would have done?

Pam: You made a big deal of it . . . like she's all fancy because she gets her own water. She really liked that.

Christina: What else?

Pam: I thought you didn't know what she wanted when she gave the water bottle back to you, but after you looked at me, I remembered what you were doing. You were trying to get her to talk. I get rushed and forget about that. It's really hard to remember to do that when I know what she wants.

Christina: Pam, you've made some really good observations. Yes. I was trying to help her feel special about having her own bottle. I used some of the strategies we've talked about in the past to encourage her to use words to get her needs met and let us know what she wants, like waiting for her to respond, using shorter sentences and phrases, repeating what she says so she can hear it said correctly, and using lots of expression with my face and my voice.

Pam: I can do those things. I really like how she's acting. She's not grabbed at my drink or even fussed about anything on the aisles. Hey . . . do you like this color of fingernail polish?

Christina: Yes, I do. So what's making the difference with Charlotte?

Pam: She's happy. She's usually fussy. It's like she thinks she's all big because of her own drink. I'm going to do this every time . . . and I'm only going to give her water or juice . . . at McDonald's I can even get her milk. Have you tried those new iced lattes at McDonald's? They're good.

Christina: I'm glad you're seeing some success with our ideas. What else do you need to purchase before you leave?

[Pam grabs a few more items. Meanwhile Charlotte is happy with her water bottle and staying in the cart. They move toward the checkout line.]

Christina: Pam, before we get in the checkout line, what should you be prepared for with Charlotte?

Pam: Well, she's going to want candy, but I'm going to say no. She'll get mad, but we're almost done so I don't really care.

Christina: How might her getting upset affect your car ride home?

Pam: Oh, #%$&! She won't even get in her car seat if she's mad.

Christina: OK. Good thinking. What are your options?

Pam: I guess I could give her candy, but that's probably the same as Mountain Dew.

Christina: Candy is an option, but you're right about the sugar. What else could you do?

Pam: You could take her outside while I pay.

Christina: That might work right now, but I won't always be with you during your shopping trips.

Pam: I don't know. I do not know. [shakes her head]

Christina: I've got an idea. How could you use talking to her as a strategy to keep her happy?

Pam: Just talk to her. OK. I can just jabber it up. She does like that. I'll tell the cashier about how fancy Charlotte is with her big girl drink and all.

Christina: Let's try it!

Pam: Hey Charlotte. Show the nice lady your big girl drink.

Cashier: Oh my! You are a big girl. You've got your own drink. Is it good?

Charlotte: [nodding her head yes] Mmmmm.

Pam: It's yummy. Yes it is.

[Pam looks to Christina for encouragement and rolls her eyes.]

Christina: [in a low voice] You're doing great Pam. Charlotte is VERY engaged.

Pam: [smiling] Charlotte, here. Help mama with this. Hold this box until the nice lady needs it.

[Charlotte accepts the box and waits.]

Pam: OK. Charlotte. Hand the lady the box.

[Charlotte hands the box to the cashier. The checkout continues without incident. As Pam, Charlotte, and Christina exit the store to the parking lot, Pam turns and gives Christina a high five.]

Pam: That was awesome! It was even kinda fun. I think the cashier lady thought Charlotte was cute.

Christina: I agree! It was fun watching YOU have fun with Charlotte.

Pam: Yeah . . . we don't really have that much fun. She's always acting out.

Christina: What made this different? Better?

Pam: She likes getting attention. I need to give her more. It was easier to be nice to her when she was acting better.

Christina: What do you think helped her to act better?

Pam: Well, the water bottle.

Christina: In addition to the water bottle, what did you do that made the difference?

Pam: I gave her more attention. Just talking to her about silly things seemed to really help.

Christina: You did a very good job. How did you come up with the idea to have her help with the checkout?

Pam: I don't know. It just popped into my head. I guess I was thinking about her being a big girl and helping is a big girl thing.

Christina: OK. So you thought about other ways you could support her good feelings about being a big girl. What a nice idea. Speaking of being a big girl . . . it's time for the car seat and ride home. What ideas do you have?

Pam: I'm gonna try something big girl again. OK?

Christina: OK by me!

Pam: Charlotte. It's time for us to go home. You've been such a big girl at the grocery store. You got your own drink.

Charlotte: Yes. Dink.

Pam: [smiling] Yes, your drink. You helped mama at the store. You're such a big girl. Can you be a big girl and climb up into your car seat and buckle up? I'll hand you your water after you're in your seat.

[Charlotte climbs into the car, but doesn't get into the car seat and reaches for her bottle of water.]

Pam: Charlotte. I'll give you your water when you get in your car seat.

[Charlotte protests and starts to fuss.]

Pam: Charlotte. If you want your own bottle of water, you have to ride in your car seat.

[Pam waits expectantly, humming, looking up at an airplane, and smiling at Charlotte. Charlotte reluctantly climbs into her car seat.]

Pam: Hey big girl! You got in your car seat! Can you buckle up like a big girl?

[Charlotte snaps the buckle into place. Pam checks on the latch and then hands Charlotte the bottle of water.]

Pam: Thank you, Charlotte. What a big girl!

Charlotte: Tank you, mama!

Pam: You're welcome.

Pam: [turns to Christina] What do you think of that?

Christina: More importantly . . . what do YOU think of that?

Pam: I think THAT was fantastic.

Christina: Me, too.

Pam: I'm going to keep up with this big-girl gig. It works.

Christina: Before we move on to our planning, I really need to ask you something. What are you going to do on the way home if Charlotte gets out of her car seat?

Pam: I'm going to pull over. She's too big to be acting out that way and I know I could get into trouble for it. I'll pull over and wait until she gets in her seat.

Christina: How long are you willing to wait for her to get back into her seat?

Pam: Hmmm . . . the way I feel right now, I could wait awhile [smiling]. I just bought that new Daughtry CD; I'll just listen to that.

Christina: OK. Now our plan . . . you had a lot of success today. What are you going to focus on between now and our next visit?

Pam: Like I said . . . this big girl thing really seems to work and it's fun for us. I'm going to try this during the day, getting her to sit at the table when we eat might be a good time. She also likes to get the mail. I'm going to let her do more of it on her own. I also think she can just do more stuff with a little help from me.

Christina: Like what?

Pam: Loading and unloading the dishwasher. I'm usually shooing her away when I do that. She can also help me feed the cat. She'll like that, too.

Christina: You've thought of a lot of great ways supporting Charlotte's independence while thinking about things she likes. It's really neat how you're thinking about her interests. When would you like me to come back for our next visit?

Pam: Hey, if the car seat is still a problem and my ideas don't work can I call you?

Christina: Yes. You've got my number.

Pam: Otherwise, I think next week would be good. Hopefully, I can show you some stuff that's working with Charlotte. I probably won't go back to the store before then so we can focus on how she's a big girl at home.

Christina: Sounds good. How about next Tuesday at this same time?

Pam: OK by me.

The scenario with Pam, Christina, and Charlotte provides insight into how a coach can support a young mother who has a tendency to jump topics and drift away from topics related to program support. In this scenario, Christina demonstrates a friendly, responsive approach, but she repeatedly guides the young parent back on topic. Christina sometimes ignores the comment, answers the parent's questions, or facilitates on-topic conversation with a reflective question. To prevent gaps in the planning process, Christina encouraged Pam to plan at the end of their conversation to wrap up the conversation with specific actions that Pam would take between coaching conversations. Figure 7.2 depicts the specificity and detail of Pam and Christina's joint planning process.

Coaching When a Parent Wants to Be Told What To Do

Some parents may have been conditioned to be told what to do, a response that is sometimes associated with their culture and/or is a reaction to previous experiences with formal resources and supports. Sometimes a parent states directly, "Just tell me what to do and I will do it." People are more likely to act on information, however, if they have a part in developing it and it is tailored to their specific situations. When a coachee asks to be told what to do, the coach should respond by letting him or her know that in order to be most helpful, the coach must know what the coachee already knows or is doing so that the information the coach shares can be matched to the coachee's interests, needs, and lifestyle. The coach also should give the coachee time to think and respond to the question being asked. Coaches should ask open-ended rather than yes/no questions and feel comfortable asking the coachee to provide specific examples or elaborate on his or her responses.

The coach must learn to be comfortable with silence. When the coachee is silent, the coach should not feel compelled to repeat the question, clarify it, fill the quiet with talking, or immediately jump to making suggestions or sharing ideas. Similarly, when coaching someone who is really quiet or shy, the coach should not be overly concerned about periods of silence. Individuals who are internal processors like to think about what they are going to say before responding. Coaches must learn to be quiet and allow silence so that the other person can get his or her thoughts together.

Consider the following scenario, in which Babe and her daughter Teeny (age 9 months) are enrolled in the local EHS program as well as the Part C Infant–Toddler Program. Babe is also supported by a case manager from the Department of Social Services. Babe is 17 years old and has an intellectual disability. Teeny qualifies for Part C services because she has global delays across all developmental domains. Babe enrolled in the EHS program during her pregnancy. The current visit is based on a joint plan that was developed at a previous visit between the practitioner, Frances, and Babe, in which they had introduced feeding Teeny pureed pears. When Frances arrives at the apartment, Babe yells from the sofa for Frances to come in. Frances observes that Babe is playing video games while Teeny is sitting on her lap.

Frances: Hi, Babe . . . it is good to see you. How is feeding Teeny pears working out?

Babe: What? Wait. I'm almost finished with this game. It's fun. My little brother told me I could play it.

Frances: It looks like you're having fun and Teeny seems to like the colors on the screen. You were going to feed Teeny pears this week. How is that going?

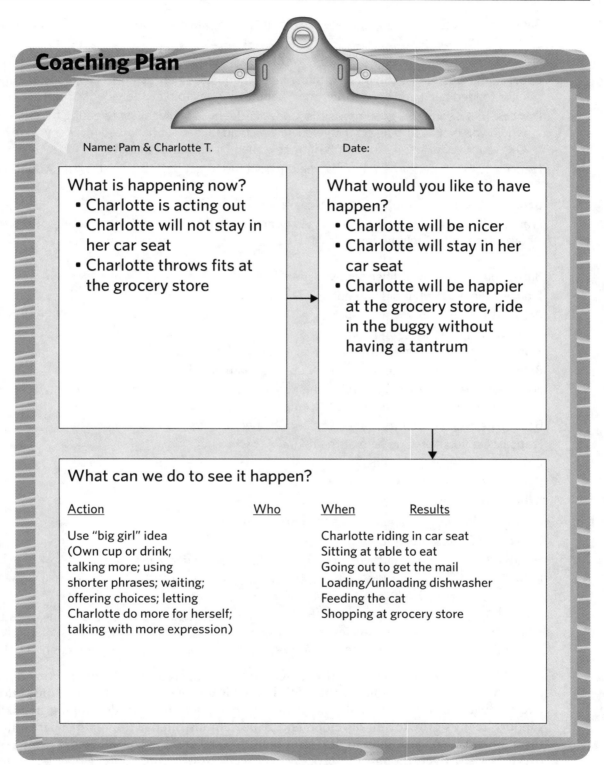

Coaching Plan

Name: Pam & Charlotte T.   Date:

What is happening now?
- Charlotte is acting out
- Charlotte will not stay in her car seat
- Charlotte throws fits at the grocery store

What would you like to have happen?
- Charlotte will be nicer
- Charlotte will stay in her car seat
- Charlotte will be happier at the grocery store, ride in the buggy without having a tantrum

What can we do to see it happen?

Action	Who	When	Results
Use "big girl" idea (Own cup or drink; talking more; using shorter phrases; waiting; offering choices; letting Charlotte do more for herself; talking with more expression)			Charlotte riding in car seat Sitting at table to eat Going out to get the mail Loading/unloading dishwasher Feeding the cat Shopping at grocery store

Figure 7.2.

Babe: Oh . . . yeah. It went good. She likes to eat pears. She likes apples, too. [Babe turns back to the video game.]

Frances: You tried apples, too! Great! How did Teeny respond?

Babe: Teeny was funny. She made a funny face when I gave her the apples. A funny, happy face. I like to feed her. I am a good momma. [Babe continues to play the video game.]

Frances: Babe, you are a good mom. It sounds like Teeny is really taking to eating the fruits. Babe, would you be OK turning off the video so we could talk about how feeding Teeny went? Babe: OK, yeah . . . it's just if I turn it off right now then I'll lose everything.

Frances: It's your decision. We did agree on this time to get back together. What would you like to do?

Babe: It's OK. I'll turn it off . . . We did make a plan.

Frances: Thanks, Babe. I'm glad our visits are important to you. Last time we met, we also talked about watching for signs for how Teeny was doing eating fruits. What did you notice?

Babe: You mean how did her poopy diapers look?

Frances: Right . . . what did you notice?

Babe: At first, her poop wasn't the same . . . just like you said it might be. It didn't get too runny, though. She did real good.

Frances: Besides her poop, what other signs did we talk about?

Babe: Throwing up . . . she didn't throw up or scream and fuss or anything.

Frances: Babe . . . nice job on trying the pears AND apples. Since it's lunch time, would you be interested in showing me how she's eating the fruits?

Babe: Sure. When can I try some veggies? She needs to try veggies. I know that.

Frances: Do you have any here at the house?

Babe: I have carrots and peas.

Frances: What would you like to try?

Babe: Carrots. I don't like peas.

[Frances observes as Babe feeds Teeny pureed carrots.]

Babe: See? She's good at it.

Frances: Babe . . . what have you done to help Teeny be so good at eating?

Babe: I feed her nice and slow. I watch to see when she wants a bite. If she spits it out, I know she's full. If she's full, I stop. I'm a good mom.

Frances: I agree. It's great to hear all the things you know about how to feed Teeny. Let's take a look at what you'll do this week feeding Teeny new fruits and veggies. We should talk a bit about how many new foods to try this week. [The joint planning discussion continues.]

This scenario demonstrates that coaching a young parent with an intellectual disability can be very successful. Frances, the EHS home visitor, used reflective questions, informative feedback, observation, and joint planning to support Babe in developing her skills to support Teeny's growth and development. Babe demonstrated action on her part following through and even expanding on the joint plan that she and the coach had developed on the previous visit. Even though the process may seem slow or the content may be somewhat limited in complexity, the coach in this scenario demonstrated how to join the parent around parent-identified priorities at a rate and depth that made sense for the parent and supported the child.

Coaching Parents When the Previous Plan Is Not Completed

When a coachee fails to complete the joint plan from the previous session between visits, the coach should first ask himself or herself whether the plan was truly a joint plan or if it was the coach's suggestion or recommendation. If the former is true, then at some point during the conversation the coach should ask the coachee whether the previous plan is still a priority and if it is, when and how the coachee will implement it. Coaches often have difficulty initiating conversations that bring up uncomfortable subjects. If the issues are left unresolved, however, they can develop into problems that most likely could have been avoided by using open and honest communication as early as possible in the coaching relationship.

One strategy that is effective in tackling tough issues is "upfronting." Upfronting is not confrontational; it is a technique used by the coach to bring up unresolved issues or topics that have been left unaddressed. Upfronting is nonjudgmental and is used without emotion. The coach should use "I" statements whenever possible during upfronting and should make it clear that he or she is seeking understanding and clarification of a specific issue. If, for example, the joint plan never seems to be a priority for the coachee, the coach may need to have an upfronting conversation by saying something like, "I've noticed that we have developed a joint plan every week for the past 3 weeks, but so far you haven't been able to implement the plan. Is this still a priority for you?" If the coachee responds that it is, the coach might say, "How can we modify the plan so that it will be useful for you?"

Similarly, if a pattern emerges that, for example, a family is seldom home when the coach arrives for scheduled visits or frequently cancels visits, the coach should self-reflect on the possible reasons for the no-show situation. Questions such as, "Have I been honoring the priorities of the family?" "How do I know my supports are helpful?" and "Have I been listening to the family?" may reveal information that is helpful to the coach. After the coach has considered possible reasons for his or her role in the no-show or cancellation situation, he or she should bring up the topic with the family as soon as possible. Exploring the family's interest in the supports and services sooner rather than later will prove to be most effective. The coach can say something like, "I've noticed that you haven't been home for the last few visits we scheduled. Could we talk about how you're feeling about the time we spend together?" or, "I noticed that you cancelled three out of our last five visits. I'd like to take a moment and talk together about how you see our visits helping you achieve your priorities. Is that OK with you?" Facilitating an open dialogue about priorities is essential for a positive and productive coaching relationship.

CONCLUSION

Using coaching as a strategy for adult interaction with families in natural learning environments offers unique benefits and challenges to early childhood intervention practitioners. As practitioners become familiar with parent priorities and child interests, the focus of the supports and content for the coaching conversations is targeted to enhance the abilities of the parent to support child participation in a variety of real-life contexts or to assist the parent in identifying and accessing resources. This chapter has illustrated through many scenarios that coaching is possible with *all* families, in *all* settings, and for *all* children regardless of the challenges that coaches and families face. A coach must always presume competence of the coachee and reflect on specific strategies or coaching skills that will ensure support for the coachee.

RESOURCES

McWilliam, R.A. (Ed.). (2010). *Working with families of young children with special needs* (pp. 127–146). New York: Guilford Press.

This edited text provides methods and tools for working with families of infants and toddlers with disabilities.

Roggman, L.A., Boyce, L.K., & Innocenti, M.S. (2008). *Developmental parenting: A guide for early childhood practitioners.* Baltimore: Paul H. Brookes Publishing Co.

This guide provides practical information for home visitors for working with parents and other care providers to improve children's learning and development.

Workgroup on Principles and Practices in Natural Environments. (2008). *Agreed upon mission and key principles for providing early intervention services in natural environments.* OSEP TA Community of Practice-Part C Settings Services in Natural Environments Documents. Retrieved from http://www.nectac.org/~pdfs/topics/families/Finalmissionandprinciples3_11_08.pdf

Workgroup on Principles and Practices in Natural Environments. (2008). *Seven key principles: Looks like/doesn't look like.* OSEP TA Community of Practice-Part C Settings. Retrieved from http://www.nectac.org/~pdfs/topics/families/Principles_LooksLike_DoesntLookLike3_11_08.pdf

Workgroup on Principles and Practices in Natural Environments. (2008). *Agreed upon practices for providing early intervention services in natural environments.* OSEP TA Community of Practice-Part C Settings. Retrieved from http://www.nectac.org/~pdfs/topics/families/AgreedUponPractices_FinalDraft2_01_08.pdf

This series of documents produced by the National Early Childhood Technical Assistance Center lists the evidence-based principles and practices for how to provide supports in natural learning environments in accordance with Part C of the Individuals with Disabilities Education Act. In addition to laying out the mission and key principles, the documents describe what the practices look like and do not look like and elaborate on the steps in the early intervention process from initial contact through transition.

Chapter 8

Coaching Teachers

As Chapter 7 emphasized, working with the adults who are involved in the lives of young children is a required skill set for an early childhood practitioner. Whereas the previous chapter focused on how to support parents and other adult family members, this chapter will focus on how to support teachers in center-based settings (e.g., EHS, Head Start, Even Start, preschools, child care centers, family child care homes). The chapter also includes specific scenarios involving young children with or at risk for developmental delays or disabilities and shows how they can be included in center-based settings and can participate successfully alongside their typically developing peers.

EARLY CHILDHOOD SETTINGS: OPERATIONALIZING NATURAL LEARNING OPPORTUNITIES

Chapter 7 noted that Part C of the Individuals with Disabilities Education Act (IDEA) of 2004 (PL 108-446) requires that early intervention services be provided in natural environments. Center-based opportunities can be natural environments for young children if these settings are inclusive of children who are typically developing rather than being created for the primary purpose of caring for, educating, or treating children with disabilities. More specifically, IDEA states that natural environments are "settings that are natural or normal for the child's same age peers without disabilities." Classrooms that are segregated, therefore, are not considered natural environments. Odom (2000) defined an inclusive setting as having two key features: critical mass and physical membership. The critical mass indicator is met when, minimally, the number of children with disabilities in the setting is less than or equal to the number of children without disabilities. Physical membership means that the children with disabilities have true group membership. In other words, the children with disabilities in the classroom spend the same amount of time in the same location and participate in the same activities as the children without disabilities (Brown, Odom, Li, & Zercher, 1999; Odom, 2000).

These features of an inclusive setting have further meaning for early childhood practitioners who are responsible for supporting a child with a disability in a classroom setting. Routinely pulling a child out of a classroom environment to provide specialized therapy or instruction violates the basic tenets of inclusive practices and does not meet the federal regulatory guide-lines for serving young children in natural environments. Many early childhood practitioners have been accustomed to supporting children in segregated settings or providing them with pull-out therapy or specialized instruction. In the past, therapists have removed children from classroom activities for decontextualized practice of delayed skills (e.g., the physical therapist [PT] takes the child out of center time classroom activities to a separate room to work on sitting balance while reaching for toys). Other specialists may not remove the child from the classroom but may take the child to a more isolated area in the classroom to set up blocked instruction or therapy sessions to work on specific skill expression (e.g., the occupational thera-pist [OT] pulls the child out of morning circle time to go to the sand table at the other end of the classroom to work on finding and retrieving small objects buried in the sand). Other prac-titioners have attempted to integrate themselves into the classroom setting and have actually taken over teaching a particular activity or component of the classroom routine (e.g., the speech-language pathologist [SLP] takes over shared reading activities in order to challenge a specific child to make certain sounds or produce specific words during the reading time). These types of traditional interventions are no longer considered best practices, and in fact, they are disruptive to early childhood classrooms and generally not conducive to child learning. This is not to say that a therapist, special education teacher, or other specialist should never interact directly with the children. The primary role, however, of the practitioner coming into a teacher's class-room or program is to build the capacity of the other teachers or caregivers in the chil-dren's lives to ensure that child learning and development is occurring on a regular basis, not just when the early childhood practi-tioner is present. The early childhood practi-tioners, therefore, may need to develop new skills in order to be helpful and be welcomed by the teachers in inclusive settings.

> **Remember**
>
> The two critical features of inclusive settings are
>
> 1. Critical mass
> 2. Physical membership
>   (Odom, 2002)

High-quality, inclusive classroom settings are chock-full of development-enhancing learn-ing opportunities that occur as part of the everyday routines and activity settings. Competent early childhood teachers work creatively and diligently to facilitate learning opportunities throughout the day that are based on the interests of the children who are enrolled in the pro-gram. In addition, early childhood teachers provide new and challenging opportunities for the children in their classrooms in order to expose them to new ideas and information. These learn-ing opportunities cross all developmental domains and provide a plethora of valuable learning experiences for children with all types of abilities. Teachers have varying attitudes, levels of expe-rience, and expertise related to teaching and supporting young children with varying abilities. Using coaching as the interaction style to support teachers in inclusive settings to successfully promote the participation of all children in the classroom environment is an effective strategy for early childhood practitioners.

On occasion, an early childhood coach may be placed in a situation in which the class-room environment is less than optimal. In such a situation, learning opportunities exist, but the situation could be improved if the teacher received coaching support. Ellen is an OT working for a local early intervention program. She has been working with Angie (age 4 months) and her mother Scotty for a few months. Scotty recently found a job and placed Angie in a family child care home in her community. Angie's child care provider, Lisa, cares for three other children who are under the age of 2 years. Scotty was nervous about leaving her baby, but she felt that she had no option. Ellen agreed to contact Lisa to see if she was interested in coaching supports. Ellen discovered that Lisa was interested in talking with her about Angie and her needs. As she entered the house for her first visit, Ellen made two observations that concerned her. First, she noticed a strong smell of cigarette smoke in the environment, and second, she saw that each of the infants was placed in an infant swing. Lisa was watching television when Ellen arrived.

Ellen: Hi, Lisa. It is nice to meet you. Thank you for inviting me to visit today.

Lisa: Hey! I'm new to all of this and I want to do right by these babies. My mom always kept kids so I've been around little kids all my life.

Ellen: Wow . . . you must really enjoy young children.

Lisa: I love babies . . . now when they get older, not so much, but I do love babies.

Ellen: Tell me more about your interest in caring for babies.

Lisa: Well . . . they're easy for one thing . . . feed 'em, change 'em, and get 'em to sleep. That's really all they need.

Ellen: Hmmm . . . it looks like they're all sleeping now. How did you manage that?

Lisa: Well, sometimes I have to let one fuss while I take care of the others, but usually if I turn on the swings they settle down. They like the swings. I like 'em, too. I've got real nice ones . . . they're all new.

Ellen: They are nice swings. Well, as you know, I'm here to talk to you specifically about Angie. She's enrolled in the early intervention program because she was born really early and had somewhat of a rough start.

Lisa: Oh, I know . . . Scotty told me about all that . . . such a shame.

[Ellen proceeds to share information about Part C services and asks Lisa what questions she has about Angie. From their discussion, Ellen learns that Angie sleeps most of the day and does not take as much formula as when she was at home with her mother all day. Lisa is concerned about this and is open to Ellen visiting on a regular basis. Ellen indicates that she will contact Angie's service coordinator so they could add information to her individualized family service plan (IFSP).]

Ellen: Lisa, tell me what you know about some of the risks that are associated with being born prematurely.

Lisa: Well, now that we've talked about her eating and gaining weight, I know that. Not sure what else.

Ellen: Sometimes the infants can have difficulty with their breathing . . . they can also be prone to getting sick easily, colds and such.

Lisa: She can be stuffy a lot. Especially when she eats . . . it's like she can't breathe and eat at the same time.

Ellen: I was wondering if it would be OK with you to bring up a sensitive subject.

Lisa: Sure . . . what you see is what you get with me.

Ellen: I like that. I'm a straight shooter, too. That works best for me. May I ask, do you smoke?

Lisa: Oh, no! I can't stand it. It's my husband. He smokes like a chimney. Does the house stink?

Ellen: To be honest, I did notice the smell of smoke when I came in.

Lisa: That is so gross. I get where I can't smell it. If he's home when the babies are here, I do not let him smoke in the house. He knows that is bad.

Ellen: That is really good. How much do you know about the effects of second-hand smoke?

Lisa: What is that?

[Ellen proceeds to share information about what the research says about smoking, second-hand smoke, and even third-hand smoke (residual smoke in furniture, rooms, and so forth). Lisa is horrified to learn this and makes it clear that her husband will no longer smoke in the home, even if the babies are not present. She also indicates an interest in learning how to rid her home of residual cigarette smoke. Due to the time and sensitive nature of their conversation, Ellen feels that it is best to close for the day. Although she was unable to address all of the issues she noted during her visit, she feels that she and Lisa are off to a good, solid start in their coaching relationship. They make a plan that Ellen will call her about the IFSP meeting and hope to get going with their visits the next week. Lisa asks Ellen to share resources with her about smoking so her husband can read the materials.]

On subsequent visits, Ellen was able to share information about infant development with Lisa. Lisa was amazed to learn about the importance of interaction and over time came to realize that putting the babies in the infant swings for short periods was OK, but that she had been relying on the swings too much. She also soaked up the information on adult–child interaction and became much more responsive and engaged with the children in her care. Ellen spent lots of time with Lisa identifying what the infants liked and how to provide them with more opportunities to enjoy their interests. Lisa took great pride in her new abilities and was filled with ideas that she wanted to share during each visit with Ellen.

The scenario with Ellen and Lisa demonstrates a situation that was not optimal initially, but in which the coach was able to build the capacity of the child care provider to consider new information, learn new skills, and implement positive changes in her child care environment. Ellen demonstrated the ability to meet Lisa at her current level of understanding and was open with her about even sensitive subjects. Over time, Lisa's confidence and competence were greatly enhanced as a result of Ellen's expertise, knowledge, and coaching skills.

TYPES OF COACHES IN GROUP SETTINGS

Because different communities have different amounts and types of formalized early childhood opportunities, early childhood practitioners must be aware of the resources that are available within a given community. Common formalized early childhood settings include but are not limited to EHS, Head Start, Even Start, private and public preschools, child care centers, family child care homes, and faith-based preschool settings. In addition, a number of communities have received Early Reading First grants or have prioritized funding in their school districts in order to infuse early literacy programs into public and private preschool settings. The early childhood coaches in a given community might include therapists and early childhood special education teachers from the Part C early intervention program, and they might work to support early childhood teachers and child care providers for children who are dually enrolled (e.g., a child with cerebral palsy enrolled in an EHS classroom). The coaches in another community might be educators from a local literacy initiative who are supporting the infusion of evidence-based early literacy practices into existing preschool programs. Coaches with special training to support programs in implementing practices that support the social–emotional growth and development of young children are increasingly common in community programs across the country (Fox, Dunlap, Hemmeter, Joseph, & Strain, 2003).

Consider Alba, a teacher in an EHS classroom in a rural community. Alba and her teaching partner Gina are both new to classroom teaching. Their classroom includes eight young children ranging in age from newborns to 3-year-olds. This year, one of the newly enrolled youngsters has severe behavioral challenges. Both Gina and Alba are very excited about having Kevin in their classroom, but they are anxious that they might not have all the skills they need to meet all of his needs. Laura, an early childhood special education teacher and coach from the local infant–toddler program, will be working with them to ensure that Kevin's EHS experience is highly successful. Laura has been trained to assist teachers in implementing positive behavior supports to ensure the successful participation of all children. Alba will be Kevin's lead teacher. To prepare for his participation in her classroom, she has asked his parents to fill out the Early Interest-Based Everyday Activity Checklists (Swanson, Raab, Roper, & Dunst, 2006) in order to identify interest-based child learning opportunities that occur as part of Kevin's everyday family and community life. After Kevin's parents return the checklist, Alba will discuss it with them to ensure that she understands the information they provide. Alba will then use the information to identify specific interest-based activities, toys, and opportunities that Kevin will need in order to enjoy his time and express his interests throughout his day at EHS. Kevin's parents indicate in the checklist that he loves playing with his toy dinosaurs. He likes to line them up, sort them by color and type, and take them in and out of the bag that he keeps with him at all times. Kevin also likes being outside, playing in water, and eating marshmallows. Kevin's parents also share that he does not like other people to touch his dinosaurs and hope that it won't be problematic to have the dinosaurs in the classroom. Alba quickly begins to think of ways to use Kevin's interests as she plans her classroom set-up and schedule.

Laura knows how important it is to understand how Alba approaches teaching in her classroom. She has observed in the classroom and understands that both Alba and Gina focus on promoting positive social interactions, use the children's interests to organize their classroom activities, and encourage parent involvement in all aspects of their program. Understanding these concepts is critical to Laura's ability to be an effective coach for Alba and Kevin. Laura also knows that although Kevin is 2 years old, he is not yet communicating clearly with others. Kevin prefers playing alone and can become physically aggressive if he is required to do something that he does not want to do. Kevin's parents are very interested in having him learn how to communicate better with others and especially to play with other children. Laura has received permission from Kevin's parents to share this information with Alba. Laura has also identified the need to revisit the IFSP to include Alba's priorities. After the IFSP planning process is complete, Laura will support Alba in feeling competent and confident in supporting Kevin's ability to participate in all aspects of the EHS classroom as well as scheduling visits at home with Kevin's parents to ensure continuity of support for his success across environments.

A few weeks later, assessments have been completed and the IFSP meeting has occurred. One of the outcomes on Kevin's IFSP is for him to be able to play on the playground safely with the other kids. Laura schedules her visits around convenient times for Alba and plans to stay for longer periods initially as Kevin is becoming accustomed to his new environment. In preparation for Kevin bringing his dinosaurs to school, Alba and Gina have pulled together all of the materials they have related to dinosaurs, including a special purchase of dinosaur toys that are very similar to Kevin's. Alba and Gina plan to leave these materials out where they are available for all of the children, in hopes of deterring any issues about Kevin's need to keep his dinosaurs organized and with him at all times. Using reflective questioning, Laura is able to assist Alba and Gina in developing some plans for including Kevin in the classroom activities as well as contingency plans if Kevin becomes physically aggressive with others. Specifically, their first visits will focus on transitions to and from outside play. Laura has shared some information with Alba and Gina about using pictures to help Kevin communicate his wants and needs as well as prepare for transitions throughout the day.

The approach taken by Laura and Alba demonstrates that they have knowledge and insight for how to use a child's interests to support his inclusion in a classroom setting. They understand the importance of teaching Kevin to be a competent play partner for the other children and of having him participate in a variety of early childhood experiences. Even though it is not detailed in this scenario, the role of the parents is also respected and included in the classroom setting. The evidence of a true partnership between Laura and Alba is already apparent in their willingness to solve problems and work together while respecting one another's expertise and abilities.

Reflect

Consider the role of Laura, the early childhood special education teacher in the previous scenario. How do her practices compare to yours or those of other practitioners with whom you have worked? Think about specific strategies that you could use to implement practices like those of the educator in this scenario.

Observe

Obtain permission to observe in an early childhood setting in your community. Specifically watch for natural learning opportunities that occur for children in the setting. Watch a specific child to see whether you can identify his or her interests.

KEY CONSIDERATIONS RELATED TO COACHING TEACHERS IN EARLY CHILDHOOD SETTINGS

In order to support teachers in early childhood settings, coaches must consider several key issues that are inherent to working in formalized early childhood settings. Just as early childhood practitioners must respect family environments when they are supporting children in their homes, coaches must also spend time developing an understanding of the teachers' or programs' philosophy of education and classroom management. Classroom environments, especially those in high-quality settings, are very busy. Coaches in early childhood settings must remember and respect the demands on the teachers' time to support and manage an active classroom environment. Although the teachers have many responsibilities, making time and setting the stage for a shared planning process regarding the coach's involvement in the classroom is critical. Preplanning and discussion will maximize the teachers' abilities to make time for coaching sessions. In addition, early discussions about teacher-specific or classroom-specific issues can lay the groundwork for administrative involvement and support in the process.

Understanding the Philosophy of the Group Setting

Developing an understanding of the educational philosophy of the program and teacher is one of the first steps in developing a partnership. In order for a coach to be successful in an early childhood classroom, he or she must gain an in-depth understanding of the guiding philosophical principles of the agency, program, and teacher. Because coaching depends on building on the coachee's current abilities, expertise, and knowledge, gathering information (i.e., talking with teachers, reading program materials, and observing teachers in their classrooms) prior to initiating coaching conversations will lay the groundwork for a collaborative partnership between the early childhood coach and teacher. If a coach lacks an understanding of the philosophical framework, he or she inadvertently could share information that conflicts with a program's standards or valued practices. In addition to not being helpful, such a coach could quickly lose credibility with the coachee, even if the coach had the best of intentions.

Consider a constructivist classroom setting where child choice and following the child's lead are preeminent principles of practice. At the end of last school year, this classroom agreed to be involved in an early literacy grant project. The teacher, Michael, was excited about bringing new resources into his classroom. Unbeknownst to Michael, the grant project required him to implement a standard curriculum that used specific children's books. When Sue, the early literacy coach, first met with Michael and discussed the grant requirements, he was shocked to learn that he would be required to include certain books in his classroom regardless of the children's interest in the books. He asked Sue to explain how this project was supporting his early literacy practices within his classroom. Sue understood the importance of following the project curriculum, knew the research supporting the shared reading activities, and had prior experience with the success of this particular curriculum. Instead of forcing the issue with Michael, however, Sue used reflective questioning to learn more about Michael's concerns, find out what he was currently doing in his classroom, identify possible options that he would feel comfortable implementing, and develop a plan to talk with the grant project director regarding flexibility of the requirements of the project. Using coaching strategies, she assisted Michael in becoming more informed and very importantly involved him in the decision-making process for the implementation of the project in his classroom.

> ### *Observe*
>
> Find out what types of philosophical approaches to early childhood education are used in the community where you work. For example, does the community have a Montessori preschool or program that is based on Reggio Emilia or Waldorf program approaches? Take time to observe in these settings to learn more about the approaches. For more information on early childhood philosophical approaches to education see Roopnarine and Johnson (2005).

Involving Teachers in the Planning Process

The example involving Sue and Michael demonstrates how to involve teachers in the planning process. Teachers in early childhood programs often learn of the involvement of an early childhood coach after the fact. When a family agrees to participate in an early intervention program, for example, their agreement to participate does not guarantee that the child care provider or preschool teacher will be interested in participating or even feel the need for support. The child care provider or preschool teacher should be included early in the planning (i.e., IFSP) process. A plan that is written by the family and that does not include the teacher or child care provider will not adequately address the needs and priorities across the child's environments. Different environments place varying demands on children and often require the child to exhibit a variety of skills and abilities in order to succeed. The adults in these environments also possess different abilities and experiences related to a child's specific needs. To ensure success for all who are involved in the process, identification of priorities across environments, as well as strengths, needs, and learning opportunities, is required. The early childhood coach can often help enhance communication between the early childhood classroom and home environment. The coach can provide specific support in both settings, and also can support parents and teachers in communicating directly with one another to maximize consistency and continuity of care for the child.

Peggy is an early childhood special education teacher who works for the local school district. She has been supporting Andrae, a little boy with global delays and a possible diagnosis of fetal alcohol syndrome (FAS) in a local Head Start classroom. Andrae lives at home with his mom, Edwina. Because Andrae has some problems related to extreme interest in his soiled diapers, both Edwina and Andrae's teacher, Vera, have identified an individualized education program (IEP) outcome for Andrae to learn how to use the toilet, especially for bowel movements. Peggy was able to support Vera's involvement with the IEP and Edwina was eager to support the toileting efforts at home. In the following dialogue, Peggy is visiting the school to meet with Vera.

Peggy: Hi, Vera! How are you today? I know you only have about 20 minutes, so let's get started. Our plan from last time . . .

Vera: [interrupts] . . . was for me to really focus on working on toileting with Andrae, specifically using a timed schedule.

Peggy: Yep . . . how's that been going?

Vera: Well, good and bad.

Peggy: How so?

Vera: Andrae is really doing well by the middle of the week. By Friday, we're down to almost no accidents and no problems with smearing bowel movements. It's great.

Peggy: . . . and the bad?

Vera: He goes home for a 2-day weekend.

Peggy: Tell me more . . .

Vera: I am absolutely convinced that Edwina is not even trying to have Andrae go on the toilet at home. On Monday when he comes back to class it's just like starting completely over. I can also tell he's gotten into his soiled diapers over the weekend because his fingernails aren't clean, so I have to clean those, too. You can probably tell that I'm frustrated.

Peggy: Yes, Vera. I can tell that you're frustrated. What have you tried to resolve this situation?

Vera: You were here a week ago Friday, right?

Peggy: Yes . . .

Vera: Well, it's happened now over two weekends. I've not said anything to Edwina.

Peggy: OK. How do you want to proceed?

Vera: I want Edwina to follow through with what she agreed to at our IEP meeting.

Peggy: I certainly understand that. Where would you like to start?

Vera: I know I need to talk with her and I don't want to do it over the phone. It's also crazy at drop-off and pick-up, so I don't have time to talk with her there like I need to.

Peggy: What are some of the possible options you can think of?

Vera: Well, of course I could call her or grab her at pick-up today and schedule a time to talk. Then she'll want to know what it's about and then we'll be off to the races!

Peggy: Just to clarify . . . you think that once you bring up the subject Edwina will want to have the conversation right then?

Vera: Yes . . . I know it. Part of it is me. I'll just want to go ahead and get the problem out on the table.

Peggy: You're saying you want to have this conversation immediately?

Vera: Yes.

Peggy: What options do you have?

Vera: I think I'll call Edwina and see if she can come in early today for pick-up. The more I think about this and the longer I let it go, the more frustrated I will get. I'll call her at lunch.

Peggy: How can I support you in having this conversation with Edwina?

Vera: What do you mean? I won't yell or anything! [laughs]

Peggy: Oh, I know that . . . I'm just asking how I can help you make the most of this conversation.

Vera: I should use coaching, right?

Peggy: Well, you know I have a biased opinion about that . . . seriously, how would that look with Edwina?

Vera: Well, first I need to find out what's been going on, even though I'm sure he's been pooping his pants at home and then playing in it. It's just so gross.

Peggy: What are some ways you can ask about the weekend activities without making assumptions?

Vera: I'll start with asking how the toileting is going at home. If she says fine, I'll need to be ready with an idea; otherwise I'll blow a gasket.

Peggy: What ideas do you have?

Vera: [thinking] . . . I could tell her about my experience and what I'm seeing. I won't bring up the fingernails . . . that would be too harsh.

Peggy: OK, then what?

Vera: I don't know. It's just such a shame that he's doing so well at school but not at home.

Peggy: What might be some reasons for the difference between home and school?

Vera: Edwina and me.

Peggy: What do you think about that?

Vera: Hmmm . . . it's really a lot of work and I have help here at school. She could have tried and run into problems. Maybe it's not so much about proving that she isn't following through at home, but figuring out how I can help or why it's not working.

Peggy: How would that look?

Vera: OK, I can do this . . . I'm sure she wants him to poop on the pot, too. Like I said, this is a LOT of work and I need to see how I can help. I could share what's working here at school. Hey . . . when you visit at home, could you help reinforce this?

Peggy: I'd be happy to. I'd like to support that follow through at home. If Edwina needs some extra support, I can make time in my schedule for that. I'll need to get some details from you about what's working with Andrae.

Vera: Just a minute . . . Allie . . . back over here please. Thank you for reminding me that it's time for us to clean up and go outside. Can you go over and get Andrae to help you? Thank you.

Peggy: I can help, too. We can get our plan together once we get everyone outside and playing on the playground.

This scenario demonstrates a situation in which the coach provided support related to communication between the early childhood teacher and the parent. Although Vera was very busy and feeling frustrated, with Peggy's assistance Vera was able to sort through her feelings and develop a plan for supporting Andrae and his mother. Peggy was also able to provide some continuity between the home and classroom environments by offering to be available to Andrae

Reflect

Early childhood practitioners often can facilitate consistency and continuity of care across home and early childhood classroom settings. Think of ways that you can support effective communication between parents and early childhood teachers for the children who are enrolled in your program.

and his mother more frequently in the home setting to help work through the challenges they were facing regarding toileting at home.

Making Time for Coaching

Identifying time for coaching to occur can be a challenge in active early childhood settings. Most preschool teachers and child care providers feel that they do not have a minute to spare in an already busy and action-packed day. Early childhood practitioners must maximize their flexibility in order to support teachers when they are available. Planning with the teacher and explaining the basics of coaching early in the process are critical components of an effective coaching partnership.

Three types of coaching conversations work effectively in interactions between practitioners and early childhood teachers: planned coaching conversations, "just-in-time coaching," and coaching "on the fly." Competent early childhood teachers are completely occupied with the children in their classrooms or with other required support activities, such as planning, organizing materials, preparing food, cleaning up, talking with parents, and meeting with other professionals; therefore, coaches must be flexible, sensitive, patient, and creative in using their time to support them. Face-to-face discussions are essential to developing a coaching relationship; however, other strategies such as following up by phone, e-mailing, and even sharing journals and logs can augment an active coaching partnership.

Planned coaching conversations are key to an effective coaching relationship and need to be scheduled at times when a teacher can converse. Early childhood practitioners often assume that nap time or after school might be sensible times to have coaching conversations, but teachers often reserve those times for planning, preparation, or scheduling other required activities for which they are responsible. Asking the teacher directly is the best way to identify a workable time to have a planned conversation. If a teacher seems vague about or even resistant to scheduling a time to meet, offering more explanation of what will happen may help the teacher carve out some available time. Offering to assist the teacher with his or her planned activities also may help to make time for a planned conversation. For example, if a teacher has a planned time to prepare materials for the children for an afternoon art activity or outdoor garden project, the coach could offer to assist with the preparation, providing more adult "hands" available for the work. If the tasks are fairly rudimentary, the coach can engage in coaching while they simultaneously prepare the materials.

Often practitioners are accustomed to an extended time frame for home visits (e.g., 30 minutes to an hour). For most early childhood teachers, carving out an hour or even 30 minutes during their day is just impossible. Coaches need to be prepared to maximize every minute and engage in shorter, maybe even segmented conversations. If coaches can be available for blocks of time (e.g., Wednesday morning) for an extended dialogue rather than scheduling a specific appointment (Wednesday from 10:30 to 11:30 a.m.), this may facilitate more functional opportunities for interaction with the teacher. An added benefit to this type of scheduling is the opportunity for real-life observations and "just-in-time" coaching supports.

"Just-in-time" coaching supports are defined as being available to support a coachee during the moment of need or naturally occurring opportunity. For example, if a teacher is struggling to maintain the attention of a very active child during morning center time, the coach's availability to observe, support, and try things with the teacher during this real-time event provides the support just in time. Using a block of time for visiting the classroom can provide multiple opportunities for just-in-time coaching throughout a morning.

Coaching "on the fly" conversations occur when the coach and teacher are working together in the moment. Coaching on the fly often involves exchanges between coach and coachee in which the characteristics of coaching play out through a series of multiple, brief interactions. For example, during real-time routines and classroom activity settings, the teacher and coach could identify a possible opportunity for support and the teacher could give it a try. The teacher would then continue carrying out his or her responsibilities while the coach observes the interactions or looks for other possible opportunities for support. The coach and teacher would then briefly interact and plan for the coach to try a strategy with the teacher in the role of observer (modeling). After modeling by the coach, the teacher and coach would reflect, and then, when the next opportunity arises, the teacher would implement the strategy while the coach observes. The effectiveness of this type of intense support is considerable compared with shorter, planned conversations that extend over weeks and months.

Seeking Administrative Involvement

When coaches are supporting teachers in formalized early childhood settings, the involvement of the administrator and supervisors is critical for success. In addition to supporting the success of individual children within a classroom, coaches can support an entire agency or program regarding the infrastructure for implementing evidence-based early childhood practices. Coaches may encounter situations in which a particular teacher needs additional supports that are beyond the role or responsibility of the assigned coach. The teacher, supervisor, and, when appropriate, the coach, can discuss the issue in order to identify needed resources or training that a coach would not be expected to provide.

Robin is a PT who is assigned to support Leilani, an early childhood educator in a community preschool program. The support is specifically intended to help a child named Toby who is learning how to use a power wheelchair. Leilani also has a classroom assistant, Cora, who has been assigned to the classroom to support Toby's success. Robin has worked closely with Leilani, Cora, Toby, and his parents to ensure that the power mobility base and seat cushion would meet Toby's needs and work well across the environments in Toby's life. During the visit today, Robin and Leilani discuss their previous plan to help Toby use the power chair within the classroom environment.

Robin: Hi, Leilani. How are you?

Leilani: I'm doing well. You?

Robin: Yes . . . no worries. Thanks for asking. Well . . . I'm excited to hear how you have been doing supporting Toby in getting around the classroom.

Leilani: First I'd like you to check something on Toby's wheelchair and then, to be honest . . . I'm having a problem.

Robin: OK. Let's talk about Toby's wheelchair. What would you like to me to check?

Leilani: Toby is leaning over to the side . . . to the right, especially when he is driving his chair.

Robin: Let's take a look. Hey Toby! How are you?

[Toby nods and smiles at Robin and Leilani.]

Leilani: Toby, can we go over to the kitchen to start getting things ready for snack?

[Toby leans over to the right and works on driving over to the kitchen area.]

Leilani: See what I mean? Don't you think he's leaning too far to the right?

Robin: I agree. Toby, can you wait a few minutes before we get your snack?

[Toby nods and smiles in agreement.]

Robin: When did Toby start leaning to the right so much?

Leilani: The past few days I think.

Robin: What has changed?

Leilani: Nothing that I know of. Here, double check me on how I'm positioning him in the seat.

[Leilani repositions Toby in the seat of the wheelchair just as she and Robin had practiced.]

Robin: I think he looks great in the seat. You're doing a nice job of making sure his hips are all the way back in the chair. I'm somewhat perplexed by this new development. Would it be OK with you if I just check out a few possibilities?

Leilani: Sure. Just talk out loud while you're thinking. It really helps me learn when you do that.

Robin: OK, thanks for sharing that. I'm such an external processor when I'm thinking that it really helps me to think out loud. Toby . . . would you mind driving around a bit for us? We're noticing that you're leaning more to the side . . . have you noticed a difference?

[Toby nods in agreement.]

Robin: Toby, while you're driving I'm going to follow behind you and provide you with some support on your body. Let's see if it helps.

[Robin and Toby move around the kitchen and play areas. Robin places lateral support on both sides of Toby's trunk while he drives.]

Robin: Leilani, what did you notice when I provided Toby with more support to his trunk while he was driving?

Leilani: He definitely wasn't leaning as much. What are you thinking? I know you can't be considering having one of us help him stay up straight in his chair.

Robin: [smiling] You're right, that wouldn't work, would it? The wheelchair manufacturer makes lateral pads that attach to the seat insert. I think Toby may need these lateral supports. The leaning is bad for the obvious reason that it impairs his driving ability, but it also can contribute to some orthopedic issues over time affecting both his spine and hips.

[Robin proceeds to explain possible problems with scoliosis and hip dislocation.]

Robin: I'm also wondering if a tray might help out. He seems to be leaning forward and a small tray would provide him with additional support that might also help keep him upright.

Leilani: I remember we talked about possibly needing a tray. I just didn't think you thought the need would arise so quickly.

Robin: You're right, but I think we need to proceed with calling the vendor about the lateral pads and a tray. How would you like to proceed?

Leilani: Do you mean regarding involving Toby's parents?

Robin: Yes. Who should talk with them?

Leilani: How about both of us? I will talk with his mom today at pick-up to tell them what we've noticed and figured out, and then you could call to talk with them about the costs and the vendor. What do you think of that plan?

Robin: I like it. I should have time to call tomorrow morning sometime.

Leilani: I'll let her know you'll be calling.

Robin: Toby . . . great work. You are really doing well with driving yourself around. I'm really proud of you.

Leilani: Me, too! OK Toby, how about you head back over to the table with Cora to have your snack? Robin, do you still have time to talk about my other issue?

Robin: Sure, what's up?

Leilani: Let's step outside for a minute. I think my problem is Cora [her classroom assistant]. She's just been really hateful about Toby's new wheelchair. She seems to resent it.

Robin: Tell me more . . . what's happened?

Leilani: She keeps making negative comments about Toby's chair . . . some are even negative about Toby. A real problem is that when he needs to move around the classroom, Cora goes over the wheelchair and actually drives it for Toby . . . not even hand-over-hand . . . she just drives it for him.

Robin: What did you do when these things happened?

Leilani: Well, I let the negative comments go. I probably shouldn't have, but you know how Cora is . . . she's been around a lot longer than me. I have trouble with her bossing me around or just ignoring the plans we make.

Robin: What did you do about her driving the wheelchair for Toby?

Leilani: I went over to her and reminded her of our plan. Remember, she was right there with us when we planned what to do. She even practiced it with both of us watching.

Robin: What happened?

Leilani: She said she wouldn't put up with him running over her feet and bumping into the other children. She also said it was ridiculous for him to have this chair and made a negative comment about how her tax dollars paid for it. I told her that we had a plan and that I certainly did not want her to be in harm's way, but that my observations did not match hers. I reminded her that you turned the speed down on the chair so low that he is really incapable of hurting anyone. She said, "I need a smoke break," and stomped out of the room.

Robin: How did you handle things after she came back?

Leilani: I haven't. I've let her steamroll me again. I'm really frustrated by this.

Robin: What do you want to do?

Leilani: Can we talk with her together?

Robin: Sure. What do you want my role to be?

Leilani: I'll start the conversation and try to get us back to our original plan.

Robin: What do you want me to do if things don't go well?

Leilani: If you feel comfortable, please step in.

Robin: Leilani, I don't want to undermine your position with Cora. I will be really cautious about how I step in. If this conversation doesn't go well, what is your next step?

Leilani: I think it's time that I talk with Deb [Leilani's program director] if this goes poorly.

Robin: Will you be letting Cora know that during this conversation?

Leilani: Yes . . . it's time, probably past time.

[Leilani calls the office to ask whether another teacher, Amy, can come to her room from the office. Amy is available and joins the class to provide supervision during the following conversation.]

Leilani: Cora, while Robin is here I wanted to revisit our plan from last time about Toby using his wheelchair in the classroom. I've told her about some of your frustrations with the situation. Would you elaborate?

Cora: [to Robin] She's probably already told you that I don't like it.

Leilani: I did tell her that. Please share why.

Cora: It's stupid. I like Toby and all, but there's no way he'll learn how to use it. It's a waste of money and of my time.

Leilani: Cora, I'm surprised by your comments about Toby's ability. This seems different from how you used to feel. What's going on?

Cora: I've got better things to do than drive that kid around the classroom. It was easier before in his old chair.

Leilani: Robin . . . can you jump in here?

Robin: Sure. Cora, as we talked when I was here last, it was easier just to push Toby around in the old chair, but we talked about all the good it would bring for Toby to use a powered wheelchair. I thought you were on board. What's changed?

Cora: [obviously upset] Everything has changed this year. Sorry, Leilani, but I liked it better before you got here. I had things down pat before and now everything is different. It's not my job to babysit Toby all day.

Leilani: Cora . . . I think it's time we have a conversation with Deb. You are obviously unhappy and I think we may need clarification from Deb regarding your role in this classroom. Can you be available today after school if Deb can see us?

Cora: Sure . . . you're right . . . you'll see. This isn't my job and I don't have to do it.

Leilani: Thanks Cora. Would you ask Amy to stay just a few more minutes for me while I finish up with Robin?

[Cora leaves to talk with Amy.]

Leilani: Geez. I'm shaking. I think that went pretty well, though, don't you?

Robin: You were very patient and calm.

Leilani: I just think it was very clear that Cora and I have a completely different understanding of her role and Deb can clear that up.

Robin: What supports do you need from me?

Leilani: I feel completely comfortable talking with Deb. She will want to see me for a few minutes prior to our discussion with Cora.

[Robin and Leilani continue their conversation. They develop a joint plan that will include what Leilani will be doing between visits and when the next visit should occur.]

This scenario demonstrates a situation in which the teacher clearly felt supported by both her program director and coach. Robin was available to help Leilani explore her options and develop a plan of action. Robin was careful not to overstep her boundaries in her role as coach or to usurp Leilani's authority as the lead classroom teacher. Leilani's comfort in discussing her concerns openly and honestly with Robin exemplifies the trust and mutual respect that has developed within this coaching relationship.

> ## Practice
>
> Make a list of tough situations that you have handled as a coach. Consider situations in which you did and did not openly discuss the concern or conflict. Write down some reflective questions that you could have used to introduce the topic. Make a plan so that you will be prepared the next time you are in a complex situation.

THE ROLE OF THE COACH WHEN SUPPORTING TEACHERS IN EARLY CHILDHOOD SETTINGS

The role of the coach when supporting teachers in early childhood settings is complex. A coach may find him or herself in situations that may not directly pertain to the initial reason for which he or she was assigned to that teacher. Early childhood teachers are faced with diverse challenges that require a vast skill set. Developing an open, trusting relationship with the coachee is imperative to a successful coaching partnership. Sometimes the coach will become the actual resource that the teacher needs. In other situations, the coach will assume the role of a mobilizer or mediator of other resources. Under these circumstances, using a resource-based approach will assist the coachee in identifying, accessing, using, and evaluating the needed resources.

Coaching More than One Teacher in a Group Setting

The scenario with Leilani, Cora, Robin, and Toby provided some insight into the role of a coach when more than one teacher is assigned to a classroom. In some situations, one of the teachers will serve in a lead teacher capacity (as Leilani did); however, in many classroom settings (e.g., EHS), the teachers have equal roles and responsibilities but may be assigned to specific children. When two teachers are present in the classroom, the coach will need to have conversations with both teachers to define their responsibilities related to the role of the early childhood coach in the classroom. It would be a rare exception where the coach would interact with only one of the teachers over the course of involvement in the classroom. Planning times for conversing becomes even more difficult when both classroom teachers are involved. Using just-in-time coaching and coaching-on-the-fly conversations increasingly becomes the norm over time. Sometimes the knowledge and expertise of the two teachers are so dissimilar that individual conversations for a short while might be required.

Confidentiality

For an early childhood practitioner who is functioning in the role of coach, it is important to maintain confidentiality of the children enrolled in the early childhood program and their parents. Because the coach is present in the classroom, he or she may be privy to information that otherwise would not be shared. Early childhood coaches must take the initiative to discuss this issue with the teacher in the classroom as well as with the parents of any child for whom the coach is providing support. Discussing possible scenarios before they happen is an excellent strategy for steering clear of future uncomfortable situations. The coach must be aware of safeguards that need to be in place to protect the privacy of all children enrolled in the program. Obtaining permission from a child's parents to explain to other parents why another adult is involved in the classroom setting is an effective strategy for managing questions from curious or concerned parents. Early childhood practitioners should not be surprised if they are asked to participate in criminal background checks or fingerprinting before they are given permission to participate in classroom activities. These are safety measures required by all licensed early childhood programs.

Involvement with a Specific Child and/or Other Children in the Classroom

Early childhood coaches who are working in classroom settings face the challenge of being available for the teacher and supportive within real-life activity settings without disrupting the classroom routine or upsetting carefully planned adult-to-child ratios. Practitioners in the field of early childhood like children and enjoy interacting with them. In classroom settings, however, many teachers work hard to promote child-to-child interaction and deemphasize adult–child interactions. When a coach enters a classroom setting, he or she must talk with the teacher beforehand about how to handle it if children approach the coach with specific requests and interaction attempts. The coach should maintain due diligence in remaining an interested and supportive observer, careful not to disrupt the normal flow of interaction between students and teachers. An action as simple as jumping in to assist a child with a request like "Tie my shoe?" or "Can I have drink?" could actually disrupt a teaching moment for the teacher or opportunity for child autonomy. The coach, of course, should be responsive and friendly to the child, and should implement evidence-based practices, but should always look to the teacher for guidance regarding how directly involved he or she should be.

When a child with special needs is included in a classroom setting, the coach may be approached by the teacher regarding other children in the classroom or may identify a need for supporting other children. For example, other children might have questions about a child's specific abilities or special equipment needs, and a teacher may need help or support to answer these questions. Recall the scenario with Andrae, Vera, and Peggy in the Head Start classroom. The first time that Andrae soiled his diaper, stripped, and began to explore the contents, the other children demonstrated an array of reactions from interest and curiosity to shock and fear. Peggy was present during this situation and Vera asked her to talk with the other children while she helped Andrae clean up. Peggy was ready to support the children, but she also planned to talk with Vera during another time about how to handle the class so that she would feel confident if this situation happened again.

Observations Beyond the Scope of the Planned Coaching Relationship

Practice

When a challenging situation occurs, be prepared to implement the following effective strategies for supporting young children in early childhood classroom settings:

- Assist the teacher in answering all of the children's questions in an open, honest manner. For example, if a child asks why Tracie screams when she gets upset, then you might support the teacher by saying, "Tracie hasn't yet learned how to use her words. When she gets upset she knows that everyone will know how she feels if she screams."

- Assist the teacher in creating situations where children can share interests. For example, you might invite other children to join an activity that is interesting to them as well as to the child who needs opportunities for side-by-side play or peer interaction.

- Support the teacher in assisting the children to invite other children to join activities. For instance, you might encourage the teacher to say, "Jorge, it looks like you're having fun playing at the light table with the dinosaurs. Kevin really likes dinosaurs. Would you like to ask him to play with you?"

- Support the teacher in creating opportunities for children to learn about personal space and preferences. A teacher could say, "Jorge, it is really nice that you like Kevin so much that you like to hug him. Remember we talked about how hugging can be scary to Kevin. How else could you show him that you like to play with him?"

- Support the teacher in encouraging the children to ask questions and share their feelings. For example, you could encourage the teacher to say, "Donette, you seem really interested in Johnna's hearing aids. What questions do you have?"

Occasionally an early childhood coach may become aware of information or practices that are not directly related to that coach's involvement in supporting the teacher. For example, an early literacy coach might be invited to support a specific teacher to infuse evidence-based early literacy practices into her classroom. Through the course of their interactions, the coach could become aware of other practices in the classroom that are incongruent with early childhood recommended practices but that are not related directly to early literacy.

The following scenario involves Lavelle, an early literacy coach, and Margene, an early childhood preschool teacher.

Margene has been teaching for 18 years in a local school district. Recently she moved to an inclusive classroom in the district. Margene was nervous about her new assignment but also was open to the possibilities. Lavelle was assigned as the early literacy coach to support Margene during her transition. During her initial observations of Margene's classroom, Lavelle was focused on the implementation of early literacy practices. A few times during her visits, Lavelle noticed that Margene often raised her voice with the children and frequently used time outs as a specific classroom management technique. Lavelle was not quite sure what to do with this information, but she only had minor concerns until yesterday. When Lavelle joined Margene's classroom yesterday, Tomas, a little boy with autism, was obviously in trouble. Margene told Lavelle that the shared reading activity would have to wait because she was working with Tomas at the moment. Lavelle observed that Tomas had been placed in a standing table. Lavelle knew that this table was designed to support children who needed assistance to stand in order to participate in classroom activities, not for children like Tomas who could stand and were independently mobile. Tomas obviously was locked in the standing table and was very angry and upset about his current situation. Lavelle was taken aback by the situation and knew that it was not her role in Margene's classroom to address topics like this one, but she also knew that the situation was not appropriate and needed to be addressed. Lavelle spoke softly to Margene.

Lavelle: Could we talk a minute?

Margene: [gruffly] I told you I needed a minute. I can't do the shared reading right now.

Lavelle: I understand, Margene. I need to talk with you about what is going on with Tomas. I am very concerned.

Margene: I'm not sure it's any of your concern, but OK . . . what are you concerned about?

Lavelle: Margene, you are obviously upset and so is Tomas. It is not appropriate for him to be locked in the standing table. You need to get him out of there and we need to call your supervisor.

Margene: I'll do no such thing. You're right. I'm upset and so is he, but he will hit me if I let him out. Also, last time I checked, this is my classroom and I will manage it the way I see fit.

Lavelle: Margene . . . I'm sorry, but I'm going to call the office right now. This is not OK.

Margene: Fine. I'll let him out, but we'll both be sorry.

[Margene goes over to Tomas and unlatches the standing table. Tomas pushes past Margene and runs over to the door to the outside playground.]

Margene: [shouting] Tomas. You are not going outside.

[Tomas runs over to the dramatic play area and grabs a fleece robe and buries his face.]

Lavelle: Margene, let's call your supervisor . . . where is Mattie [teacher assistant]?

Margene: Mattie had to run an errand. She should be back anytime. I'm not calling my supervisor.

Lavelle: OK. I will.

[At this point, Mattie enters the room apologizing for being gone.]

Lavelle: Mattie, we've had an incident with Margene and Tomas. Do you feel comfortable watching Tomas to make sure he is OK?

Mattie: Yes. I'll check on him. What happened?

Lavelle: Margene can explain while I go to the office.

[Lavelle heads to the office to speak with Margene's supervisor.]

That evening on her way home, Lavelle reflected on how she handled the situation with Margene. She critically assessed what she could have done differently and tried to think about what could have prevented this from happening. Lavelle decided that in the future if something happened that raised concerns for her, like the time outs she had noticed Margene using, she would bring it up on the spot. Lavelle wondered if the situation with Tomas could have been avoided had she mentioned her concerns about the use of time outs and Margene's raising of her voice sooner. Lavelle also planned to check in with Margene's supervisor prior to rescheduling early literacy visits. Lavelle understood at this point that Margene needed additional supports that were outside her own area of expertise as an early literacy coach.

In this scenario, the coach found herself in a situation that no doubt required action, but her choice to involve the teacher's supervisor will most likely limit her future effectiveness as a coach with the coachee. Due to the serious nature of this scenario, the coach really only had one option, to contact supervisory staff. The coach acted quickly to intervene, and she also developed a plan for the future in case she found herself in a similar situation. Sometimes coaches are not so sure about how to respond. The content area or situation may be less black and white and may require contemplation or discussion. Coaches are encouraged to talk with coachees when they find themselves in situations in which they feel uncomfortable or unsure what course of action to take. A simple request to include a supervisor in a conversation may open up dialogue for an action plan. If the coach is concerned about a classroom issue and the coachee is hesitant to discuss the situation, the coach should share the concern with the coachee and explain the need for the supervisor to become involved. Coaching is based on open, honest communication and requires courage from the participants to address tough situations. A coach should understand boundaries of responsibility in order to form an effective coaching partnership.

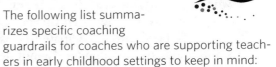

Remember

The following list summarizes specific coaching guardrails for coaches who are supporting teachers in early childhood settings to keep in mind:

- Schedule visits at a time that is convenient for the teacher.
- Respect the philosophical approach and authority of the teacher.
- Always involve the teacher in the planning process (e.g., IFSP, IEP).
- Be mindful of the teacher's ongoing responsibilities while he or she is engaged in conversations.
- Use just-in-time coaching and coaching on-the-fly for efficient use of time.
- Be responsive to the other children in the environment, but be careful not to disrupt the classroom routine or adult–child ratios.
- Help the teacher . . . offer to assist with planning or preparatory activities to maximize time for coaching conversations.
- When you are interacting directly with a child, be sure to use the situation as an intentional modeling opportunity for the teacher and/or assessment to determine how best to support both the child and the teacher(s).
- Support teachers to involve and engage parents in their child's classroom experiences.
- Be prepared for and open to frequent changes in staff and plan accordingly.
- Know your role as the coach, but if concerns arise that are outside your area of coaching, discuss those concerns with the coachee and the coachee's supervisor.

DEALING WITH TEACHER RETENTION ISSUES

A confounding issue for early childhood coaches in some early childhood settings is frequent staffing changes (Bruder, 1993; Odom, 2000). A coach must be prepared for the possibility or even probability of classroom staff leaving the organization or being assigned to a different group within a center during the time that the coach is involved in the child care setting. The nature of coaching requires the coach to be directly involved with the child care provider or teacher during every visit, unlike the situation in other approaches that feature practitioner–child interventions. Because coaching is a relationship-based interaction style, the coach goes to the center or classroom to support the child care provider or teacher, not just the child. A teacher, therefore, who is planning a move or anticipating a probable change of assignment within the program is likely to mention this possibility to the coach rather than having the coach show up for the next planned visit and find the teacher gone or reassigned. If the coach is notified of an impending change, he or she can help the child, family, and new teacher if available to anticipate the ramifications of the change. On a positive note, when teacher assignments change, coaches have a wonderful opportunity to influence additional early childhood professionals by implementing their support and capacity-building practices.

CONCLUSION

Early childhood classroom teachers play an important role in the lives of the children who are enrolled in their programs. Group opportunities provide young children with opportunities to learn and interact with same-age peers that sometimes are unavailable to children in home or other community settings. Coaches may work within these classrooms to support inclusion of children with or at risk for disabilities or to infuse specific content into an early childhood setting. Coaches can play an important role in building the capacity of teachers and child care providers who have a variety of knowledge, skills, and experience. The coaching scenarios in this chapter were designed to provide examples of real-life situations that an early childhood coach is likely to encounter and strategies for successfully supporting teachers, child care providers, and the children in their care.

RESOURCES

Head Start Center on Inclusion: http://depts.washington.edu/hscenter/

This web site provides current research for including children with disabilities in regular classrooms and programs. Information is also available related to research on professional development and knowledge utilization.

Toll, C.A. (2005). *The literacy coach's survival guide*. Newark, DE: International Reading Association.

This book details the rationale and process for coaching teachers in the area of early literacy. A special section is included on how to coach in particularly difficult situations.

Wolery, R.A. & Odom, S.L. (2000). *An administrator's guide to preschool inclusion*. Chapel Hill, NC: University of North Carolina, FPG Child Development Center, Early Childhood Research Institute on Inclusion.

This text provides program administrators with a step-by-step guide for how to develop and implement an inclusive early childhood program.

Zero to Three: National Center for Infants, Toddlers, and Families: http://www.zerotothree.org

This web site provides current research, practice information, and resources for parents and other care providers. The web site also includes a specific section on early care and education.

Chapter 9

Coaching as Part of Professional Development

Previous chapters have described coaching as an interaction style for working with family members and teachers to build their capacity related to using their existing knowledge, as well as to obtain and use new knowledge and skills. The process of coaching for these individuals is an adult learning strategy, but the sharing of new information by the coach and learning by the coachee occurs only within the context of the coachee's actual life activities (i.e., family and community activities when family members are coachees and classroom-based activities when teachers are coachees). This use of coaching generally occurs as the need or priority occurs, similar to just-in-time training and learning, rather than as a follow-up to a training event.

This chapter will place coaching within the broader context of professional development. Within this context, coaching is used for the purposes of 1) enhancing knowledge use as part of the process of learning transfer from a training environment to real-life situations, 2) providing just-in-time learning that is based on an immediate need and that does not necessarily follow a formal training opportunity, and 3) ensuring fidelity to program practice standards.

PURPOSES OF COACHING

The purpose of coaching for professional development is decided on the basis of the type of content, who initiates the coaching conversation or relationship, and the coach's and coachee's perspectives regarding breadth of the topic and amount of time required to accomplish the intended objectives (see Table 9.1).

When the purpose of coaching related to professional development is transfer of training, the content of coaching conversations and practice opportunities directly relates to the topic of a recently attended formal learning experience (e.g., workshop, training, conference presentation). Coaching for transfer of training is generally initiated or needed by the learner, who becomes the coachee, in order to apply the knowledge and skills to his or her current practices. In this type of professional development opportunity, the coachee requests and receives the support of a peer, supervisor, program administrator, or internal or external expert (e.g., literacy specialist) to serve as the coach. The role of the coach is to assist the coachee in applying the knowledge and skills from the formal learning experience to the coachee's work setting. The coach and coachee may view the coaching relationship as a short-term or long-term one depending on the complexity of the innovation learned and its application to the work setting

Table 9.1.   Purposes of coaching for professional development

Purpose	Type of content	Who initiates	Perspective
Transfer of training	Newly acquired knowledge or skills from a formal learning experience	Learner/coachee	Short term or long term; narrow or broad topic
Just-in-time learning	Immediate need, question, or priority	Learner/coachee	Short term; narrow topic
Fidelity to practice standards	Program or discipline standards; evidence-based practices	Learner/coachee; coach (i.e., colleague, supervisor, or administrator)	Long term; broad topic

and the number of different formal learning opportunities that occur. The perspective of the coach and coachee may be narrow (focused on a single skill or set of skills), or broad (in the case of a comprehensive change in practices or curricula).

Consider the example of a teacher named Shebala who attended a workshop on how to start a fatherhood initiative as part of an Early Head Start (EHS) program. Shebala shared what she had learned with her supervisor, Monica, the EHS program coordinator, and asked for assistance with using what she had learned from the workshop to start a fatherhood initiative. Monica contacted her colleague, Brad, who has a successful history of developing other programs for parents, and asked him if he would be willing to serve as Shebala's coach. Brad agreed. Starting a fatherhood program would require a long-term, broad-based perspective because this initiative would involve operationalizing many of the different aspects of what Shebala learned from her training, including needs assessment, curriculum development, marketing or advertising, development of skills related to small group facilitation, and data collection. Shebala and Brad set a timeframe of 1 year to apply what Shebala learned in order to plan and initiate the fatherhood program. In addition, Monica worked with Shebala to attend other trainings about EHS fatherhood initiatives, and Brad continued to serve as her coach to assist her with incorporating the new information into the program that she was developing.

When the purpose of coaching as professional development is providing just-in-time learning, the coaching content is based on an immediate learning need, question, or priority as it occurs within the context of the coachee's work. Coaching for just-in-time professional development is generally initiated by the learner. That individual approaches a colleague, supervisor, administrator, or content expert with a question or immediate need. The perspective of the coach and coachee for this type of coaching is generally short term and narrowly focused. The coaching interaction only needs to last long enough for the coachee to obtain the knowledge or develop the needed skill. Although this purpose and type of coaching may occur as part of a long-term coaching relationship, more often these types of professional development opportunities are spontaneous situations that last only long enough for the new learning to occur and be infused into practice.

Consider the following example of a just-in-time professional development opportunity that occurred one day when Kate, a first-year teacher in an early intervention program, asked Linda, who had over 20 years of teaching experience, how to help a parent be more responsive to her child's learning. Kate shared with Linda that she had just returned from a home visit during which the mother was reading a book to her child. The mother kept asking the

> ### Reflect
>
> Recall the last professional development opportunity that you attended. How could coaching have been used to support your new learning?

child to label the pictures and would not turn the page until the child tried to say the word. Even though this activity was related to the child's interest in books, both the child and mother became increasingly frustrated during this activity, and the child tried to close the book and run away. Kate wanted to share information with the parent about being responsive and following the child's lead as a way to promote interest-based child learning.

Linda began the conversation by asking Kate what she already knew, had read, or had observed other staff members do to promote parent responsiveness. Kate shared her current understanding of the practice. Linda asked Kate to analyze what she had seen other teachers do in similar situations and how she might use that knowledge in this situation with the parent reading the book. Kate shared her analysis, and then she and Linda developed a plan for how Kate would share information about responsiveness related to book reading with the mother on her next home visit. Linda asked what additional support Kate wanted from her. Kate asked Linda to go with her on the next visit to observe her explain the information to the mother, model responsiveness, and then support the parent in being responsive during book reading. Linda agreed to go with Kate and they planned to debrief the visit on the way back to the office.

When the purpose of coaching in professional development is ensuring fidelity to practice, the coaching content is based on program or discipline practice standards and evidence-based practices in early childhood (e.g., early intervention, early literacy development, inclusion). The coaching opportunity may be initiated by the coachee, his or her previously assigned coach, or someone in an administrative role. The program administrator or supervisor may serve as the coach if he or she has the necessary level of knowledge regarding the targeted evidence-based practices or standards. Otherwise, the coachee or administrator may seek someone who has the appropriate knowledge and skills to serve as the coach. Whereas some learners self-reflect and self-assess to the point of identifying that they need coaching supports to help them use program standards or evidence-based practices, other individuals may not realize that a gap in understanding or practice exists until another person brings it to his or her attention. The coach and coachee usually take a long-term perspective as the coach works closely with the coachee to acquire the necessary knowledge and/or skills over time. The perspective may be either narrowly focused or broad based depending on the number, type, and depth of practices to be addressed.

Reflect

When was the last time you could have benefited from just-in-time learning? Who could have served as your coach?

Consider the example of Sarah, a supervisor in an early intervention program who attended a home visit with Brenda, an early childhood teacher, as part of a routine supervisory observation. When the parent told Brenda that she was concerned about her child's diet and was afraid that he was not eating well, Brenda simply replied that a lot of children his age were picky eaters. Immediately after the visit, Sarah shared her observation with Brenda related to the conversation about the child's diet and asked Brenda how she decided on her response and how it fit with program standards related to child nutrition. Brenda admitted that the parent's question caught her by surprise and she could not remember the program standards on child nutrition nor what was developmentally appropriate for a child that age. Brenda told Sarah that she would check the program standards as soon as she got back to the office and would obtain resources on child nutrition and healthy eating. Brenda shared some specific resources that she would check and Sarah added a few additional options for her consideration. Sarah also asked Brenda to reflect on criteria that she would use to determine whether the program standards and the resources were evidence based.

Sarah's and Brenda's plan included getting back together the following day to review what Brenda had learned from the program standards and nutrition resources. At that time, they would also discuss how Brenda could return to this conversation with the parent and how she might find out more about the parent's interest in child nutrition.

BACKGROUND ON PROFESSIONAL DEVELOPMENT

A common component of most early childhood programs, whether their function is early intervention, early literacy, Head Start, or EHS, is professional development. In fact, most of these initiatives require ongoing training of staff, and the federal and/or state regulations that govern the programs ensure that the programs meet training requirements. Professional development may be divided into two broad categories: preservice training, which usually takes the form of academic coursework and practicum experiences, and in-service training, which is conducted after individuals enter the professional workforce. In-service training opportunities may include, but are not limited to, conferences, workshops, training sessions, communities of practice, study groups, just-in-time training, journal clubs, mentoring programs, and coaching programs. Specific methods of professional development include lecture, guided design, accelerated learning, web-based training (synchronous and asynchronous), coaching, consultation, technical assistance, and mentoring. In spite of the training requirements and the varied options for training delivery, the field of early childhood has not reached consensus on a common definition of professional development (Buysse, Winton, & Rous, 2009).

Programs tend to define the audience, content, and process for professional development in many different ways. In order to more effectively provide technical assistance to states in the area of early childhood as part of a federally funded grant, staff of the National Professional Development Center on Inclusion (NPDCI) developed and validated a definition of professional development. As part of the literature review, the NPDCI identified six key assumptions about professional development that ultimately was used to craft the definition (Buysse et al., 2009):

1. Professional development includes a number of different types of guided learning experiences.

Reflect

In your organization or discipline, which practices could be supported or enhanced through the use of coaching? Who in your organization or within your discipline could provide coaching related to fidelity to practice or use of evidence-based practices? In your organization, what are the opportunities for promoting fidelity to practices?

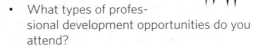

Reflect

If you are a consumer of professional development,

*   What types of professional development opportunities do you attend?
*   What methods of professional development are typically used?
*   How do these methods support you in implementing the new knowledge and skills once you return to your practice setting?

If you are responsible for providing professional development,

*   What types of professional development opportunities do you offer?
*   What methods of professional development do you typically use?
*   How do you help ensure that participants are able to implement their new knowledge and skills after they return to their practice settings?

2. Practitioners in the field of early childhood have a wide range of roles and responsibilities, education levels, experience, and diverse backgrounds and work with children who also are from diverse backgrounds.

3. Family members are key allies in professional development.

4. Recipients of professional development are responsible for acquiring and applying knowledge and skills through professional development opportunities.

5. The job of persons providing professional development is to facilitate learning opportunities that directly meet the needs of child development professionals and are based on current research and recommendations from the field.

6. The framework for planning and evaluating professional development includes three overlapping components: *who, what, and how.*

Using these assumptions, the NPDCI defined professional development as follows:

> Professional development is facilitated teaching and learning experiences that are transactional and designed to support the acquisition of professional knowledge, skills, and dispositions as well as the application of this knowledge in practice. The key components of professional development include: (a) the characteristics and contexts of the learners (i.e., the "who" of professional development, including the characteristics and contexts of the learners and the children and families they serve), (b) content (i.e., the "what" of professional development; what professionals should know and be able to do; generally defined by professional competencies, standards, and credentials); and (c) the organization and facilitation of learning experiences (i.e., the "how" of professional development; the approaches, models, or methods used to support self-directed, experientially-oriented learning that is highly relevant to practice. (NPDCI, 2008, p. 3)

The "how" described in the NPDCI definition of professional development is further delineated as learning opportunities that "are intensive, are sustained over time, and include guidance and feedback on how to apply specific practices through methods such as coaching, consultation or facilitated collaboration" (Buysse et al., 2009, p. 240). The professional development literature is clear that even though workshops are the primary means of in-service training, workshops alone are not effective (Fixen, Naoom, Blasé, Friedman, & Wallace, 2005; Guskey, 1986; Joyce & Showers, 2002; Reiss, 2007; Winton & McCollum, 2008). Though workshops are not effective in isolation, when coaching is added to them as a follow-up activity and/or for purposes of maintaining fidelity to interventions, workshops can be a factor in achieving positive outcomes (Fixen et al., 2005; Joyce & Showers, 2002).

Critical to training effectiveness is the manner in which the workshop content is delivered and supported beyond the initial training event. In a research synthesis of four adult-learning approaches (accelerated learning, coaching, guided design, and just-in-time training), which was completed in order to promote changes in the way that in-service training is provided, Trivette, Dunst, Hamby, and O'Herin (2009) provided five conclusions about in-service training:

1. Training that is most effective uses the learners' experiences in planning and application to promote deep understanding.

2. The more that the adult-learning characteristics of introduce, illustrate, practice, evaluate, reflect, and mastery are used in the training or practice opportunities, the greater the likelihood of positive benefits.

3. Active learner participation is the most effective component of adult-learning methods.

4. The most effective training opportunities include many learning experiences, multiple opportunities for learner self-assessment, and instructor-guided learner assessment against established standards.

5. Training should include a small number of participants over multiple sessions to allow the instructor to provide more focused attention on the learners and provide more occasions for processing, reflecting, and mastery assessment.

The authors of this research synthesis summarized their findings by reporting that the most effective types of professional development ensure that learners receive guidance, feedback, and the types of support that ensure deeper understanding and mastery of the training content (Trivette et al., 2009).

Prominent education researchers Beverly Joyce and Bruce Showers (2002) identified four components of training: theory, demonstration or modeling by the instructor, practice of the skill by the learner within the training environment, and coaching during application of the new knowledge and skills back in the classroom. The training instructor may use readings, discussion, lecture, or other means of information sharing in order to provide the learner with the background and rationale of a particular learning innovation. The training instructor may demonstrate or model within simulated situations during the training or by showing video of the innovation used in real-life settings. Practice by the learner within the context of the training event allows the learner to use the newly learned knowledge or skill in a simulated setting to gain some experience and confidence. Coaching during application provides opportunities for the learner to practice the new knowledge or skills in the environment in which the knowledge or skills will actually be used. During such practice the learner receives the supports of either a peer who is also in the process of learning and using the new knowledge or skills or a person who is already expert at using the new innovation.

As seen in Table 9.2, research (Joyce & Showers, 2002; Showers, Joyce, & Bennett, 1997) indicates that for knowledge acquisition, presentation of theory alone has a minimal effect on assisting learners to achieve training outcomes. Theory in combination with demonstrations by the instructor, practice opportunities within the training, and instructor feedback yielded modest gains in the percentage of training participants who achieved the intended outcomes. For *skill* acquisition, presentation of theory alone resulted in only 5% of participants achieving the training outcomes, but use of theory, demonstration, practice, and feedback combined resulted in 60% participant achievement. When *knowledge utilization and transfer of training* was the

Table 9.2.   Percentage of participants who attain outcomes, by training component

Components of training	Outcomes of training		
	Knowledge	Skill acquisition	Utilization/transfer to real-life context
Theory	10	5	0
Demonstration by instructors	30	20	0
Practice by participants with feedback from instructors	60	60	5
Coaching in real-life contexts	95	95	95

From Joyce, B., and Showers, B. (2002). *Student achievement through staff development: Fundamentals of school renewal.* White Plains, NY: Longman; adapted by permission.

intended outcome, use of theory in isolation had no effect on training participants, and theory combined with demonstration, practice, and feedback provided only a slight effect. When coaching was added and provided in the actual context in which the newly learned knowledge and skills were to be used, almost all of the participants demonstrated strong knowledge, consistent demonstration of the skills, and appropriate transfer of the knowledge and skills to the real-life context. The use of coaching enabled almost all of the subjects in this body of research to transfer the innovation from the training setting to the classroom setting (Joyce & Showers, 1982, 2002). Coaching is one strategy that may be used for the "how" described in the NPDCI definition of professional development. Coaching as a means for professional development is consistent with the five conclusions about in-service training that were provided by Trivette and colleagues (2009) to promote change in the way that in-service training is currently conducted. In accordance with these five implications, coaching 1) builds on the coachee's experiences in order to promote deep understanding; 2) uses the adult-learning characteristics of *introduce* (sharing informative feedback), *illustrate* (modeling by the coach), *practice* (action/practice by the coachee), *evaluate* (self-reflection or self-assessment by the coachee and affirmative, evaluative, and informative feedback by the coach), *reflect*, and *mastery* (indicated by self-attribution by the coachee and affirmative and evaluative feedback by the coach); 3) promotes active participation on the part of the learner; 4) provides many opportunities for coaching conversations over time, including reflection (self-assessment) and feedback by the coach; and 5) generally involves only the coach and coachee. As described by Joyce and Showers (2002), coaching is a strategy for transfer of training to the environment in which the knowledge and skills will actually be used (i.e., knowledge utilization).

Transfer of Training: Knowledge Utilization

Winton and McCollum defined knowledge utilization as "systematic strategies to promote the adaptation, implementation, and institutionalization of practices based on research" (2008, p. 9). Like Trivette and colleagues (2009), other authors indicate that knowledge utilization is enhanced when opportunities for practice, feedback, support, reflection, critical thinking, and mastery over time occur in the context in which the knowledge and skills typically will be used (Joyce & Showers, 2002; Snyder & Wolfe, 2008; Winton & McCollum, 2008). As highlighted in Chapter 2 and further substantiated by Snyder and Wolfe (2008) in their description of professional development follow-up strategies, coaching is one of the few strategies for transfer of training that has been empirically established as effective (Fixen et al., 2005; Joyce & Showers; Trivette et al., 2009).

Knowledge utilization occurs in both the preservice and in-service arenas of professional development. Knowledge utilization begins as students in preservice training practice within the context of the classroom environments using simulations or approximations of what might occur when the knowledge or skill could be used in a real-life setting. Knowledge utilization also occurs for preservice students during practicum experiences when they have the opportunity to practice what they have learned in their university or college classrooms within community-based contexts. As seen in Chapter 2, coaching by faculty or practitioners within these community settings has been shown to be effective in promoting the preservice students' learning (Anderson & Radencich, 2001; Bowman &

Observe

How do professional development opportunities that you attend or plan for your organization address the five conclusions about in-service training that were identified by Trivette and colleagues (2009)?

McCormick, 2000; Kurtts & Levin, 2000). Research has shown that when coaching was used as a strategy for transfer of knowledge and skills from in-service training, teachers who received ongoing support through coaching used newly learned practices more frequently and more appropriately than did teachers who did not receive coaching. They also showed more long-term retention of the new knowledge and skills than did teachers who did not receive coaching support (Joyce & Showers, 2002).

A recent synthesis of the literature on implementation research (Fixen et al., 2005) indicates that evidence supports coaching as an effective means for knowledge transfer and utilization. Because change is difficult for most individuals, Fixsen and colleagues list three problems that individuals encounter when they attempt to use newly learned knowledge and skills back in their work settings. First, learners tend to use new behaviors in an unsophisticated way compared with experts who have been demonstrating the behavior for quite some time. Over time and with the support of a coach, the learner can integrate the new skills into his or her practices and personalize them while still adhering to the characteristics of the evidence-based practice.

Second, the learner lacks confidence in use of the new behaviors or skills. The learner, therefore, requires support in using the skills and dealing with the response of the recipients of supports and services as well as other colleagues. The monograph of the results of the implementation research synthesis states

> "When practitioners change their behavior the reactions from consumers and stakeholders initially may not be positive, effectively punishing the practitioner for making a change. For fragile, new behavior the negative reaction may be enough to discourage the practitioner from persisting. One role of a coach is to prepare the practitioner for potential reactions and support the practitioner through the early stages of implementation until the new behavior is more skillfully embedded in the clinical environment." (Fixen et al., 2005, p. 44)

Reflect

Think about a time since your preservice training when you have tried to learn a new evidence-based practice. How did you feel when others questioned your use of the skill, either how you were doing it or why you were doing it at all? What did you do? Did you stop trying to use the practice and go back to your old ways? If so, what types of support would have helped you to become more competent and confident in the use of the new practice? If not, what kept you from returning to your previous practices?

Third, in relation to the use of coaching to support transfer of training, the implementation research synthesis revealed that the learning of new behaviors and skills is unfinished at the conclusion of the initial training event. Further assistance is needed, therefore, to help apply the learning to the context in which the knowledge and skills will be used (Fixen et al., 2005). In the summary of information related to the use of coaching to promote transfer of training, the synthesis authors conclude,

> "Coaching makes clear contributions to the preparation of practitioners, both in the experimental and other research literature. The core coaching components seem to be teaching (i.e., sharing information) and reinforcing evidence-based skill development and adaptations of skills and craft knowledge to fit the personal styles of the practitioners (changing form, not function)." (Fixen et al., 2005, p. 47)

Fullen (2001) refers to the problem that individuals encounter when they attempt to use newly learned knowledge and skills in the work setting as the *implementation dip*. This is the period during which the implementer of new practices is working to shift to the new practices, but the use of the new practices does not come as easily yet as the old practices did. He or she realizes that going back to the old practices would be easier than continuing to become more competent and confident in the use of the new practices. This is a particularly critical time for the person trying the new practices to have the support of a coach.

Peer Coaching and Expert Coaching

A common question that arises when coaching is used as a follow-up to a formal professional development program for the purposes of knowledge transfer and utilization is who should serve as the coach. Ackland (1991) reviewed 29 studies of coaching and divided coaching programs into two basic types, coaching by experts and reciprocal peer coaching. *Experts*, as defined by Ackland, were teachers with particular areas of knowledge and skills who had been specifically trained to provide feedback and support to other teachers. *Reciprocal peer coaching* involved teachers who had a similar level of expertise observing and coaching each other on targeted skills.

According to the synthesis of coaching in Chapter 2, current literature defines three types of coaching: reciprocal peer, peer, and expert. Reciprocal peer is defined similarly to the way that Ackland defined it. Peer coaches are defined as individuals who have the same or similar role as the person who is being coached, but who have particular knowledge and skills regarding which they coach the other. Experts are persons with specific content knowledge or skills who are generally from outside the organization and whose role is to provide coaching to specific individual(s) as part of the program or project. Experts may be workshop trainers, researchers, higher education faculty members, or other individuals who have the content and/or coaching expertise and who have received specific training on how to use coaching to facilitate knowledge transfer and utilization. All three types of coaching have been found to be effective (Bowman & McCormick, 2000; Hasbrouck, 1997; Kohler, Crilley, Shearer, & Good, 1997; Kurtts & Levin, 2000; Peterson, Luze, Eshbaugh, Jeon, & Kantz, 2007; Slater & Simmons, 2001; Tschantz & Vail, 2000). Which type of coaching is the most effective remains an empirical question (Fixen et al., 2005).

Practice

Before you go to your next professional development opportunity, arrange with your organization for someone who is knowledgeable about the content to serve as your coach when you return to assist you in applying the new knowledge and skills to your practices.

Alternatively, if you have content expertise and another individual from your program is participating in a professional development opportunity, offer to serve as that person's coach to help him or her apply the newly learned knowledge and skills to the work setting.

Consider the example of Joan, a teacher who attended a 1-day workshop on positive behavior supports for early childhood classrooms. She hoped to learn some techniques at the workshop to help one of her students, Caleb, more fully participate in classroom activities. Caleb was recently diagnosed with autism. He loves books, bugs, and soft fabrics. He tends to be very active and his passion for touching material that is soft is not always welcomed by his classmates or teachers. Although Caleb likes circle time because it involves books, he has some difficulty staying in the same location as the rest of the class during this activity, and his hands seem to find their way to his friends' clothing, especially during the cooler months when they wear fleece fabrics. During the workshop, Joan learned about using children's interests to promote learning and positive behaviors. She also found the technique of using social stories intriguing and decided it was something she might like to try.

As part of the workshop follow up, a coach was assigned to each participant to help him or her blend the practices learned at the workshop into his or her work setting. Doris, a teacher who had 10 years of experience working in early childhood classrooms, was selected as Joan's coach. Doris has a degree in special education, and she has supported many children with autism to successfully participate in fully inclusive classroom environments. Joan and Doris began their first meeting by having Joan share what she had learned from the workshop. Doris helped Joan identify a classroom activity, circle time, which already contained some of Caleb's interests as a place for Joan to begin supporting him through the use of some of the techniques that she had learned at the workshop. They agreed that during this activity, Doris would come into the classroom to observe and provide more direct coaching supports for Joan.

Joan decided that she was going to use a social story about circle time with Caleb. Joan took the lead in developing the social story. Doris assisted Joan in reflecting on the content and visuals to ensure that it would match Caleb's level of understanding. As a result of these reflections, Joan decided to use actual photographs of children in the classroom, including Caleb, rather than line drawings or clip art from a computer program.

Joan remained concerned about what Caleb would do with his hands during the story time other than touching his friends. Doris asked Joan to think about how she could use Caleb's interests in a positive way to address this challenge. After brainstorming several options, Joan decided that she would make Caleb a handkerchief out of fleece material with images of bugs on it that Caleb could either attach to his belt or keep in his pocket. Whenever he wanted to touch a friend, either Joan or the assistant teacher would redirect Caleb to his handkerchief.

Joan implemented the plan she had developed with support from Doris while Doris observed. Immediately after the circle time, Doris supported Joan in reflecting on how the activity had worked for both her and Caleb. Joan identified some areas for improvement on which she and the assistant teacher wanted to focus. Doris provided some additional feedback about what she had seen that worked and about Joan's ideas for improvement. Joan and Doris developed their joint plan and scheduled a time for Doris to come back the following week to observe circle time again. Doris also planned to work with Joan on finding some other times during the day when she could use social stories and Caleb's interests to promote positive behavior, learning, and social interactions with his classmates.

Just-in-Time Learning Based on Immediate Need or Priority

Just-in-time learning occurs in response to an identified need for knowledge or skills within the context in which the knowledge or skill can be used. As a result, the learning can be individualized to the person who is requesting the support and immediately contextualized within the real-life activity. Using the work of Bersin and O'Leonard (2005), Trivette and colleagues (2009) define the characteristics of this type of professional development opportunity as 1) either providing or promoting the acquisition of knowledge or skills necessary to perform a specific task, 2) showing contextualized use of the new knowledge or ability, and 3) having access to the support of a supervisor, mentor, or coach when necessary. For example, a teacher might require just-in-time learning when he or she needs assistance with one of the children as they are preparing to go outside and play. The child typically becomes so excited that he tends to push and shove the other children. A coach could support this teacher on how to engage the child so that his energy is directed positively during the transition. The child could be given line leader duties or asked to help the assistant teacher pull the riding toys out of the shed. For an early intervention practitioner, just-in-time learning could occur on a joint visit. For example, the physical therapist (PT) (i.e., coach) assists the speech-language pathologist (SLP) in recognizing the need for better positioning of a child in her highchair. The PT could engage the SLP in brainstorming ways that they can help the mother adjust and maintain the child's position in the chair.

Consider the example of Caitlyn, a new graduate who has a degree in physical therapy and a desire to work with young children and their families. Her only experience working with or even being around infants and toddlers was one practicum experience during her undergraduate training. She is extremely bright and quickly learned the program standards and practices of her new employer. Although she still lacks confidence, her knowledge of physical therapy practices is extremely good. After she had been working for the program for 1 month, Caitlyn approached her supervisor and explained that she felt she was not being helpful to the families on her early intervention caseload. After reflection with her supervisor, she realized that her feelings of inadequacy resulted directly from questions that parents would ask her about typical child development beyond the domain of motor development. Parents often described behaviors of their children that were related to toileting, play, and other areas of development and asked her whether the behaviors were normal. Caitlyn found herself at a loss for information to share in those moments. She knew that other members of her team and her supervisor were very knowledgeable about these and other topics related to parenting and typical child development, but she wanted to learn more for herself. Caitlyn and her supervisor developed a plan to give Caitlyn more experience being around young children so that she could observe their development, interactions, and caregiver routines in some preschool and child care classrooms. Caitlyn's supervisor served as her coach to help facilitate the observations and debrief with her about what she was learning. After Caitlyn's observations concluded, her supervisor continued in the coaching role to assist her in further developing her skills in being able to make observations and answer questions about typical development and parenting issues. The coaching relationship continued until Caitlyn reached a point of increased competence and confidence that included knowing when to go back to her supervisor for additional coaching support.

> ## Practice
>
> What is a pressing issue or question within the context of your work regarding which you need some immediate support? Arrange with your organization for someone knowledgeable about the content to serve as your coach.
>
> Alternatively, the next time someone asks you for immediate support around some specific knowledge or skill, use a coaching interaction style to build on what the person already knows or is doing and to explore alternatives together.

Fidelity to Practice Standards

Being a reflective practitioner means continually examining one's practices in light of new research and agreed-on standards for practice and then applying this new learning in order to increase effectiveness and promote continuous professional growth (Daniels, 2002; Ferraro, 2000; Pedro, 2005; Schon, 1987). At one time, program administrators assumed that everyone who was working for the organization, either through direct employment or as a contract provider, used the most current research available to guide and refine practices. In contrast, many early childhood professionals continue to practice in the way that they learned in their preservice training (Campbell & Halbert, 2002; Campbell & Sawyer, 2007; Harris, 1997; McLean & Cripe, 1997).

Increasingly, professional organizations, grant funding agencies, and individual programs are establishing practice standards that are intended to guide the planning, implementation, and evaluation of both programs and specific practices (American Speech-Language-Hearing Association, 2008; Pilkington, 2006; Sandall, Hemmeter, Smith, & McLean, 2005; Vanderhoff, 2004; Woods, 2008; Workgroup on Principles and Practices in Natural Environments, 2007). This move to standards-based practice is due at least in part to a shift toward increased accountability and use of evidence-based practices (Winton & McCollum, 2008).

Evidence-based practices are defined as "practices that are informed by research, in which the characteristics and consequences of environmental variables are empirically established and the relationship directly informs what a practitioner can do to produce a desired outcome" (Dunst, Trivette, & Cutspec, 2002, p. 3). The literature from the field of early childhood contains multiple references to the importance of using evidence-based practices and to translating research into practice (Buysse & Wesley, 2006; Dollaghan, 2004; Jette et al., 2003; Law, 2000; Meline & Paradiso, 2003).

Early childhood professionals need assistance and support to ensure that their practices are current with research-based literature, discipline practice standards, and program practice standards (i.e., intervention fidelity). *Intervention fidelity* is defined as "the extent to which end-users adopt and use instructional methods and procedures (processes) for implementing targeted practices mirroring the evidence-based characteristics of the practices (adoption)" (Dunst, Trivette, McInerney, et al., 2008, p. 5). Supervision is one method for promoting intervention fidelity. Many programs, however, do not have supervisory systems in place, or if they do, the design of the supervision does not provide direct support beyond initial orientation and basic training. In many venues, supervision is used merely to ensure compliance with program policies but does not guide or support the way that an individual practitioner implements the technical aspects of his or her discipline.

Coaching as professional development is another method that can be used to support intervention fidelity. This support can be accomplished by having supervisors coach supervisees, assigning experienced peers to coach early childhood professionals who are working on adherence to practice standards, or creating a position in order to hire an individual whose job it is to assist colleagues in obtaining and maintaining fidelity to practices. For example, the primary role of an early literacy coach would be to support classroom teachers with the implementation of an early literacy curriculum.

The need for coaching regarding fidelity to practice standards may be identified by the coachee or by a supervisor, administrator, or individual in a dedicated coaching role. If a supervisor or other administrator recognizes the need for this type of professional development opportunity, it would occur when the administrator directly observes the individual's practices or engages in a discussion of the practices with the individual. The next step would be for the supervisor or administrator to invite the coachee to participate in coaching as a professional development opportunity specifically related to adherence to program practice standards. If the individual declines the assistance and support of a coach, the program administrator may use a more traditional supervisory

Practice

Review the program standards of your organization and new evidence-based practices from your discipline or field of practice. Ask a colleague or administrator to then serve as your coach to assist you with evaluating your fidelity to the practice standards or evidence-based practices.

Alternatively, if you are a supervisor or administrator and you observe an individual practicing in a way that is contrary to your program practice standards or evidence-based practices, offer to coach the individual in aligning current practices to the standards or to assign a knowledgeable colleague to do so.

process to ensure practice fidelity, as use of practice standards and evidence-based practices is not optional.

Consider the example of Jodelle, an early literacy coach who has just started working with Stacia, a preschool teacher who has 5 years of experience. During a recent visit, Jodelle brought a box full of materials that she and Stacia had ordered using some of their Early Reading First grant start-up funds, including a lot of new books. On her regular visit the following week, Jodelle slipped into the back of the classroom just as Stacia was finishing reading a story to the children. Naturally, Jodelle excitedly scanned the classroom to see how Stacia had arranged some of the new books and other materials. Although Stacia was in fact reading one of the new books, Jodelle did not see the other books easily accessible to the children in the library area or strategically placed in the centers around the room. Finally she saw the books neatly arranged according to size and shape on a shelf above Stacia's work area, clearly out of the reach of little hands.

The assistant teacher, Amber, began facilitating the transition from book reading time to the centers as Stacia joined Jodelle at the back of the room. Jodelle commented on Stacia's use of the new book and shared her observation that the rest of the books were on the high shelf. Stacia confirmed Jodelle's assumption that she had placed the books up high so that the children could not reach them. Stacia had been so happy to receive the new materials that she wanted to make sure they were protected and would last a long time. Jodelle asked Stacia to analyze how putting the books on the shelf out of the children's reach matched the early literacy program's standards that they had recently discussed and had been working to implement in her classroom. Stacia explained that the book for the shared reading activity was available to the children, but that she was protecting all of the others. Jodelle shared information with Stacia about the importance of having all the books available to the children and together they generated several reasons why and how that system helped to promote the children's early literacy development. They also reflected together on Stacia's concern about the books being destroyed and identified strategies for Stacia to use to help the children learn to explore and use the books. Jodelle and Stacia developed a plan for how they would continue comparing the early literacy program practice standards to the classroom environment. Their plan also included working on Stacia's and Amber's practices related to early literacy when working directly with the children in the classroom.

CONCLUSION

Coaching may be used as part of professional development in both preservice and in-service arenas through the use of expert or peer-to-peer coaching approaches. Coaching can promote knowledge utilization and transfer of new knowledge and skills to the work environment, provide just-in-time learning in response to an immediate need for support, and ensure adherence to program practices and standards. Coaching is a critical component of professional development activities that ensures immediate use and ongoing adherence to the most current research-based practices.

RESOURCES

Dunst, C.J., & Trivette, C.M. (2009). Let's be PALS: An evidence-based approach to professional development. *Infants & Toddlers, 22*(3), 164–176.

This article is based on a number of syntheses and meta-analyses of the research on adult learning methods and provides specific information related to learner and trainer roles and implications for professional development.

Joyce, B., & Showers, B. (2002). *Student achievement through staff development: Fundamentals of school renewal.* White Plains, NY: Longman Publishers.

This text examines the research base behind staff development in education and provides guidance for how to structure professional development activities to maximize teacher transfer of new knowledge and skills to the classroom setting.

National Professional Development Center on Inclusion: http://community.fpg.unc .edu/resources/topics/professional-development

This web site provides a variety of up-to-date resources related to professional development in early childhood and inclusion of children with disabilities in settings with their typically developing peers.

Trivette, C.M., Dunst, C.J., Hamby, D.W., & O'Herin, C.E. (2009). Characteristics and consequences of adult learning methods and strategies. *Practical Evaluation Reports, 2*(1), 1–32.

This report is a research synthesis of the effectiveness of four adult-learning methods (accelerated learning, coaching, guided design, and just-in-time training) compared with six adult learning method characteristics from *How People Learn* (Bransford, Brown, & Cocking, 2000). It includes specific recommendations for training and technical assistance.

Chapter 10

The Future of Coaching in Early Childhood Intervention

The type of coaching discussed in this handbook is expert based (Ackland, 1991), context based (Stober & Grant, 2006), and goal oriented (Ives, 2008) and is used to promote adult learning (Cox, 2006). (See Chapter 1 for more details.) The purpose of using a coaching interaction style is to recognize the current knowledge, ideas, and strengths of the coachee and enhance existing knowledge and practices, help the coachee develop new skills, and promote continuous learning by the coachee. Across varying content, the role of the coach is to provide a supportive and encouraging environment in which the coach and coachee can explore and reflect on the current situation, generate and consider new ideas and feedback, and develop and strengthen abilities to problem solve prioritized topics or situations. The coach strives to build the capacity of the coachee to engage in self-reflection, self-correction, and generalization of new skills rather than developing dependence on the coach for ideas, direction, praise, and sustained success. As was established in Chapter 1, a challenge related to coaching exists across disciplinary boundaries, intervention contexts, and lines of work because practitioners have not embraced a common definition of coaching (Berg & Karlsen, 2007; Ives, 2008). Although burgeoning discussions about coaching are beneficial and critical to expanding the use of the practice, the lack of specificity and clarity surrounding these discussions has created confusion and misunderstanding about what coaching in early childhood looks like (Rush & Shelden, 2008) and especially how coaching practices can be implemented with coachees who have diverse backgrounds and priorities (Schwartz & Sandall, 2010). Further complexity is added to the situation by the wide range of roles and responsibilities of the practitioners who serve as coaches in the field of early childhood.

As discussed in Chapters 1 and 8, different types of early childhood coaches are emerging across content areas with the role of supporting young children through a variety of evidence-based intervention approaches, but all have the same primary

> ### Remember
>
>
>
> The type of coaching described in this text is
>
> - Expert-based
> - Context-based
> - Goal-oriented
> - Used to promote adult learning

target for support, interaction, and intervention: the adults who are involved in the
lives of young children (e.g., parents, teachers, other care providers). More and more
research is confirming the irrefutable concept that the development of children is
enhanced when parents and adult care
providers are engaged with and responsive
to the children in their care (Mahoney,

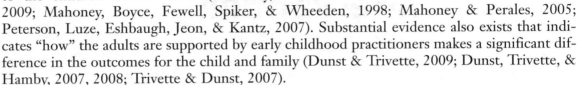

Reflect

How do your practices
match the type of coaching
that is described in this text?
What might you do to adjust your coaching
practices for your intended purpose?

2009; Mahoney, Boyce, Fewell, Spiker, & Wheeden, 1998; Mahoney & Perales, 2005;
Peterson, Luze, Eshbaugh, Jeon, & Kantz, 2007). Substantial evidence also exists that indicates "how" the adults are supported by early childhood practitioners makes a significant difference in the outcomes for the child and family (Dunst & Trivette, 2009; Dunst, Trivette, &
Hamby, 2007, 2008; Trivette & Dunst, 2007).

Coaching requires adult engagement, and several hallmark initiatives use coaches to facil-
itate adult interaction, engagement, and responsiveness with children, such as the P.L.A.Y.
Project (Solomon, Necheles, Ferch, & Bruckman, 2007), the DIR/FT approach (Greenspan &
Wieder, 1998), Parent–Child Interaction Therapy (Brinkmeyer & Eyberg, 2003), the Pyramid
Model for Supporting Social Emotional Competence in Infants and Young Children (Center on
the Social and Emotional Foundations for Early Learning, 2010), and Evidence-Based Early
Intervention (Shelden & Rush, 2010). Although these approaches, as well as a long list of studies that support parent-implemented interventions during everyday learning opportunities, are
clear about the positive outcomes that may be attained, the information about *how* practitioners
teach, support, and coach parents and other adults is inconsistent. The global use of the term
coaching is becoming more common, yet it is not actually helpful for practitioners, researchers,
parents or other care providers. According to a review of substantial data, many studies that
include the use of the term coaching do not specifically state the characteristics of the practice
or describe the specific strategies that the coach uses to promote the coachee's ability to implement evidence-based strategies, techniques or actions. Some studies include descriptors of
coaching actions such as providing encouragement, direct teaching, asking questions, sharing
affirmation, delivering feedback, and engaging in active listening. Other studies, however,
describe strategies such as telling the parent what to do without mentioning a reflective process
to precede or at least accompany the provision of directive feedback (e.g., Brinkmeyer &
Eyberg, 2003; Seifer, Clark, & Sameroff, 1991).

Alternatively, a study by Woods, Kashinath, and Goldstein (2004) examined caregiver-
implemented teaching strategies that were used in daily routines, the authors described in
detail how the caregivers were supported to learn new responsive teaching strategies.
Although the study does not mention coaching, the detailed description in the procedures
section of the article (pp. 181–182) clearly depicts the use of practices that employ observation, feedback, reflection, action/practice, and joint planning. The type of description provided by Woods and colleagues helps to identify specific characteristics of the practices that
were implemented during the study and is a recommended format for future studies. The field
of early childhood intervention clearly sees positive outcomes associated with the use of
coaching (Dunst, Trivette, Hamby, & O'Herin, 2009; Peterson et al., 2007); however, significant progress cannot occur without acceptance of a standard definition of coaching that is
based on identified evidence-based characteristics.

This text has provided an operational definition of coaching delineated by a set of evidence-based characteristics that, when implemented over time, build the capacity of the

coachee to self-reflect, generate new ideas and solutions, implement desired actions, and evaluate the effectiveness of his or her efforts. The use of coaching as an interaction style is not a new concept (Campbell, 1997; Dinnebeil, McInerney, Roth, & Ramasway, 2001; Hanft & Pilkington, 2000; Rush, 2000; Rush, Shelden, & Hanft, 2003). Additional questions and challenges, however, remain beyond the step of identifying an agreed-upon definition of the practice. These inquiries are not about whether coaching is effective; it is. (See Chapter 2 for more information regarding evidence-based characteristics of coaching.) Nor are the challenges insurmountable; they are not. Rather, they are discussed to provide further understanding of specific coaching strategies and techniques, expand information about the uses of coaching, and identify additional information to assist practitioners in being successful coaches across a wide variety of environments. This chapter will explore these questions and challenges and propose recommendations for deepening the understanding of coaching as an evidence-based practice in early childhood intervention.

QUESTIONS FROM THE FIELD

Answers to questions about specific nuances of coaching practices are important to support practitioners in the field of early childhood intervention. Typically, as practitioners learn more about coaching, new questions from the field arise. Answers to questions about the evidence-based characteristics of coaching that yield favorable outcomes for young children and their families will not only help practitioners, but will support continued research about the use of coaching in early childhood intervention.

Question 1: Use of Observation and Action Characteristics over Time

The characteristics of evidence-based coaching are clear. (See Chapters 1, 2, and 5 for more details.) Additional information is needed, however, regarding the benefits of the presence of specific characteristics of coaching over time. For example, research shows that the coach must use observation during the course of a coaching relationship. Limited information is available about the optimal frequency of observation and action/practice characteristics that are related to maximizing outcomes for the coachee and the children in his or her care. In a recent meta-analysis, Kaminski, Valle, Filene, and Boyle (2008) reported that parent training programs in which parents practiced skills in sessions with their children in the presence of a practitioner had larger treatment effects than those that did not. Peterson and colleagues (2007) reported enhanced parental engagement when coaches used observation during home visits. These studies provide meaningful data to inform early childhood practices. Additional studies, however, are needed to expand the understanding of frequency of observation during coaching conversations.

Reflect

How frequently do you use the characteristics of observation and action over time, and how does this practice assist you and the coachee to achieve the intended outcomes?

Question 2: Understanding Nuances of Joint Planning During Coaching Conversations

Joint planning is a required characteristic of coaching during every coaching conversation. Additional information about the nuances of developing a joint plan would be helpful to practitioners. For example, it seems reasonable that having the coachee rather than the coach state the plan for what will happen between visits would provide more opportunity for follow-through and assist in the coachee's implementation of the plan. Studies that examine specific joint planning strategies would provide helpful informa-

> **Reflect**
>
> How do you document, the joint plan and what strategies do you find to be most effective for the coachees whom you support?

tion to early childhood practitioners across a wide variety of environments. Another question related to joint planning is whether coachees with particular characteristics respond more positively or rapidly when a joint plan is written down between visits. If differences exist in responses among different types of coachees, then who should physically write the plan, the coach or coachee? These are examples of a few questions about coaching characteristics that require further study in order to better inform early childhood coaches about effective implementation of coaching.

Question 3: Coaching in Group Settings: On-the-Fly and Just-in-Time

When they are learning about coaching, most early childhood practitioners are quick to question how one can coach a teacher who is busy managing his or her classroom or a child care provider who might be less than enthusiastic about the coach's presence in the child care setting. As described in Chapter 8, coaching teachers has challenges that are most often due to the very busy nature of the environment. Teachers frequently cannot carve out time in their schedule to focus exclusively on having a coaching interaction. Experience and observation has shown that the strategies of coaching-on-the-fly and just-in-time coaching are effective methods of working with teachers in early childhood settings. More information is needed, however, to assist practitioners in developing a deeper understanding of how to implement these strategies. Practitioner factors also affect their ability to coach teachers in group settings. Coaches must be flexible and patient in order to support teachers in busy environments where many variables exist that cannot be controlled (e.g., child needs, classroom schedules, teacher preferences) and to assist teachers in managing the environmental demands while also providing them with effective support. (See Chapter 3 for more information on characteristics of coaches.)

> **Reflect**
>
> What are the characteristics of your coaching practices and interactions with teachers that make the experiences more or less successful?

Question 4: Supervisors' Use of Coaching

As was discussed in Chapter 4, reflective supervision has features and characteristics in common with coaching. Chapter 4 also established that supervisors can and do use coaching and that reflective supervision can bring many benefits to both the coach and coachee (Dinnebeil, Buysse, Rush, & Eggbeer, 2008; Fenichel, 1992). Coaching, however, is a nonhierarchical interaction style. When a coach is the coachee's supervisor, a hierarchical nature is inherent in the relationship. Studies that provide additional information about how supervisors can use coaching strategies would help to support supervisors in the field of early childhood intervention.

Question 5: Additional Data Regarding Characteristics of Effective Coaches

Reflect

If you serve in a supervisory role, how do you distinguish between coaching conversations and supervisor/supervisee interactions?

As was explored in Chapter 3, more data are needed about specific characteristics of effective coaches. Developing a true partnership is key to having an effective coaching relationship. Challenges to developing a coaching partnership (e.g., time, language barriers, payment issues, parent trust) are easy to identify. Interpersonal attributes of the coach, however, may be a primary obstacle influencing parent–practitioner communication, which is of course an essential element to any coaching relationship (Blue-Banning, Summers, Frankland, Nelson, & Beegle, 2004; Brady, Peters, Gamel-McCormick, & Venuto, 2004; McWilliam, Tocci, & Harbin, 1998). McWilliam (2010) provides an excellent discussion on strategies for promoting effective communication with families.

Coaching is an interaction style that requires less directiveness on the part of the practitioner. Coaching promotes two-way reflective conversations that meet parents, teachers, and other care providers where they are and focus on topics they have prioritized. The interpersonal characteristics of the coach are important factors that contribute significantly to a coach's ability to coach. Clearly, some individuals find it easier to learn and use coaching than do others. Learning more about the specific characteristics that a good coach needs will assist practitioners to engage in deeper self-reflection regarding both their natural propensities and behaviors and skills that they may need to learn, which will assist them in coaching families and professional colleagues.

Reflect

What characteristics of effective coaches do you exhibit, and how will you modify your current interaction style to be an even more effective coach?

The level of education required to be an effective coach is a common issue. Due to flexible program requirements, early childhood coaches may have a variety of educational backgrounds and levels of preservice preparation (Stayton et al., 2009). For example, depending on the program, the position of "teacher" may be occupied by an individual with a doctoral degree or by someone with no formal postsecondary education. Limited data exist on the effect of a coach's educational level on the intended outcomes. As was discussed in Chapters 1 and 2, data exist to support the effectiveness of peer coaches across a variety of levels of education (e.g., students, teachers, parents, physicians). Additional information regarding education of expert coaches would clarify the effects of content knowledge on outcomes of coaching, the types of training and technical assistance that should be required for use of coaching, and the relationship between overall ability to implement coaching and level of education.

CHALLENGES TO THE FIELD

Several challenges are present across a variety of contexts in which early childhood practitioners serve as coaches. The challenges discussed in this section are not related solely to the use of coaching in early childhood intervention, as many programs have faced these or similar issues since their initial implementation. Coaching practices, however, bring many of the challenging issues to the forefront of program implementation and test the systems' abilities to adapt and change in light of new evidence that requires attention to a host of practice and fiscal implications.

Challenge 1: Coaching Families from a Variety of Cultures

Many programs and practitioners across the country are faced with a changing demographic of the children and families enrolled in early childhood programs. More families who do not speak English and/or come from a variety of diverse backgrounds are receiving formalized services and supports (Hanson & Lynch, 2010; U.S. Census Bureau, 2010). Appreciating cultural diversity is a huge challenge for many programs and practitioners (Hanson & Lynch, 2010; Lynch, 2004; Lynch & Hanson, 2004). Coaches must understand the beliefs and social mores of the families they support in order to provide family-centered services.

Effective use of a coaching interaction style requires clear and effective communication between coaching partners. If an early childhood practitioner does not speak the language of the family involved in the program, then the coach must partner with an interpreter. Acceptance of and programmatic support for the required use of interpreters is a necessary change for many early childhood programs. Programs often view the use of interpreters as a luxury or rely solely on informal resources that a particular family or community may have identified. Programs also report the use of grant funds or donations to support limited budgets for interpreting services. Interventionists who are not using coaching practices have described writing notes, drawing pictures, and even relying on nonverbal communication as the primary means of interacting with parents of the children they are supporting. These descriptions, however, are associated with practitioner–child-focused practices or models and will not suffice when practitioners use coaching as the interaction style with parents and other care providers. The fiscal implications related to the required provision of interpreter services must be addressed at a systems level to ensure that programs are effectively supporting families from a variety of diverse backgrounds.

The increased use of interpreters in early childhood programs not only has fiscal implications for national programs, state agencies and community programs, it also spurs questions related to the programs' and practitioners' abilities to understand the unique needs of families across different cultures and recognize how to partner with them effectively around supporting their children (Barrera & Kramer, 2009). Learning more about how families from a variety of cultures view the role of early childhood practitioners is an important aspect for programs and practitioners using coaching. Coaches may ask more and different types of questions than practitioners who are not using coaching; therefore, they need to understand how this interaction style might be perceived by individuals whose cultures differ from that of the coach. Coaches use strategies and engage in conversations that encourage the coachee to generate, implement, and evaluate his or her own ideas. This approach may be different from what is expected or understood by people from other cultures or backgrounds. Additional research on the impact of using coaching as the adult interaction style with families whose cultures differ from that of the coach is needed to enhance the ability of early childhood programs to maximize outcomes for all young children and families in their care. Hanson and Lynch (2010) provide more information regarding communicating effectively with families from diverse backgrounds.

> ### *Reflect*
>
> How do you come to understand the values, beliefs, and cultures of families, teachers, or other care providers with whom you work?

Specific information regarding the effects of coaching when using interpreters is needed to improve practitioners' abilities to effectively partner with parents and teachers from a variety of diverse backgrounds. Common sense suggests that the use of an interpreter will make the coaching process more complicated and lengthy simply because an additional communication partner has been added to the mix. Guidelines for successful interactions using interpreters are available for practitioners (Ohtake, Santos, & Fowler, 2001). No data are available, however, to inform early childhood practitioners about how the presence of an interpreter affects coaching strategies. Observation and experience have shown that practitioners tend to use an increased number of closed, yes/no questions when partnering with interpreters to support family members who do not speak English. These yes/no questions often have suggestions embedded within them, such as "Would you be willing to put him in his highchair to eat meals?" or "Will you let him walk down the steps instead of carrying him?" These types of coaxing questions increase the directiveness of the conversations and limit the coachee's opportunities for reflection. (See Chapter 5 for more information.) Due to the increased time that is required to have coaching conversations when interpreters are involved, coaches may neglect to save adequate time for true joint planning. The result may be no plan being developed or a directive statement from the coach to the coachee stating what the plan will be. Additional research about coaching using interpreters would be of great benefit to many programs and practitioners who are working with non–English-speaking families.

Challenge 2: Billability

In the field of early childhood intervention, therapists frequently are required to obtain reimbursement for their services by billing private insurance or Medicaid. Third-party payers reimburse for medically necessary services that require expertise to remediate deficits and promote skill acquisition, which is one of the ultimate outcomes of early intervention. When therapists are faced with information about using coaching in early intervention, they often comment initially about a perceived inability to obtain reimbursement if coaching is being used. Coaching is not a service delivery model. Coaching is a style of interaction used by a coach to build the capacity of the coachee to maximize his or her competence and confidence in supporting a child's participation in real-life settings or obtaining needed resources. In other words, coaching is the way that an early childhood practitioner interacts with or communicates with the adults in the life of the child who is enrolled in early invention. For physicians, the term *bedside manner* is defined as the way that a physician interacts with or communicates with his or her patients (Wikipedia, 2010). The manner in which a physician interacts with a patient cannot be dictated by a third-party payer. Hence, the way that an early childhood practitioner interacts with the adults in the lives of children who are enrolled in the program (e.g., parents, teachers, child care providers) cannot be dictated by the payer as reimbursable or not.

Part C of the Individuals with Disabilities Education Improvement Act of 2004 (PL 108-446) requires that supports and services for eligible children be provided in the child's natural environments and be designed to promote the competence and confidence of care providers to enhance the child's growth and development through participation in everyday activities. Coaching is an evidence-based strategy that the practitioner uses to interact with parents and care providers to maximize child progress when the practitioner is and is not present. In early intervention, however, the practitioner is not billing the third-party payer for how he or she interacts with the parent or care provider (i.e., coaching), but rather for the time and expertise that are necessary to achieve the developmental progress of the child or to assist a parent in identifying needed resources.

Mediating parents' knowledge and skills is an added benefit of coaching practices. Other strategies create dependency on service providers, but coaching builds the capacity of a parent or care provider. Due to this added benefit, one might expect coaching to be the interaction style that is preferred by third-party payers. Billability of services is a systems issue that must be addressed in order to ensure that programs and practitioners are supporting the adults in the lives of the children enrolled in a variety of programs. The upshot of the actual challenge is the understanding that coaching support for parents and other care providers is a required component of medically necessary services and that therapist–child-focused interventions (which are most commonly paid for by third-party payers) do not capitalize on what is known about infant and toddler learning, growth, and development.

Challenge 3: Professional Development

One of the major challenges facing the field of early childhood is the issue of professional development, both at preservice and in-service levels (Bruder, 2010; Bruder, Mogro-Wilson, Stayton, & Dietrich, 2009; Campbell, Chiarello, Wilcox, & Milbourne, 2009; Clark, Polichino, Jackson, & the Commission on Practice, 2004; Dunst, 2009; Stayton et al., 2009; Woods & Snyder, 2009). An ongoing challenge for institutions of higher learning is bridging the evidence-based information gap and ensuring that new graduates, regardless of their discipline or level of education, are prepared to enter a work force with the most current skill set that is available. Practice standards are available from professional organizations, special interest groups, and academic councils that were developed to provide guidance, accountability, and evaluation of professional practices (American Federation of Teachers, 2002; American Speech-Language-Hearing Association, 2008; Chiarello & Effgen, 2006; Council for Exceptional Children, 2003; Hyson, 2003; Sandall, Hemmeter, Smith, & McLean, 2005; Workgroup on Principles and Practices in Natural Environments, 2007). Due to a complex set of issues in the realm of higher education, however, great variability continues to exist regarding the curricular content for professionals who are training to work in an early childhood arena, in spite of increased efforts for accountability and use of evidence-based practices. (See Chapter 9 for more details.)

In addition, the adoption of an evidence-based framework for practicing interventionists remains an obstacle in the early childhood work force (Bruder, 2010; Bruder et al., 2009; Campbell et al., 2009; Dunst, 2009; Trivette et al., 2009). Valid reasons exist for this mismatch, including but not limited to lack of access to evidence-based professional development activities, fiscal constraints limiting provision and requirements for ongoing training and credentialing, and competing requirements in preservice education programs (Bruder, 2010). Detailed information about how to provide evidence-based professional development activities is available (Fixen, Naoom, Blasé, Friedman, & Wallace, 2005; Guskey, 1986; Joyce & Showers, 2002; Reiss, 2007; Trivette et al., 2009; Winton & McCollum, 2008). Early intervention practitioners indicate, however, that their preferred (and most frequently accessed) venues for continuing education are workshops and conferences, rather than other options that are more consistent with the evidence base for adult learning and implementation of a new practice or innovation (Campbell et al., 2009; Fixen et al., 2005; Trivette et al., 2009).

Regardless of their disciplinary background, information about how to empower families is a core area of knowledge and skill that practitioners who are entering the field of early childhood need in order to effectively support young children and their families (Dunst, 2009). Yet data exist indicating that family-centered practices are not easily accepted or learned by early intervention practitioners, especially therapists (Lawlor & Mattingly, 1998;

Wilkins, Pollock, Rochon, & Law, 2001). Substantial information is available on the powerful impact of parents on child outcomes (Dunst et al., 2008; Mahoney, 2009; Shonkoff & Phillips, 2000). The data on the effectiveness of implementation of capacity-building strategies for supporting families are particularly well respected and well founded (Dunst et al., 2008; Turnbull et al., 2007). Early childhood coaches, however, need a strong conceptual framework of family-centered care regardless of their background (e.g., therapists, literacy coaches, teachers). Understanding promotional strategies that build the confidence and competence of parents and other care providers is essential to providing evidence-based supports and to being a good coach. University programs that prepare occupational therapists (OTs), physical therapists (PTs), speech-language pathologists (SLPs), early childhood teachers, early literacy specialists, and early childhood special education (ECSE) teachers to work with young children and their families must make time in the curricula to support the knowledge, skills, and understanding of promoting practitioner–parent partnerships. Early childhood practitioners should graduate with a strong, foundational knowledge of what works. Empowering families works, and the information is available to teach practitioners how to do it.

CONCLUSION

In 2008, the National Early Childhood Technical Assistance Center published the guidance document *Seven Key Principles: Looks Like/Doesn't Look Like* (Workgroup on Principles and Practices in Natural Environments). One of the key principles states that the primary role of the service provider in early intervention is to work with and support the family members and care-

> ### Reflect
>
> What additional training and support do you need in order to become a more successful coach, and what is your plan for meeting those needs?

givers in a child's life. The document states that intervention "looks like" coaching and supporting the family to carry out strategies and activities that are developed with team members in order to support everyday learning opportunities for the child, instead of therapist–child focused sessions. Mounting evidence of the effectiveness of parent-implemented strategies used as a natural part of everyday learning for young children and their families leads to an important implication for the use of coaching in early childhood (Dunst, 2006; Kaiser, Hancock, & Nietfeld, 2000; McCollum & Hemmeter, 1997; Mahoney, 2009; Mahoney et al., 1998; Mahoney & Perales, 2003, 2005; Moes & Frea, 2002; Peterson et al., 2007; Schertz & Odom, 2007).

What, however, are the characteristics of effective interventions for teaching parents parent-implemented strategies? How are practitioners approaching teachers who are interested in learning new strategies or enhancing existing skills? This handbook is about using evidence-based characteristics of coaching as an intervention for supporting parents and teachers in learning and implementing high-quality parent or teacher-mediated practices and strategies to support child learning, growth, and development. In order to effectively implement evidence-based coaching in early childhood, specific characteristics must be present over time to build the capacity of the coachee. Use of coaching to support parents and teachers in implementing parent- or teacher-mediated practices requires the use of joint planning, observation of the coachee and the coach (including intentional modeling), action or practice between visits on the part of the coachee, feedback, and most importantly guided opportunities for reflection.

A promotional way of thinking may be a new and challenging way of practicing for many early childhood professionals. When they embrace it, however, they may find that it is an empowerment mindset that can result in a career-altering shift. Believing that all coachees have strengths, competence, and the capacity to learn is essential for an effective coaching relationship. A coach must understand, furthermore, that when a coachee lacks competence, it is not the fault of that individual, but a consequence of lack of opportunity or adequate support from a social system (Dunst & Trivette, 1994). When coaches function using this paradigm or philosophy, options for success are magnified. A reflective coach continually searches for new ways and opportunities to support the competence and confidence of the coachee, no matter what content or topic is being addressed.

Learning is an exciting journey. Viewing the journey with anticipation, curiosity, and perseverance adds to the enjoyment of the experience. Recall the SLP and PT who were mentioned in Chapter 1: We have come a long way in developing our understanding of providing evidence-based, family-centered services. Learning how to effectively partner with families has been both energizing and humbling for us. Although we are very different in our approaches, this SLP and PT have much in common, especially a commitment to lifelong learning. We hope that this book will prove to be a helpful and beneficial tool for early childhood practitioners who themselves are lifelong learners, dedicated to implementing evidence-based practices to support young children and their families.

RESOURCES

The following are web sites of other initiatives, programs, and approaches that use coaches to facilitate adult interaction, engagement, and responsiveness with children:

DIR/Floortime approach: http://www.icdl.com/dirFloortime/overview/index.shtml

Parent–Child Interaction Therapy (PCIT): http://pcit.phhp.ufl.edu/

P.L.A.Y. Project: http://www.playproject.org/

Pyramid Model for Supporting Social Emotional Competence in Infants and Young Children at the Center on the Social and Emotional Foundations for Early Learning: http://www.vanderbilt.edu/csefel

References

Ackland, R. (1991). A review of the peer coaching literature. *Journal of Staff Development, 12*(1), 22–27.

American Federation of Teachers. (2002). *At the starting line: Early childhood education programs in the 50 states.* Washington, DC: American Federation of Teachers. Retrieved from http://www.aft.org/pdfs/ece/startingline1200 .pdf

American Speech-Language-Hearing Association (ASHA). (2008). *Roles and responsibilities of speech-language pathologists in early intervention: Guidelines* [Technical Report]. Rockville, MD: Author. Retrieved from http://www .asha.org/docs/html/gl2008-00293.html

Anderson, N.A., & Radencich, M.C. (2001). The value of feedback in an early field experience: Peer, teacher and supervisor coaching. *Action in Teacher Education, 23*(3), 66–74.

Auerbach, J.E. (2006). Cognitive coaching. In D.R. Stober & A.M. Grant (Eds.), *Evidence-based coaching handbook: Putting best practices to work for your clients* (pp. 103–128). Hoboken, NJ: John Wiley & Sons.

Augustus F. Hawkins-Robert T. Stafford Elementary and Secondary School Improvement Amendments of 1988. PL 100-297, §1(a), April 28, 1988, 102 Stat. 130.

Bailey, D.B., Jr., Hebbeler, K., Scarborough, A., Spiker, D., & Malik, S. (2004). First experiences with early intervention: A national perspective. *Pediatrics, 113*, 887–896.

Bailey, D.B., Jr., Palsha, S.A., & Huntington, G.S. (1990). Preservice preparation of special educators to serve infants and toddlers with handicaps and their families: Current status and training needs. *Journal of Early Intervention, 14*, 43–54.

Bailey, D.B., Jr., Simeonsson, R.J., Yoder, D.E., & Huntington, G.S. (1990). Preparing professionals to serve infants and toddlers with handicaps and their families: An integrative analysis across eight disciplines. *Exceptional Children, 57*, 26–35.

Bandura, A., & Locke, E.A. (2003). Negative self-efficacy and goal effects revisited. *Journal of Applied Psychology, 88*(1), 87–99.

Barrera, I., & Kramer, L. (2009). *Using skilled dialogue to transform challenging interactions: Honoring identity, voice, and connection.* Baltimore: Paul H. Brookes Publishing Co.

Barrick, M.R., & Mount, M.K. (1991). The big five personality dimensions and job performance; a meta-analysis. *Personnel Psychology, 44*, 1–26.

Beckwith, L., Rodning, C., & Cohen, S. (1992). Preterm children at early adolescence and continuity and discontinuity in maternal responsiveness from infancy. *Child Development, 63*(5), 1198–1208.

Bell, S.T. (2004). *Setting the stage for effective teams: A meta-analysis of team design variables and team effectiveness.* Unpublished doctoral dissertation, Texas A & M University, College Station, TX.

Berg, M.E., & Karlsen, J.T. (2007). Mental models in project management coaching. *Engineering Management Journal, 19*(3), 3–13.

Bersin, J., & O'Leonard, K. (2005). Performance support systems. *T + D, 59*(4), 67–69.

Black, L.L., Suarez, E.C., & Medina, S. (2004). Helping students help themselves: Strategies for successful mentoring relationships. *Counselor Education & Supervision, 44*, 44–55.

Blue-Banning, M., Summers, J.A., Frankland, H.C., Nelson, L.L., & Beegle, G. (2004). Dimensions of family and professional partnerships: Constructive guidelines for collaboration. *Exceptional Children, 70*, 167–184.

Bornstein, M.H., Tamis-LeMonda, C.S., & Haynes, O.M. (1999). First words in the second year: Continuity, stability, and models of concurrent and predictive correspondence in vocabulary and verbal responsiveness across age and context. *Infant Behavior and Development, 22*(1), 65–85.

Bowman, C.L., & McCormick, S. (2000). Comparison of peer coaching versus traditional supervision effects. *The Journal of Educational Research, 93*(4), 256–261.

Brady, S.J., Peters, D.L., Gamel-McCormick, M., & Venuto, N. (2004). Types and patterns of professional–family talk in home-based early intervention. *Journal of Early Intervention, 26*, 146–159.

Brandt, R. (1987). On teachers coaching teachers: A conversation with Bruce Joyce. *Educational Leadership, 44*, 12–17.

Bransford, J.D., Brown, A.L., & Cocking, R.R. (2000). *How people learn: Brain, mind, experience, and school.* Washington, DC: National Academies Press.

Brewer, E.J., Jr., McPherson, M., Magrab, P., & Hutchins, V. (1989). Family-centered, community-based, coordinated care for children with special health care needs. *Pediatrics, 83,* 1055–1060.

Brinkmeyer, M.Y., & Eyberg, S.M. (2003). Parent–child interaction therapy for oppositional children. In A.E. Kazdin & J.R. Weisz (Eds.), *Evidence-based psychotherapies for children and adolescents* (pp. 204–223). New York: Guilford Press.

Brown, W.H., Odom, S.L., Li, S., & Zercher, C. (1999). Ecobehavioral assessment in early childhood programs: A portrait of preschool inclusion. *Journal of Special Education, 33,* 138–153.

Bruce, C.D., & Ross, J.A. (2008). A model for increasing reform implementation and teacher efficacy: Teacher peer coaching in grades 3 and 6 mathematics. *Canadian Journal of Education, 31*(2), 346–370.

Bruder, M. (1993). The provision of early intervention and early childhood special education within community early childhood programs: Characteristics of effective service delivery. *Topics in Early Childhood Special Education, 13,* 19–37.

Bruder, M.B. (2010). Early childhood intervention: A promise to children and families for their future. *Exceptional Children, 76*(3), 339–355.

Bruder, M.B., & Dunst, C.J. (1999/2000, December/January). Expanding learning opportunities for infants and toddlers in natural environments: A chance to reconceptualize early intervention. *Zero to Three, 20*(3), 34–36.

Bruder, M.B., Mogro-Wilson, C.M., Stayton, V.D., & Dietrich, S.L. (2009). The national status of in-service professional development systems for early intervention and early childhood special education practitioners. *Infants and Young Children, 22*(1), 13–20.

Burley-Allen, M. (1995). *Listening: The forgotten skill.* New York: John Wiley & Sons.

Buysse, V., & Wesley, P.W. (2004). *Consultation in early childhood settings.* Baltimore: Paul H. Brookes Publishing Co.

Buysse, V., & Wesley, P. (2006). *Evidence-based practice in the early childhood field.* Washington, DC: Zero to Three Press.

Buysse, V., Winton, P., & Rous, B. (2009). Reaching consensus on a definition of professional development for the early childhood field. *Topics in Early Childhood Special Education, 28,* 235–243.

Campbell, P.H. (2004). Participation-based services: Promoting children's participation in natural settings. *Young Exceptional Children, 8,* 20–29.

Campbell, S.K. (1997). Therapy programs for children that last a lifetime. *Physical and Occupational Therapy in Pediatrics, 17*(1), 1–15.

Campbell, P.H., Chiarello, L., Wilcox, M.J., & Milbourne, S. (2009). Preparing therapists as effective practitioners in early intervention. *Infants and Young Children, 22*(4), 21–31.

Campbell, P.H., & Halbert, J. (2002). Between research and practice: Provider perspectives on early intervention. *Topics in Early Childhood Special Education, 22,* 213–226.

Campbell, P.H., & Sawyer, L.B. (2007). Supporting learning opportunities in natural settings through participation-based services. *Journal of Early Intervention, 29*(4), 287–305.

Cegelka, P., Fitch, S., & Alvarado, J. (2001, March). *The coach-of-coaches model for preparing rural special education teachers.* Paper presented at the Growing Partnerships for Rural Special Education, San Diego.

Center on the Social and Emotional Foundations for Early Learning. (2010). Retrieved from http://www.vanderbilt.edu/csefel

Chai, A.Y., Zhang, C., & Bisberg, M. (2006). Rethinking natural environment practice: Implications from examining various interpretations and approaches. *Early Childhood Education Journal, 34,* 203–208.

Chiarello, L., & Effgen, S.K. (2006). Updated competencies for physical therapists working in early intervention. *Pediatric Physical Therapy, 8*(2), 148–67.

Clark, G., Polichino, J., Jackson, L., & the Commission on Practice. (2004). Occupational therapy services in early intervention and school-based programs. *American Journal of Occupational Therapy, 58*(6), 681–685.

Costa, A.L., & Garmston, R.J. (1994). *Cognitive coaching: A foundation for renaissance schools.* Norwood, MA: Christopher-Gordon.

Council for Exceptional Children. (2003). *What every special educator must know: Ethics, standards, and guidelines for special educators* (5th ed.). Arlington, VA: Author.

Cox, E. (2006). An adult learning approach to coaching. In D.R. Stober & A.M. Grant (Eds.), *Evidence-based coaching handbook: Putting best practices to work for your clients* (pp. 193–217). Hoboken, NJ: John Wiley & Sons.

Cox, E., & Ledgerwood, G. (2003, Summer). Editorial: The new profession. *International Journal of Evidence Based Coaching and Mentoring, 1*(1).

Daniels, D.C. (2002, May). Becoming a reflective practitioner. *Middle School Journal, 52–56.*

Davis, K., Middaugh, D., & Davis, R. (2008). First down! Keeping your team in the game with great coaching. *Nursing Management, 17,* 434–436.

DeGangi, G.A., Wietlisbach, S., Poisson, S., Stein, E., & Royeen, C. (1994). The impact of culture and socioeconomic status on family-professional collaboration: Challenges and solutions. *Topics in Early Childhood Special Education, 14,* 503–520.

Delany, J.C., & Arredondo, D.E. (1998, October). *Using collegial coaching and reflection as mechanisms for changing school cultures,* Paper presented at the Annual Meeting of the University Council for Educational Administration, St. Louis. (ERIC Document Reproduction Service No. ED430903)

Dinnebeil, L.A., Buysse, V., Rush, D., & Eggbeer, L. (2008). Skills for effective collaboration. In P. Winton, J. McCollum, & C. Catlett (Eds.), *Effective professionals: Evidence and application in early childhood and early intervention* (pp. 227–245). Washington, DC: Zero to Three Press.

Dinnebeil, L.A., Hale, L.M., & Rule, S. (1996). A qualitative analysis of parents' and service coordinators' descriptions of variables that influence collaborative relationships. *Topics in Early Childhood Special Education, 16,* 322–347.

Dinnebeil, L.A., Hale, L.M., & Rule, S. (1999). Early intervention program practices that support collaboration. *Topics in Early Childhood Special Education, 19,* 225–235.

Dinnebeil, L.A., McInerney, W.F., Roth, J., & Ramasway, V. (2001). Itinerant early childhood special education services: Service delivery in one state. *Journal of Early Intervention, 24,* 35–44.

Dollaghan, C.A. (2004). Evidence-based practice in communication disorders: What do we know, and when do we know it? *Journal of Communication Disorders, 37,* 391–400.

Donovan, M.S., Bransford, J.D., & Pellegrino, J.W. (Eds.). (1999). *How people learn: Bridging research and practice.* Washington, DC: National Academies Press.

Doyle, J.S. (1999). *The business coach: A game plan for the new work environment.* New York: John Wiley & Sons.

Dunst, C.J. (2006). Parent-mediated everyday child learning opportunities: I. Foundations and operationalization. *CASEinPoint, 2*(2), 1–10. Retrieved from http://www.fippcase.org/caseinpoint/caseinpoint_vol2_no2.pdf

Dunst, C.J. (2009). Implications of evidence-based practices for personnel preparation development in early childhood development. *Infants and Young Children, 22*(1), 44–53.

Dunst, C.J., Bruder, M.B., Trivette, C.M., & Hamby, D.W. (2006). Everyday activity settings, natural learning environments, and early intervention practices. *Journal of Policy and Practice in Intellectual Disabilities, 3,* 3–10.

Dunst, C.J., Hamby, D.W., & Brookfield, J. (2007). Modeling the effects of early childhood intervention variables on parent and family well-being. *Journal of Applied Quantitative Methods, 2,* 268–288.

Dunst, C.J., Hamby, D., Trivette, C.M., Raab, M., & Bruder, M.B. (2000). Everyday family and community life and children's naturally occurring learning opportunities. *Journal of Early Intervention, 23,* 151–164.

Dunst, C.J., Herter, S., & Shields, H. (2000). Interest-based natural learning opportunities. In S. Sandall & M. Ostrosky (Eds.), *Natural Environments and Inclusion* (Young Exceptional Children Monograph Series No. 2) (pp. 37–48). Longmont, CO: Sopris West.

Dunst, C.J., & Trivette, C.M. (2009). Capacity-building family-systems intervention practices. *Journal of Family Social Work, 12,* 119–143.

Dunst, C.J., & Trivette, C.M. (1994). What is effective helping? In C.J. Dunst, C.M. Trivette, & A.G. Deal (Eds.), *Supporting and strengthening families: Methods, strategies and practices* (pp. 162–170). Cambridge, MA: Brookline Books.

Dunst, C.J., & Trivette, C.M. (1996). Empowerment, effective help-giving practices and family-centered care. *Pediatric Nursing, 22,* 334–337, 343.

Dunst, C.J., Trivette, C.M., & Cutspec, P.A. (2002). Toward an operational definition of evidence-based practices. *Centerscope, 1*(1), 1–10.

Dunst, C.J., Trivette, C.M., & Deal, A.G. (1994). Resource-based family-centered intervention practices. In C.J. Dunst, C.M. Trivette, & A.G. Deal (Eds.), *Supporting and strengthening families: Methods, strategies, and practices* (pp. 140–151). Cambridge, MA: Brookline Books.

Dunst, C.J., Trivette, C.M., & Hamby, D.W. (2006). *Family support program quality and parent, family and child benefits* (Winterberry Monograph Series). Asheville, NC: Winterberry Press.

Dunst, C.J., Trivette, C.M., & Hamby, D.W. (2007). Meta-analysis of family-centered help-giving practices research. *Mental Retardation and Developmental Disabilities Research Reviews, 13,* 370–378.

Dunst, C.J., Trivette, C.M., & Hamby, D.W. (2008). *Research synthesis and meta-analysis of studies of family-centered practices.* Asheville, NC: Winterberry Press.

Dunst, C.J., Trivette, C.M., Humphries, T., Raab, M., & Roper, N. (2001). Contrasting approaches to natural learning environment interventions. *Infants and Young Children, 14*(2), 48–63.

Dunst, C.J., Trivette, C.M., & Johanson, C. (1994). Parent-professional collaboration and partnerships. In C.J. Dunst, C.M. Trivette, & A.G. Deal (Eds.), *Supporting and strengthening families: Vol. 1. Methods, strategies, and practices* (pp. 197–211). Cambridge, MA: Brookline Books.

Dunst, C. J., Trivette, C. M., & LaPointe, N. (1994). Meaning and key characteristics of empowerment. In C.J. Dunst, C.M. Trivette, & A.G. Deal (Eds.), *Supporting and strengthening families: Methods, strategies, and practices* (pp. 12–28). Cambridge, MA: Brookline Books.

Dunst, C.J., Trivette, C.M., McInerney, M., Holland-Coviello, R., Masiello, T., Helsel, F., et al. (2008). Measuring training and practice fidelity in capacity-building scaling-up initiatives. *CELLpapers, 3*(1), 1–11.

Economic Opportunity Act of 1964, PL 88-452, 42 U.S.C. §§ 2701 *et seq. Statutes at large, 63.*

Education of the Handicapped Act Amendments of 1986, PL 99-457, 20 U.S.C. §§ 1401 *et seq.*

Elementary and Secondary Education Act of 1988 (PL 100-297)

Ellinger, A.D., Hamlin, R.G., & Beattie, R.S. (2008). *Coaching, HRD, and OD: Towards three 'silo' fields of practice or a single 'unified' profession?* Paper presented at the Academy of Human Resource Development International Research Conference in the Americas, Panama City, FL. (ERIC Document Reproduction Service No. ED501611)

Fenichel, E. (1992). *Learning through supervision and mentorship to support the development of infants, toddlers, and their families: A sourcebook.* Washington, DC: Zero to Three.

Ferraro, J.M. (2000). *Reflective practice and professional development.* Washington, DC: ERIC Clearinghouse on Teaching and Teacher Education. (ERIC Document Reproduction Service No. ED449120)

Fixen, D.L., Naoom, S.F., Blasé, K.A., Friedman, R.M., & Wallace, F. (2005). *Implementation research: A synthesis of the literature.* Tampa, FL: University of South Florida.

Flaherty, J. (1999). *Coaching: Evoking excellence in others.* Boston: Butterworth-Heinemann.

Forunies, F.F. (2000). *Coaching for improved work performance.* New York: McGraw-Hill.

Fox, L., Dunlap, G., Hemmeter, M.L., Joseph, G.E., & Strain, P.S. (2003). The teaching pyramid: A model for promoting social competence and preventing challenging behavior in young children. *Young Children* (July), 48–52.

Fullen, M. (2001). *Leading in a culture of change.* San Francisco: Jossey-Bass.

Gallacher, K.K. (1997). Supervision, mentoring and coaching: Methods for supporting personnel development. In P.J. Winton, J.A. McCollum, & C. Catlett (Eds.), *Reforming personnel preparation in early intervention: Issues, models, and practical strategies* (pp.191–214). Baltimore: Paul H. Brookes Publishing Co.

Gersten, R., Morvant, M., & Brengelman, S. (1995). Close to the classroom is close to the bone: Coaching as a means to translate research into classroom practice. *Exceptional Children, 62,* 52–66.

Gilkerson, L. (2004). Reflective supervision in infant mental health programs: Adding clinical process to nonclinical settings. *Infant Mental Health Journal, 25,* 424–439.

Goldberg, L.R. (1990). An alternative "description of personality": A big-five factor structure. *Journal of Personality and Social Psychology, 59,* 1216–1229.

Goldsmith, M. (2000). Coaching change. *Executive Excellence, 17*(6), 4.

Gordon, S.P., Nolan, J.F., & Forlenza, V.A. (1995). Peer coaching: A cross-site comparison. *Journal of Personnel Evaluation in Education, 9,* 69–91.

Grant, A.M. (2006). An integrative goal-focused approach to executive coaching. In D.R. Stober & A.M. Grant (Eds.), *Evidence-based coaching handbook: Putting best practices to work for your clients* (pp. 153–192). Hoboken, NJ: John Wiley & Sons.

Greenspan, S., & Wieder, S. (1998). *The child with special needs: Encouraging intellectual and emotional growth.* Reading, MA: Perseus Publishing.

Guskey, T.R. (1986). Staff development and the process of teacher change. *Educational Leadership, 15*(5), 5–12.

Hanft, B.E., & Pilkington, K.O. (2000). Therapy in natural environments: The means or end goal for early intervention? *Infants and Young Children, 12*(4), 1–13.

Hanft, B.E., Rush, D.D., & Shelden, M.L. (2004). *Coaching families and colleagues in early childhood.* Baltimore: Paul H. Brookes Publishing Co.

Hanson, J., Johnson, B., Jeppson, E., Thomas, J., & Hall, J. (1994). *Moving forward with family-centered care.* Bethesda, MD: Institute for Family-Centered Care.

Hanson, M.J. (2004). Ethnic, cultural, and language diversity in intervention settings. In E.W. Lynch & M.J. Hanson (Eds.), *Developing cross-cultural competence: A guide for working with children and their families* (pp. 3–18). Baltimore: Paul H. Brookes Publishing Co.

Hanson, M.J., & Lynch, E.W. (2010). Working with families from diverse backgrounds. In R.A. McWilliam (Ed.), *Working with families of young children with special needs* (pp. 147–174). New York: Guilford Press.

Harris, S.R. (1997). The effectiveness of early intervention for children with cerebral palsy and related motor disabilities. In M.J. Guralnick (Ed.), *The effectiveness of early intervention* (pp. 327–347). Baltimore: Paul H. Brookes Publishing Co.

Harrison, P.J., Lynch, E.W., Rosander, K., & Borton, W. (1990). Determining success in interagency collaboration: An evaluation of processes and behaviors. *Infants and Young Children, 3,* 69–78.

Harry, B. (1992). Developing cultural self-awareness: The first step in values clarification for early service providers. *Topics in Early Childhood Special Education, 12,* 333–350.

Hasbrouck, J.E. (1997). Mediated peer coaching for training preservice teachers. *The Journal of Special Education, 31*(2), 251–271.

Hasbrouck, J.E., & Christen, M.H. (1997). Providing peer coaching in inclusive classrooms: A tool for consulting teachers. *Intervention in School and Clinic, 32,* 172–178.

Head Start Transition Project Act PL 101–501, title I, subtitle B (§131 *et seq.*), Nov. 3, 1990, 104 Stat. 1238, (42 U.S.C. 9855 *et seq.*).

Hebbeler, K., Spiker, D., Bailey, D., Scarborough, A., Malik, S., Simeonsson, R., et al. (2007). *Early intervention for infants and toddlers and their families: Participants, services, and outcomes.* Final Report of the National Early Intervention Longitudinal Study (NEILS) (No. SRI 11247). Menlo Park, CA: SRI International.

Hendrickson, J.M., Gardner, N., Kaiser, A., & Riley, A. (1993). Evaluation of a social interaction coaching program in an integrated day-care setting. *Journal of Applied Behavior Analysis, 26*(2), 213–225.

Homa, K., Regan-Smith, M., Foster, T., Nelson, E.C., Liu, S., Kirkland, K.B., et al. (2008). Coaching physicians in training to lead improvement in clinical microsystems: A qualitative study on the role of the clinical coach. *The International Journal of Clinical Leadership, 16,* 37–48.

Horowitz, J.A., Bell, M., Trybulski, J., Munro, B.H., Moser, D., Hartz, S.A., et al. (2001). Promoting responsiveness between mothers with depressive symptoms and their infants. *Journal of Nursing Scholarship, 33*(4), 323–329.

Hosack-Curlin, K. (1988, April). *Measuring the effects of a peer coaching project.* Paper presented at the annual meeting of the American Educational Research Association, New Orleans.

Humphrey, R., & Wakeford, L. (2008). Development of everyday activities. A model for occupation-centered therapy. *Infants and Young Children, 21*(3), 230–240.

Huntington, D., Anderson, D., & Vail, C.O. (1994). The effects of peer coaching on practicum students in a supervised field experience. *Issues in Teacher Education, 3*(1), 37–49.

Hyson, M. (2003). *Preparing early childhood professionals: NAEYC's standards for programs.* Washington, DC: National Association for the Education of Young Children.

Individuals with Disabilities Education Improvement Act (IDEA) of 2004, PL 108-446, 20 U.S.C. §§ 1400 *et seq.*

International Coach Federation (ICF). (n.d.). *Frequently asked questions—ICF code of ethics.* Retrieved from http://www.coachfederation.org/about-icf/ethics-&-regulation/faq/

Ives, Y. (2008). What is coaching? An exploration of conflicting paradigms. *International Journal of Evidence Based Coaching and Mentoring, 6*(2), 100–113.

Jackson, P. (2004). Understanding the experience of experience: A practical model of reflective practice for coaching. *International Journal of Evidence Based Coaching and Mentoring, 2*(1), 57–67.

Jette, D.U., Bacon, K., Batty, C., Carlson, M., Ferland, A., Hemingway, R.D., et al. (2003). Evidence-based practice: Beliefs, attitudes, knowledge, and behaviors of physical therapists. *Physical Therapy, 83,* 786–805.

Johnson, B. (1990). The changing roles of families in health care. *Children's Health Care, 19*(4), 234–241.

Joyce, B., & Showers, B. (1982). The coaching of teaching. *Educational Leadership, 40*(1), 4–8, 10.

Joyce, B., & Showers, B. (2002). *Student achievement through staff development: Fundamentals of school renewal.* White Plains, NY: Longman.

Judge, T.A., Higgins, C.A., Thoresen, C.J., & Barrick, M.R. (1999). The big five personality traits: General mental ability and career success across the lifespan. *Personnel Psychology, 52,* 621–652.

Jung, L.A. (2010). Identifying families' supports and other resources. In R.A. McWilliam (Ed.), *Working with families of young children with special needs* (pp. 9–26). New York: Guilford Press.

Kaiser, A.P., Hancock, T.B., & Nietfeld, J.P. (2000). The effects of parent-implemented enhanced milieu teaching on the social communication of children who have autism. *Early Education and Development, 11,* 423–446.

Kaiser, A.P., Hancock, T.B., & Trent, J.A. (2007). Teaching parents communication strategies. *Early Intervention Services: An Interdisciplinary Journal of Effectiveness, 1*(2), 107–136.

Kaminski, J.W., Valle, L.A., Filene, J.H., & Boyle, C.L. (2008). A meta-analytic review of components associated with parent training program effectiveness. *Journal of Abnormal Child Psychology, 36,* 567–589.

Keilty, B., & Galvin, K.M. (2006). Physical and social adaptations of families to promote learning in everyday experiences. *Topics in Early Childhood Special Education, 26,* 219–233.

Kellegrew, D.H. (2000). Constructing daily routines: A qualitative examination of mothers with young children with disabilities. *American Journal of Occupational Therapy, 54,* 252–259.

Kim, J.M., & Mahoney, G. (2005). The effects of relationship focused intervention on Korean parents and their young children with disabilities. *Research in Developmental Disabilities, 26*(2), 101–201.

Kinlaw, D.C. (1999). *Coaching for commitment: Interpersonal strategies for obtaining superior performance from individuals and teams.* San Francisco: Jossey-Bass.

Knowles, M.S., Holton, E.F., & Swanson, R.A. (1998). *The adult learner.* Woburn, MA: Butterworth-Heinemann.

Kohler, F., Crilley, K., Shearer, D., & Good, G. (1997). Effects of peer coaching on teacher and student outcomes. *Journal of Educational Research, 90,* 240–250.

Kohler, F.W., Ezell, H.K., & Paluselli, M. (1999). Promoting changes in teachers' conduct of student pair activities: An examination of reciprocal peer coaching. *The Journal of Special Education, 33*(3), 154–165, 188.

Kohler, F.W., McCullough, K., & Buchan, K. (1995). Using peer coaching to enhance preschool teachers' development and refinement of classroom activities. *Early Intervention and Development, 6,* 215–239.

Kolb, D.A. (1984). *Experiential Learning: Experience as the Source of Learning and Development.* Englewood Cliffs, NJ: Prentice Hall.

Kurtts, S.A., & Levin, B.B. (2000). Using peer coaching with preservice teachers to develop reflective practice and collegial support. *Teaching Education, 11,* 297–310.

Law, M. (2000). Strategies for implementing evidence-based practice in early intervention. *Infants and Young Children, 13*(2), 32–40.

Lawlor, M., & Mattingly, C. (1998). The complexities embedded in family-centered care. *American Journal of Occupational Therapy, 52*(4), 259–267.

Lowenthal, B. (1992). Interagency collaboration in early intervention: Rationale, barriers, and implementation. *The Transdisciplinary Journal, 2,* 103–111.

Lynch, E.W. (2004). Developing cross-cultural competence. In E.W. Lynch & M.J. Hanson (Eds.), *Developing cross-cultural competence: A guide for working with children and their families* (pp. 41–75). Baltimore: Paul H. Brookes Publishing Co.

Lynch, E.W., & Hanson, M.J. (1993). Changing demographics: Implications for training in early intervention. *Infants and Young Children, 6*(1), 50–55.

Lynch, E.W., & Hanson, M.J. (2004). Steps in the right direction: Implications for service providers. In E.W. Lynch & M.J. Hanson (Eds.), *Developing cross-cultural competence: A guide for working with children and their families* (pp. 449–466). Baltimore: Paul H. Brookes Publishing Co.

Mahoney, G. (2009). Relationship focused intervention (RFI): Enhancing the role of parents in children's development intervention. *International Journal of Early Childhood Special Education, 1*(1), 79–94.

Mahoney, G., Boyce, G., Fewell, R., Spiker, D., & Wheeden, C.A. (1998). The relationship of parent-child interaction to the effectiveness of early intervention services for at-risk children and children with disabilities. *Topics in Early Childhood Special Education, 18*(1), 5–17.

Mahoney, G., & Perales, F. (2003). Using relationship-focused intervention to enhance the social-emotional functioning of young children with autism spectrum disorders. *Topics in Early Childhood Special Education, 23*(2), 77–89.

Mahoney, G., & Perales, F. (2005). A comparison of the impact of relationship-focused intervention on young children with pervasive developmental disorders and other disabilities. *Journal of Developmental and Behavioral Pediatrics, 26*(2), 77–85.

Mallette, B., Maheady, L., & Harper, G. (1999). The effects of reciprocal peer coaching on preservice general educators' instruction of students with special learning needs. *Teacher Education and Special Education, 22*(4), 201–216.

Marchant, M., & Young, K.R. (2001). The effects of a parent coach on parents' acquisition and implementation of parenting skills. *Education and Treatment of Children, 24*(3), 351–373.

McBride, S., Brotherson, M., Joanning, H., Whiddon, D., & Demmitt, A. (1993). Implementation of family-centered services: Perceptions of families and professionals. *Journal of Early Intervention, 17,* 414–430.

McCollum, J.A., & Hemmeter, M.L. (1997). Parent–child interaction intervention when children have disabilities. In M.J. Guralnick (Ed.), *The effectiveness of early intervention* (pp. 549–576). Baltimore: Paul H. Brookes Publishing Co.

McCrae, R.R., & Costa, P.T. (1987). Validation of the five-factor model of personality across instruments and observers. *Journal of Personality and Social Psychology, 52,* 81–90.

McLean, L.K., & Cripe, J.W. (1997). The effectiveness of early intervention for children with communication disorders. In M.J. Guralnick (Ed.), *The effectiveness of early intervention.* Baltimore: Paul H. Brookes Publishing Co.

McWilliam, P.J. (2010). Talking to families. In R.A. McWilliam (Ed.), *Working with families of young children with special needs* (pp. 127–146). New York: Guilford Press.

McWilliam, R.A. (1996). *Rethinking pull-out services in early intervention: A professional resource.* Baltimore: Paul H. Brookes Publishing Co.

McWilliam, R.A. (2000). It's only natural . . . to have early intervention in the environments where it's needed. *Young Exceptional Children Monograph Series No. 2: Natural Environments and Inclusion,* 17–26.

McWilliam, R.A., & Clingenpeel, B. (2003, August). *Functional intervention planning: The routines-based interview.* Retrieved from http://ectc.education.ne.gov/rbi/functional_intervention_planning.pdf

McWilliam, R.A., & Scott, S. (2001). A support approach to early intervention: A three-part framework. *Infants and Young Children, 133*(4), 55–66.

McWilliam, R.A., Tocci, L., & Harbin, G.L. (1998). Family-centered services: Service providers' discourse and behavior. *Topics in Early Childhood Special Education, 18,* 206–211.

Meline, T., & Paradiso, T. (2003). Evidence-based practice in schools: Evaluating research and reducing barriers. *Language, Speech, and Hearing Services in Schools, 34,* 273–283.

Miller, S.P. (1994). Peer coaching within an early childhood interdisciplinary setting. *Intervention in School and Clinic, 30,* 109–113.

Miller, S.P., Harris, C., & Watanabe, A. (1991). Professional coaching: A method for increasing effective and decreasing ineffective teacher behaviors. *Teacher Education and Special Education, 14,* 183–191.

Mink, O.G., Owen, K.Q., & Mink, B.P. (1993). *Developing high performance people: The art of coaching.* Reading, MA: Addison-Wesley.

Moes, D.R., & Frea, W.D. (2002). Contextualized behavioral support in early intervention for children with autism and their families. *Journal of Autism and Developmental Disorders, 32,* 519–534.

Morgan, R.L., Gustafson, K.J., Hudson, P.J., & Salzberg, C.L. (1992). Peer coaching in a preservice special education program. *Teacher Education and Special Education, 15,* 249–258.

Morgan, R.L., Menlove, R., Salzberg, C.L., & Hudson, P. (1994). Effects of peer coaching on the acquisition of direct instruction skills by low-performing preservice teachers. *The Journal of Special Education, 28*(1), 59–76.

Morgesen, F.P., Reider, M.H., & Campion, M.A. (2005). Selecting individuals in team settings: The importance of social skills, personality characteristics, and teamwork knowledge. *Personnel Psychology, 58,* 583–611.

Mott, D.W., & Dunst, C.J. (2006). Influences of resource-based intervention practices on parent and child outcomes. *CASEinPoint, 2*(6), 1–8. Retrieved from http://www.fippcase.org/caseinpoint/caseinpoint_vol2_no6.pdf

Munro, P., & Elliott, J. (1987). Instructional growth through peer coaching. *Journal of Staff Development, 8*(1), 25–28.

National Professional Development Center on Inclusion (NPDCI). (2008). *What do we mean by professional development in the early childhood field?* Chapel Hill, NC: The University of North Carolina, FPG Child Development Institute, Author.

Nolan, J.F., & Hillkirk, K. (1991). The effects of a reflective coaching project for veteran teachers. *Journal of Curriculum and Supervision, 7*(1), 62–76.

O'Connor, B. (1995). Challenges of interagency collaboration: Serving a young child with severe disabilities. *Physical & Occupational Therapy in Pediatrics, 15,* 89–109.

Odom, S. L. (2000). Preschool inclusion: What we know and where we go from here. *Topics in Early Childhood Special Education, 20,* 20–27.

Ohtake, Y., Santos, R.M., & Fowler, S.A. (2001). It's a three-way conversation: Families, service providers, and interpreters working together. *Infants and Young Children, 4*(1), 12–18.

Park, J., & Turnbull, A.P. (2003). Service integration in early intervention: Determining interpersonal and structural factors for success. *Infants and Young Children, 16*(1), 48–58.

Parsloe, E., & Wray, M. (2000). *Coaching and mentoring: Practical methods to improve learning.* London: Kogan Page.

Passmore, J. (2008). *Psychometrics in coaching: Using psychological and psychometric tools for development.* Philadelphia: Kogan Page.

Pedro, J.Y. (2005). Reflection in teacher education: Exploring pre-service teachers' meanings of reflective practice. *Reflective Practice, 6*(1), 49–66.

Peterson, C.A., Luze, G.J., Eshbaugh, E.M., Jeon, H., & Kantz, K.R. (2007). Enhancing parent-child interactions through home visiting: Promising practice or unfulfilled promise? *Journal of Early Intervention, 29*(2), 119–140.

Peterson, D.B. (2006). People are complex and the world is messy: A behavior-based approach to executive coaching. In D.R. Stober & A.M. Grant (Eds.), *Evidence-based coaching handbook: Putting best practices to work for your clients* (pp. 51–76). Hoboken, NJ: John Wiley & Sons.

Peterson, S.K., & Hudson, P.J. (1989). Coaching: A strategy to enhance preservice teacher behaviors. *Teacher Education and Special Education, 12*, 1–2, 56–60.

Phillips, M.D., & Glickman, C.D. (1991). Peer coaching: Developmental approach to enhancing teacher thinking. *Journal of Staff Development, 12*(2), 20–25.

Pilkington, K.O. (2006). Side by side: Transdisciplinary early intervention in natural environments (Electronic Version). *OT Practice, 11*(6), 12–17.

Raab, M. (2005). Interest-based child participation in everyday learning activities. *CASEinPoint, 1*(2), 1–5.

Rappaport, J. (1981). In praise of paradox: A social policy of empowerment over prevention. *American Journal of Community Psychology, 9*, 1–25.

Reiss, K. (2007). *Leadership coaching for educators.* Thousand Oaks, CA: Corwin Press.

Roberts, J. (1991). Improving principals' instructional leadership through peer coaching. *Journal of Staff Development, 12*(4), 30–33.

Roopnarine, J.L., & Johnson, J.E. (2005). *Approaches to early childhood education.* Upper Saddle River, NJ: Pearson.

Ross, J.A. (1992). Teacher efficacy and the effects of coaching on student achievement. *Canadian Journal of Education, 17*(1), 51–65.

Rush, D.D. (2000). Perspective. *Infants and Young Children, 13*(2), vi–ix.

Rush, D.D., & Shelden, M.L. (2008). Common misperceptions about coaching in early intervention. *CASEinpoint, 4*(1), 1–4.

Rush, D.D., Shelden, M.L., & Hanft, B.E. (2003). Coaching families and colleagues: A process for collaboration in natural settings. *Infants and Young Children, 16*, 33–47.

Sandall, S., Hemmeter, M.L., Smith, B.J., & McLean, M.E. (2005). *DEC recommended practices: A comprehensive guide for practical application in early intervention/early childhood special education.* Longmont, CA: Sopris West.

Schertz, H.H., & Odom, S.L. (2007). Promoting joint attention in toddlers with autism: A parent-mediated developmental model. *Journal of Autism and Developmental Disorders, 37*, 1562–1575.

Schon, D.A. (1983). *The reflective practitioner: How professionals think in action.* New York: Basic Books.

Schon, D.A. (1987). *Educating the reflective practitioner.* San Francisco: Jossey-Bass.

Schwartz, I.S., & Sandall, S.R. (2010). Is autism the disability that breaks Part C? A commentary on "Infants and toddlers with autism spectrum disorder: Early identification and early intervention," by Boyd, Odom, Humphreys, and Sam. *Journal of Early Intervention, 32*(2), 105–109.

Seifer, R., Clark, G.N., & Sameroff, A.J. (1991). Positive effects of interaction coaching on infants with developmental disabilities and their mothers. *American Journal on Mental Retardation, 96*(1), 1–11.

Sekerka, L.E., & Chao, J. (2003). Peer coaching as a technique to foster professional development in clinical ambulatory settings. *The Journal of Continuing Education in the Health Professions, 23*, 30–37.

Shanley, J.R., & Niec, L.N. (2010). Coaching parents to change: The impact of in vivo feedback on parents' acquisition of skills. *Journal of Clinical Child & Adolescent Psychology, 39*(2), 282–287.

Shelden, M.L., & Rush, D.D. (2001). The ten myths about providing early intervention services in natural environments. *Infants and Young Children, 14*(1), 1–13.

Shelden, M.L., & Rush, D.D. (2010). A primary-coach approach to teaming and supporting families in early childhood intervention 175–202. In R.A. McWilliam (Ed.), *Working with families of young children with special needs* (pp. 175–202). New York: Guilford Press.

Shelton, T., Jeppson, E., & Johnson, B. (1987). *Family-centered care for children with special health care needs.* Bethesda, MD: Association for the Care of Children's Health.

Shelton, T., & Stepanek, J.S. (1994). *Family-centered care for children needing specialized health and development services.* Bethesda, MD: Association for the Care of Children's Health.

Shelton, T., & Stepanek, J.S. (1995). Excerpts from "Family-centered care for children needing specialized health and development services." *Pediatric Nursing, 21*, 362–364.

Shonkoff, J.P., & Phillips, D.A. (2000). *From neurons to neighborhoods: The science of early development.* Washington, DC: National Academies Press.

Showers, B. (1982). *Transfer of training: The contribution of coaching.* Eugene, OR: Center for Educational Policy and Management, University of Oregon. (ERIC Document Reproduction Service No. ED231035)

Showers, B. (1984). *Peer coaching: A strategy for facilitating transfer of training.* A CEPM R&D Report. Eugene, OR: Center for Educational Policy and Management, University of Oregon.

Showers, B., & Joyce, B. (1996). The evolution of peer coaching. *Educational Leadership, 53*, 12–17.

Showers, B., Joyce, B., & Bennett, B. (1987). Synthesis of research on staff development: A framework for future study and state-of-the-art analysis. *Educational Leadership, 45*(3), 77–87.

Slater, C.L., & Simmons, D.L. (2001). The design and implementation of a peer coaching program. *American Secondary Education, 29*(3), 67–76.

Snyder, P., & Wolfe, B. (2008). The big three process components for effective professional development: Needs assessment, evaluation, and follow-up. In P. Winton, J. McCollum, & C. Catlett (Eds.), *Effective professionals: Evidence and application in early childhood and early intervention* (pp. 13–51). Washington, DC: Zero to Three Press.

Solomon, R., Necheles, J., Ferch, C., & Bruckman, D. (2007). Pilot study of a parent training program for young children with autism: The P.L.A.Y. Project Home Consultation program. *Autism, 11*(3), 205–224.

Soodak, L.C., & Erwin, E.J. (2000). Valued member or tolerated participant: Parents' experiences in inclusive early childhood settings. *The Journal of the Association for Persons with Severe Handicaps, 25*, 29–41.

Spagnola, M., & Fiese, B.H. (2007). Family routines and rituals. A context for development in the lives of young children. *Infants and Young Children, 20*(4), 284–299.

Sparks, G.M. (1986). The effectiveness of alternative training activities in changing teaching practices. *American Educational Research Journal, 23*, 217–225.

Stayton, V.D., Dietrich, S.L., Smith, B.J., Bruder, M.B., Mogro-Wilson, C., & Swigart, A. (2009). State certification requirements for early childhood special educators. *Infants and Young Children, 22*(1), 4–12.

Stichter, J.P., Lewis, T.J., Richter, M., Johnson, N.J., & Bradley, L. (2006). Assessing antecedent variables: The effects of instructional variables on student outcomes through in-service and peer coaching professional development models. *Education and Treatment of Children, 29*(4), 665–692.

Stober, D.R. (2006). Coaching from the humanistic perspective. In D.R. Stober & A.M. Grant (Eds.), *Evidence-based coaching handbook: Putting best practices to work for your clients* (pp. 17–50). Hoboken, NJ: John Wiley & Sons.

Stober, D.R., & Grant, A.M. (2006). Toward a contextual approach to coaching models. In D.R. Stober & A.M. Grant (Eds.), *Evidence-based coaching handbook: Putting best practices to work for your clients* (pp. 355–365). Hoboken, NJ: John Wiley & Sons.

Stremel, K., & Campbell, P.H. (2007). Implementation of early intervention within natural environments. *Early Intervention Services: An Interdisciplinary Journal of Effectiveness, 1*(2), 83–105.

Swanson, J., Raab, M.R., Roper, N., & Dunst, C.J. (2006). Promoting young children's participation in interest-based everyday learning activities. *CASEtools, 2*(5), 1–22. Retrieved from http://www.fippcase.org/casetools/casetools_vol2_no5.pdf

Toll, C.A. (2005). *The literacy coach's survival guide.* Newark, DE: International Reading Association.

Trivette, C.M., & Dunst, C.J. (2007). *Capacity-building family-centered help-giving practices.* Winterberry Research Reports Vol. 1, No. 1. Asheville, NC: Winterberry Press.

Trivette, C.M., Dunst, C.J., & Hamby, D. (2004). Sources of variation in and consequences of everyday activity settings on child and parenting functioning. *Perspectives in Education, 22*(2), 17–35.

Trivette, C.M., Dunst, C.J., Hamby, D.W., & O'Herin, C.E. (2009). Characteristics and consequences of adult learning methods and strategies. *Practical Evaluation Reports, 2*(1), 1–32.

Tschantz, J.M., & Vail, C.O. (2000). Effects of peer coaching on the rate of responsive teacher statements during a child-directed period in an inclusive preschool setting. *Teacher Education and Special Education, 23*, 189–201.

Turnbull, A.P., Summers, J.A., Turnbull, R., Brotherson, M.J., Winton, P., Roberts, R., et al. (2007). Family supports and services in early intervention: A bold vision. *Journal of Early Intervention, 29*(3), 187–206.

Turnbull, A., Turbiville, V., & Turnbull, H. (2000). Evolution of family-professional partnerships: Collective empowerment as the model for the early twenty-first century. In J. Shonkoff & S. Meisels (Eds.), *Handbook of early childhood education* (2nd ed.). New York: Cambridge University Press.

U.S. Census Bureau. (2010). *Language and English use and English-speaking ability: 2000.* Retrieved from http://factfinder.census.gov/servlet/ACSSAFFPeople

Valvano, J. (2004). Activity-focused motor interventions for children with neurological conditions. *Physical and Occupational Therapy in Pediatrics, 24*(12), 79–107.

Vanderhoff, M. (2004). Maximizing your role in early intervention. *PT: Magazine of Physical Therapy, 12*(12), 48–54.

Vereijken, C.M.J.L., Ricksen-Walraven, M., & Kondo-Ikemura, K. (1997). Maternal sensitivity and infant attachment security in Japan: A longitudinal study. *International Society for the Study of Behavioural Development, 21*(1), 35–49.

Wesley, P.W., & Buysse, V. (2004). Consultation as a framework for productive collaboration in early intervention. *Journal of Educational and Psychological Consultation, 15*(2), 127–150.

Whitmore, J. (2002). *Coaching for performance.* London: Nicholas Brealey.

Wikipedia. (2010). *Bedside manner.* Retrieved from en.wikipedia.org/wiki/Bedside_manner#Bedside_manner

Wilkins, S., Pollock, N., Rochon, S., & Law, M. (2001). Implementing client-centered practice: Why is it so difficult to do? *Canadian Journal of Occupational Therapy, 68*(2), 70–79.

Williamson, L.S., & Russell, D.S. (1990). Peer coaching as a follow-up to training. *Journal of Staff Development*, *11*(3), 2–4.

Wilson, L.L., Holbert, K., & Sexton, S. (2006). A capacity-building approach to parenting education. *CASEinPoint*, *2*(7), 1–9. Retrieved from http://www.fippcase.org/caseinpoint/caseinpoint_vol2_no7.pdf

Wilson, L.L., & Mott, D.W. (2006). Asset-based context matrix: An assessment tool for developing contextually-based child outcomes. *CASEtools*, *2*(4), 1–12. Retrieved from http://www.fippcase.org/casetools/casetools_vol2_no4.pdf

Wineburg, M. (1995). *The process of peer coaching in the implementation of cooperative learning structures*. Paper presented at the Annual Meeting of the American Educational Research Association, San Francisco.

Winton, P.J., & McCollum, J.A. (2008). Preparing and supporting high-quality early childhood practitioners: Issues and evidence. In P. Winton, J. McCollum, & C. Catlett (Eds.), *Effective professionals: Evidence and application in early childhood and early intervention* (pp. 1–12). Washington, DC: Zero to Three Press.

Woods, J. (2008, March 25). Providing early intervention services in natural environments. *The ASHA Leader*, *13*(4), 14–17, 23.

Woods, J., Kashinath, S., & Goldstein, H. (2004). Effects of embedding caregiver-implemented teaching strategies in daily routines on children's communication outcomes. *Journal of Early Intervention*, *26*(3), 175–193.

Woods, J.J., & Kashinath, S. (2007). Expanding opportunities for social communication into daily routines. *Early Intervention Services: An Interdisciplinary Journal of Effectiveness*, *1*(2), 137–154.

Woods, J.J., & Snyder, P. (2009). Interdisciplinary doctoral leadership training in early intervention. Considerations for research and practice in the 21st century. *Infants and Young Children*, *22*(1), 32–43.

Workgroup on Principles and Practices in Natural Environments (2007, November). *Mission and principles for providing services in natural environments*. OSEP TA Community of Practice-Part C Settings. Retrieved from http://www.nectac.org/topics/families/families.asp

Wynn, M.J., & Kromrey, J. (1999). Paired peer placement with peer coaching in early field experiences: Results of a four-year study. *Teacher Education Quarterly*, *26*(1), 21–38.

Zwart, R.C., Wubbels, T., Bohuis, S., & Bergen, T.C.M. (2008). Teacher learning through reciprocal peer coaching: An analysis of activity sequences. *Teacher and Teacher Education*, *24*, 982–1002.

Index